All knowledge is contained in fandom.

—Anthony Boucher

The HEIRS of ANTHONY BOUCHER

A History of Mystery Fandom

by

MARVIN LACHMAN

Dedication

This book is dedicated to the memory of William F. Deeck, who epitomized mystery fandom at its best. He spent countless hours preparing indexes to the major fan magazines, making research into the mystery far easier than it might otherwise have been. He helped those who wrote books, especially Ellen Nehr in her *Doubleday Crime Club Compendium* and me in *The American Regional Mystery*.

Bill Deeck was important in making Malice Domestic one of the most successful mystery conventions. He also did a superb job of programming for the 1986 Bouchercon. He was a frequent—invariably witty—speaker at both conventions.

The dry sense of humor that made Bill such a delight to talk to was also present in the hundreds of reviews and articles he wrote for fan magazines. His writing on James Corbett brought laughter, as did his talks about that infamous writer.

Bill's death in 2004 left a huge gap in mystery fandom. He will not be forgotten.

Acknowledgments

At risk of committing the sin of omitting someone, I should like to thank the following individuals who shared reminiscences or material pertinent to this history: Jackie Acampora, Geoff Bradley, Jon L. Breen, Robert E. Briney, Jan Burke, Lianne Carlin, J. Randolph Cox, Bill Crider, the late Bill Deeck, Kate Derie, George Easter, Sue Feder, Beth Fedyn, Vallery Feldman, Elizabeth Foxwell, Bill and Toby Gottfried, Doug Greene, Edward D. Hoch, Allen J. Hubin, Andy Jaysnovitch, George Kelley, Jiro Kimura, Deen Kogan, Ely Liebow, Peter Lovesey, Mary Mason, Jeff Meyerson, Fiske Miles, Len and June Moffatt, Richard Moore, Iwan Hedman-Morelius, Cap'n Bob Napier, Al Navis, Francis M. (Mike) Nevins, Gary Warren Niebuhr, Barry and Terry Phillips, Janet A. Rudolph, Tom and Enid Schantz, Art Scott, Mark Segal, Ruth Sickafus, Kevin Burton Smith, Steve Stilwell, Kate Stine, Bruce Taylor, and Sarah Weinman.

Also, I wish to thank my wife Carol for her continued support. Though seldom a mystery reader, she has attended many of the conventions about which I've written.

Contents

Contents

The Nineteen-Nineties and Twenty-First Century

Introduction: The Making of a Mystery Fan

by Edward D. Hoch
Past President of Mystery Writers of America and
Recipient of its Grand Master Award

When Marv Lachman first told me of his plans for this book and asked me to write an introduction for it, I was pleased to be part of the project. I've known Marv for some thirty-five years, and can think of no one better equipped to tell the story of mystery fandom. And the more I thought about it the more I realized that I too have always been a mystery fan.

I've written elsewhere that the first adult novel I ever read was the Pocket Books edition of Ellery Queen's *The Chinese Orange Mystery*, purchased at the corner drugstore for twenty-five cents. The year was 1939. I was nine years old and a faithful listener to the weekly Ellery Queen radio show since it had become a Sunday night fixture a few months earlier. About a year later, when I was bedded down with chicken pox, my grandfather brought me the complete Sherlock Holmes, another radio favorite. I read both books eagerly, and a whole new world opened to me.

Some time after that I discovered Green Dragon books, a series of monthly digest size paperbacks that I read and collected for almost three years. When they were joined by a companion series, Black Knight books, I read those too. The authors were unknown to me, and years later I discovered that many of the titles were reprinted from Phoenix Press and Mystery House hardcovers, not exactly the cream of the mystery crop.

It wasn't until 1945, when I answered an ad and joined the new Unicorn Mystery Book Club, that I started discovering writers I liked almost as much as Queen and Doyle. The first four-in-one Unicorn volume introduced me to Margaret Millar and Thomas B. Dewey, and many others followed. By this time I was beginning to realize that I loved a mystery, to paraphrase another favorite radio title. I subscribed to *Ellery Queen's Mystery Magazine* and started searching used bookstores for the issues I'd missed. I went on to discover Carr, Christie, Chesterton, Chandler, Cain and Charteris, and the "C" section in my bookcase began to sag.

In 1949 Clayton Rawson invited Unicorn subscribers to join Mystery Writers of America as affiliate members, an offer I readily accepted. I'd started writing short stories while still in high school, and though I didn't become a published author until 1955 I found myself attending MWA meetings in New York when my army service took me there during the Korean War. After my discharge I worked a year for Pocket Books in New York, continuing my close ties to MWA.

I'd never attended an Edgar Awards dinner until I won the Edgar myself in 1968. This intensified my relationship with both writers and fans. Already a regular contributor to *EQMM* and other mystery magazines, I sold my first novel and quit my advertising job in Rochester to write full time. I believe it was in 1971 that my wife Patricia and I were invited to a party of mystery fans at the Bronx apartment of Carol and Marv Lachman. It was attended by Al Hubin, Otto Penzler, Chris Steinbrunner, Charles Shibuk and others who were to become important cornerstones of mystery fandom. These parties, held after the Edgar dinners in late April, were an event that I still remember fondly.

When the first Bouchercon was announced for Santa Monica, California in 1970 we skipped it only because it was held in May, shortly after the Edgar Awards dinner. Patricia and I were at the second one in Los Angeles, and we have now attended twenty-six of those thirty-five annual events. In many ways Bouchercon has become the perfect mystery convention, a seamless blending of writers and fans that not only helps publicize the mystery and encourage new writers but also provides a lively meeting place for practitioners of a sometimes lonely profession.

I think there are times when many writers wonder if there's really anyone out there reading their words, caring about the characters and plots they shape from their imagination. At Bouchercon and other fan events I'm always pleased when someone tells me they've enjoyed a recent story. I often seek out authors myself, to express my pleasure at their latest book. Though I've been a published writer for fifty years now, I'm still a fan.

The history of mystery fandom is a story that needed to be told. Many readers, and even some writers, are unaware of what has gone before. They know little or nothing of the fans from the past, and what they contributed to the genre. It is, after all, mystery fandom that keeps alive all those great names from yesterday while discovering the new classic writers of our own day. With this book Marv Lachman has done an amazing job of chronicling it all, from the earliest Sherlockians through the popular fanzines and mystery conventions to the latest internet websites.

Read it, and rejoice!

Preface

This history of mystery fandom is called *The Heirs of Anthony Boucher* because it was to Boucher's column that fans turned before what I consider "The Fan Revolution" was launched in 1967. There were fans before 1967, and I shall discuss them in my first chapter. However, it was in 1967 that the mystery developed a fandom that was not limited to specific authors or characters such as Sherlock Holmes.

Boucher was an excellent mystery novelist, but he gave up writing novels—though he continued to write the occasional short story—to review for the *San Francisco Chronicle* in 1942. In 1951 he became the mystery critic for the *New York Times Book Review*. In addition, he reviewed for *Ellery Queen's Mystery Magazine*. He was considered the outstanding reviewer of crime fiction in America and on three occasions received Edgars from Mystery Writers of America for his criticism.

Boucher mentioned in his column fan activities relating to Patricia Wentworth, John D. MacDonald, and, of course, Sir Arthur Conan Doyle and Sherlock Holmes. He also reviewed what was perhaps the earliest general fan work, *A Preliminary Check List of the Detective Novel and Its Variants* (1966), an annotated list of recommendations by Charles Shibuk. In 1966 he publicized a bibliography of the works of John Dickson Carr compiled by Rick Sneary of California.

I had been reading mysteries for almost twenty-five years before I wrote or spoke to another fan. In 1967 I was only one of millions of mystery *readers*, but I also considered myself a *fan*. I kept notes of the books I read, prepared checklists of favorite authors, and compiled brief biographies of them and their series detectives. They were only for my own use.

My isolation was ended in 1967 when Allen J. Hubin of White Bear Lake, Minnesota, wrote to people who had requested Sneary's work, asking if they were interested in a journal *about* mystery fiction. The answers he received were positive. I was one of those replying enthusiastically, and those interested in Hubin's journal provided enough articles and reviews to fill the first issue. *The Armchair Detective*—and the fan revolution—was launched.

Hubin also wrote to me of a mystery fan, Charles Shibuk, living, as I did then, in the Bronx, and I telephoned him. We spoke of mysteries for an hour, my first conversation with another fan, and it was the start of a long friendship. Since I was there at the beginning and have continued to be active in fandom to the present, it would be false modesty not to mention myself in this history. (In 1997 Mystery Writers of America awarded me its Raven for my fan-related activities.) I have tried to be objective in this history, but because I care about the mystery, both its past and its future, I did not avoid expressing opinions on some subjects.

In 1967 Boucher's advice and strong encouragement were major factors in Hubin's deciding to go ahead with *The Armchair Detective*. Boucher then enthusiastically reviewed the first issue of *The Armchair Detective* on December 3, 1967. He spoke for mystery fans when he described it as the kind of journal for which he had been looking for many years. He wrote letters that were published in the second and third issues of *TAD*.

We expected Boucher would play a major role in the newly born fandom, but that was not to be. I can still recall the shock of reading Boucher's obituary in the newspaper on May 1, 1968. It was as if a friend had died. I had read his column on Sundays for almost twenty years. Everything that has been done in mystery fandom since he died is part of Anthony Boucher's legacy.

The book you are reading had its roots in a brief article I wrote for *CADS* in 1992: "An Informal (and Personal) History of American Fans." I concluded by saying that there will never be more than a relatively small number of people who enjoy reading and talking *about* mysteries as much as they enjoy reading them. If you're reading this book, you're one of them.

Marvin Lachman
February 1, 2005

1 Fandom Before "The Revolution"

Mystery fandom followed many of the paths trod by science fiction fandom, but it was over thirty years behind. In 1930, inspired by Hugo Gernsback's *Amazing Stories*, fans began forming organizations, beginning with the Science Correspondence Club, and publishing "fanzines," their term for fan magazines. In 1939 they held the first World Science Fiction Convention (Worldcon) in New York City, where a world's fair emphasizing the future was being held. Worldcons have been held annually since 1946, and beginning in 1953, Hugo Awards (named after Gernsback) have been presented by fans. The Science Fiction Writers of America started presenting the Nebula Awards in 1966. If science fiction fans were ahead, their writers were behind, because Mystery Writers of America (MWA) first presented its Edgar Allan Poe Awards in 1946.

There has been speculation as to the reasons for the relatively slow start by mystery fandom. It is probably because science fiction fans are younger, have fewer responsibilities, have more energy for fandom, and are less inhibited. Wearing costumes is important at science fiction gatherings. A few mystery conventions have attempted costume events, with indifferent results. The fedora and trench coat do not permit much variation. *Star Wars* and *Star Trek* appeal to the young more than crime stories. There have been significant increases in the size of the World Mystery Convention, but it still lags far behind its science fiction cousin. In 2004, when 1,350 people attended Bouchercon, 6,000 attended Worldcon.

The first history of science fiction fandom published in book form was *The Immortal Storm* (1954) by Sam Moskowitz, chairman of the first Worldcon. As far as I can determine, the book you are reading is the first history of general mystery fandom.

Sherlockian Fandom (1934–)

The "revolution" to which I have referred was in 1967, and this book is primarily about fandom since then. However, no history of fandom is complete without mentioning fans of Sherlock Holmes. Their history has been published; one volume of Jon L. Lellenberg's multi-volume history of Sherlockians devotes 508 pages to the years 1947–1950 alone.

In 1934, author Christopher Morley founded the **Baker Street Irregulars** (BSI), an organization of fans of Sherlock Holmes. Its name is that of the London street urchins who help Holmes in his cases. In June 1934 their first meeting was held in New York City, followed in December by the first BSI dinner. Now, to celebrate Holmes's "birthday" as suggested in Doyle's writings, the BSI dines on the Friday closest to that date, January 6th. At first, the banquets were for males, with the exception of a token female who represented "The Woman," as Holmes called Irene Adler. Many women now attend the dinners.

The Irregulars circulated among themselves writing debating various aspects of the Holmes canon. Of these, Vincent Starrett wrote, "a very considerable literature has accumulated, for the most part essays in fantastic scholarship—solemn tongue-in-cheek fooling in the fields of textual criticism and imaginary biography." Typical of these was Rex Stout's "Watson Was a Woman," in which he purported to show that a female shared the rooms at 221B Baker Street, and John D. Clark's theory, also advanced by William S. Baring-Gould, that Nero Wolfe was the illegitimate offspring of Holmes and Adler.

In 1944, Edgar W. Smith, a leading Irregular—in his business life he was a vice-president at General Motors—edited a collection of these essays in *Profile by Gaslight: An Irregular Reader About the Private Life of Sherlock Holmes*, which Simon & Schuster published. Smith had enough material left over to edit a second collection, *A Baker Street Four-Wheeler*, published by his own private press, Pamphlet House. The favorable reaction to these books led Smith to edit a magazine, *The Baker Street Journal*, which first appeared in January 1946 and whose purpose was to continue this speculation and scholarship. The publisher was Ben Abramson, owner of Manhattan's Argus Book Shop. Circulation never went beyond 2,000. As Morley said, "Never has so much been written by so many for so few."

The list of BSI members included "ordinary" fans, but also noted mystery authors Vincent Starrett, August Derleth, Frederic Dannay (Ellery Queen), and John Dickson Carr. Anthony Boucher was leader of The Scowrers, the BSI group in the San Francisco Bay area, one of many "scions" (local chapters) that had sprung up.

Franklin D. Roosevelt was made an honorary member of the BSI in 1942, and in a letter (later published in *The Baker Street Journal*) he proved himself adept at mock scholarship, postulating that Holmes was born in America to a criminal father but chose to go to England to fight crime. Roosevelt dubbed a portion of "Shangri-La," the Presidential retreat, "Baker Street." His successor, Harry S Truman, was made an honorary member, and he too was a knowledgeable Sherlockian fan.

Abramson's financial resources proved inadequate for what had become a 132-page, typeset, quarterly journal, and he suspended publication after the January 1949 issue. Smith began publishing it himself in January 1951 as a more modest, 40-page, mimeographed magazine. Dr. Julian Woolf became editor in 1960. In 1975 Fordham University began publishing it, returning it to its status as a typeset, illustrated journal. It is now published and edited by Steven Rothman of Philadelphia. The *Journal* is also on the internet (www.bakerstreetjournal.com), and a searchable set of CD-ROMs reproduces its first fifty years.

At about the time Holmes's American fans organized in 1934, their British counterparts formed the **Sherlock Holmes Society**. It was a casualty of World War II, but in 1951, inspired by the popular Sherlock Holmes Exhibition at the Marylebone Public Library during the Festival of Britain, it was resurrected thanks to Anthony Howlett, a young barrister. Howlett spent considerable time helping the exhibition, though he admitted also being attracted by Freda Pearce, the assistant librarian and his future wife. He was joined by some of the original British Sherlockians. Renamed the **Sherlock Holmes Society of London**, it held its first meeting at the Victoria and Albert Museum on July 17, 1951. In May 1952 it started publishing *The Sherlock Hol-*

mes Journal, and over a half-century later, despite many changes of editors, it is still published semiannually.

The Sherlock Holmes Journal started as a mimeographed magazine, but as membership increased, the society was able to publish it on slick paper, using, appropriately, the Baskerville typeface, and including illustrations. There have been news, reviews, poetry, articles, and much material on Doyle, including a 1959 issue honoring the centennial of his birth. James Edward Holroyd, the original co-editor, started a column of short items, titled "The Egg-Spoon," in the first issue.

Howlett appeared in that issue with film reviews and continued his work on the magazine until his death in 2003. He was instrumental in a statue of Holmes being placed near the Baker Street Underground station, and he was a major force in the society's 1968 pilgrimage to Switzerland that included a re-creation, in Victorian costume, of the battle between Holmes and Professor Moriarty at the Reichenbach Falls. (At the end of the battle, two clothed dummies fell off the cliff into the Falls.)

The 2003 obituary for Anthony Howlett gave a positive view of Sherlockian fandom in England, as, at first, did the death notices in 2004 for Richard Lancelyn Green, former Chairman of the Sherlock Holmes Society of London. Green had joined the society at age twelve in 1965, after reading his first Holmes story. He was an obsessive collector of material relating to Doyle and Holmes, owning one of the few surviving copies of *Beeton's Christmas Annual* for 1887, the first printing of *A Study in Scarlet.* Green was also a scholar, earning an Edgar for his bibliography of Doyle. Ten days after Green's obituary was published, a Reuters dispatch reported there were mysterious circumstances concerning Green's death, saying he had been garroted with a shoelace. There was an inquest, and the coroner was quoted as saying there was insufficient evidence to rule whether Green's death was murder, suicide, or a mistake.

The popularity of Sherlock Holmes continues, and it is an international phenomenon. Peter Blau, who maintains a list of Sherlockian societies, reports, according to the website Sherlockian.net, that there have been over 800 at one time or another, with 277 active as of November 2004. Twenty nations have Sherlockian groups, including twenty-two in Japan alone. There is even one in Kyrgyzstan! Forty-one of the states in the US have these groups, with California, Illinois, and New York each having more than twenty. They invariably have names imaginatively derived from the Holmes tales, for example, Mrs. Hudson's Cliffdwellers in New Jersey and the Sons of the Copper Beeches of Philadelphia.

The Edgar Allan Poe Society of Baltimore (1923–)

There was fandom before Sherlockians organized. Honoring the man credited with writing the first detective story, the Edgar Allan Poe Society of Baltimore started in 1923 and remains active. Its object: "promoting the understanding of Poe's life and writings, and his associations with Baltimore." An annual lecture about Poe is given on the first Sunday of each October. There have also been academic societies devoted to Poe, and their newsletters sometimes included material of interest to fans.

Happy Hours Magazine (1925–1936) and *Dime Novel Round-Up* (1931–)

The term "Dime Novel" refers to paper-covered books, usually priced at a dime, that were popular in the United States from 1860 through 1915, when they were replaced by pulp magazines. Thousands of titles were published, with detective stories especially popular. After they were no longer published and were becoming increasingly scarce, their fans began to organize. Ralph F. Cummings founded the Happy Hours Brotherhood, a group of dime novel readers and collectors in 1924. In 1925 he began a bimonthly, *Happy Hours Magazine*. In January 1931 that magazine was succeeded by *Dime Novel Round-Up*, with Cummings as editor-publisher. However, *Happy Hours Magazine* was soon revived by Ralph P. Smith and published until June 1936. Cummings published *Dime Novel Round-Up* until July 1952 when Edward T. LeBlanc, of Fall River, Massachusetts, took over. LeBlanc presided for an incredible forty-two years and 390 issues, until J. Randolph Cox of Dundas, Minnesota, replaced him after the June 1994 issue. Cox, a scholar of the mystery also, continues as editor-publisher. Among mystery-related articles to appear over the years have been those about early series detectives "Old Sleuth" and King Brady, and Cox's monumental bibliography of the most famous dime novel detective, Nick Carter.

The Saint Club (1936–)

The first non-Sherlockian group devoted to one character was The Saint Club, founded in 1936 for those interested in Leslie Charteris and his creation, Simon Templar ("The Saint"). Charteris was active in its founding, and in addition to providing publicity for him, it has always had a charity component, with the club, which is still active, contributing to hospitals in its early days and now to youth facilities. Yet, it has always been irreverent, and the back of its membership card says:

The bearer of this card is probably a person of hideous antecedents and low moral character, and upon apprehension for any cause should be immediately released in order to save other persons from contamination.

The club publishes a newsletter, *The Epistle,* on an irregular basis and sells Saint-related merchandise. There is a branch of the club, OzSaint, in Queensland, Australia.

The Pulp Era (1950–1971, 1993)

Fans of dime novels are often fans of the pulps. (Pulps were fiction magazines printed on untrimmed pulpwood paper, with colorful covers, that were popular from 1915 through 1950.) Lynn Hickman began publishing fanzines for them in 1950 while a few pulps were still published. He produced fifty-nine issues, under several titles, of a magazine once jokingly titled *JD-Argassy (The Pulp Era)*. It began as a fanzine for fans of *Argosy,* the most varied of pulps, which though known for adventure fiction, generally had a mystery story in each issue. In the winter of 1963 Hickman changed the title to simply *The Pulp Era* and continued that fan magazine until spring 1971. It was revived briefly in 1993, but then Hickman died.

Patricia Wentworth Fan Club (1961)

Fans of Patricia Wentworth, the British writer who created that most unusual private detective, Maude Silver, an elderly, white-haired lady who knitted booties while interviewing her clients, formed a fan club in 1961. They printed a newsletter that was published in Newport, Rhode Island. However, no other information is available regarding this club, which is no longer active.

JDM Bibliophile (1965–1999)

A more hard-boiled writer became the subject of a fan magazine in March 1965 when Len and June Moffatt of Downey, California, first published *JDM Bibliophile*, devoted to the work of John D. MacDonald. MacDonald started writing for pulp magazines in 1946 during their waning days. He then switched to paperback originals, mostly for Fawcett's Gold Medal line. In 1964 Gold Medal launched the series that made MacDonald famous when they issued four novels about Florida adventurer-detective Travis McGee.

JDMB, a mimeographed magazine at the time, was described in its initial issue as a "non-profit amateur journal devoted to the readers of John D. MacDonald and related matters." A goal was to obtain complete bibliographic information on all of MacDonald's writings, and this was partly achieved with *The JDM Master Checklist*, published in 1969 by the Moffatts. They had help from many people, including the author himself. Though he kept good records, he, like most authors, didn't have complete publishing data on his work. Especially helpful to the Moffatts were William J. Clark and another couple, Walter and Jean Shine of Florida. The Shines published an updated version of the *Checklist* in 1980, adding illustrations, a biographical sketch, and a listing of articles and criticism about MacDonald.

Len and June Moffatt, creators of *JDM Bibliophile*.

JDMB offered news and reviews of MacDonald's writings and their adaptation to various media. There were also contributions from MacDonald, including reminiscences and commentary. The Moffatts contributed a column ("& Everything"), as did the Shines ("The Shine Section"), and other JDM fans sent articles, letters, and parodies.

After the Moffatts had published twenty-two issues of *JDMB*, it was transferred in 1979 to the University of South Florida in Tampa, with Professor Edgar Hirshberg as editor. It continued until 1999. One issue, #25 in 1979, included the Shines's "Special Confidential Report, a Private Investigators' File on Travis McGee," describing much gleaned from the McGee canon about his past, interests, cases, and associates. MacDonald once said of Walter Shine, "He knows more about Travis than I do."

On February 21, 1987 about one hundred McGee fans gathered at his "address," Slip F-18 at the Bahia Mar Marina, in Fort Lauderdale, Florida. The mayor of that city unveiled a plaque honoring McGee. Under the sponsorship of the University of South Florida, at least six conferences about John D. MacDonald were held in Florida, beginning in 1988.

Bronze Shadows (1965–1968)

In 1964, Bantam began reprinting the Doc Savage pulp stories as paperback original books. In October 1965, this inspired a fan magazine, *Bronze Shadows*, edited and published by Fred Cook, devoted to the hero and weird menace pulps, but especially to Savage. *Bronze Shadows* only lasted fifteen issues, until November 1968. However, Michael L. Cook (no relation) said in 1983, "It was within the pages of *Bronze Shadows* that pulp fandom, as it is known today, first began to form." That fandom led to other magazines and an annual convention.

Edgar Wallace Organizations (1965–)

The **Edgar Wallace Club** was not started by a fan; it was organized by Penelope Wallace, daughter of the popular and prolific English author. (About 1930 it was estimated that one of every four books published in England was by Wallace.) The Edgar Wallace Club first met in December 1965 at the National Book League in London. A souvenir program from that meeting was reprinted as part of the first *Edgar Wallace Club Newsletter*, published in January 1969. One feature of the newsletter was a listing of Wallace in print, and in 1969, thirty-seven years after Wallace died, fifty-three of his books were still in print, mainly in England, but also in Germany where he was very popular. The newsletter facilitated exchanges of Wallace books and also published lost Wallace material, including poems, short stories, and even his lyrics to a song.

American fans who never attended a meeting of the club (whose name was changed to the Edgar Wallace Society in 1972) became members, including Lianne Carlin, Allen J. Hubin, Randy Cox, Luther Norris, and Jim Goodrich. By 1972 there were 120 members. Beginning in 1970, Penelope Wallace, though listed as "Organiser," no longer produced the newsletter, which was published by the Peter Shipton firm. John Hogan took over as "Organiser" with *Newsletter* #65, and the format changed from several sheets stapled in the top corner to that of a booklet. In February 1986 the newsletter became *The Crimson Circle*, the new title coming from a famous Wallace novel. Hogan died after issue 98, and his widow, Betty, took over for two issues. Then Neil Clark became "Organiser" for another two issues. Kai Jorg Hinz of Germany became editor in August 1994 and remained through May 1998 when the Society became inactive. In August 2000, *The Crimson Circle* resumed, with Penny Wyrd, Wallace's granddaughter, now "Organiser/Administrator" and Pim Koldewijn of the Netherlands editor. Issues were brief and sporadic, compared to the earlier days of the club, though one appeared in summer 2004.

During the hiatus of the Edgar Wallace Society, Alan Carter set up the **Edgar Wallace Appreciation Society**, issuing six issues of its newsletter, *The Edgar Wallace Journal*, in 1999–2000; it resumed in December 2003.

The Praed Street Irregulars and *The Pontine Dossier* (1966–)

Long before the Sherlockian popularity of the 1970s, created by Nicholas Meyer's bestseller pastiche *The Seven-Percent Solution* (1974), August Derleth began a series of pastiches about a Holmes-like detective, Solar Pons, and his friend and chronicler, Dr. Lyndon Parker. Pons was created in 1928 after Derleth confirmed, through correspondence with Doyle, that there would be no more Sherlock Holmes adventures. Upon the death of Derleth in 1971, the series was continued by Basil Copper. Eventually, there were almost one hundred novels and short stories about Pons, more than about Holmes.

Luther Norris of California founded a society in 1966 devoted to this pastiche character, using the name Praed Street Irregulars (PSI) after the street on which Pons lived. In February 1967 Norris founded a journal for the society, *The Pontine Dossier*, which he published until his death in January 1978. The PSI had annual dinners in the Los Angeles area, beginning in April 1967.

The John Dickson Carr Bibliophile (1966)

There was only one issue of *The John Dickson Carr Bibliophile*, published by Rick Sneary for the August 1966 mailing of FAPA (the Fantasy Amateur Press Association), but because Anthony Boucher mentioned it in his column, it played a vital role in mystery fandom. Members of FAPA were fans of the mystery too, and early issues of the *JDMB* were part of FAPA mailings.

The Journal of Popular Culture (1967–)

The Journal of Popular Culture, published by Bowling Green State University of Ohio and edited by Ray Browne, first appeared in the summer of 1967, shortly before the first general-interest mystery fan magazines, and it is still published. It is an academic journal (the official publication of the Popular Culture Association) but its editors consider crime fiction an important part of popular culture. Most issues have one or more articles of interest to mystery fans. They have ranged from the "academic" such as Elliot G. Gilbert's "The Detective as Metaphor in the Nineteenth Century" to Francis M. Nevins's article on uncollected pulp stories by Erle Stanley Gardner.   In 2002, upon the retirement of Ray Browne, the *Journal* moved to Michigan State University, where it continues under editor Gary Hoppenstand.

2 The Armchair Detective (1967–1997)

The Armchair Detective was the *catalyst* to mystery fandom, an appropriate term considering that its founder was a chemist. It gave fans an outlet for their enthusiasm about mystery fiction and led to other fan publications. *TAD* encouraged fans to write scholarly works about the mystery, many of which won MWA's Edgar Awards. It brought the mystery a degree of academic respectability reflected in dissertations for Ph.D.s and courses taught at the university level. It brought fans together, first in informal gatherings, then in increasingly large meetings such as Bouchercon.

If Al Hubin had trepidations about starting the magazine, his experience after Boucher's rave review only increased them. He expected some responses a few days after the Sunday on which Boucher was published, but come Wednesday his mailbox was empty. Some detective work on his part led him to a nearby playground where he found that neighborhood children had—for the first and only time—plundered his mailbox and scattered his mail there. Fortunately, Hubin was able to retrieve all forty new subscriptions. More came, and soon all 200 copies he had printed were gone, necessitating a second printing.

The early issues of *TAD* show what fans wanted to read—and what they were willing to write. Because most books *about* the mystery were out of print and because bibliographic material was in short supply, fans wanted to read about favorite authors, and they wanted checklists that would allow them to complete their collections of these authors and their series detectives. Furthermore, though the "Golden Age" of detective fiction (usually dated from 1920 through 1939) was more than twenty-five years ago, *TAD's* early readers seemed primarily interested in the past, especially writers who flourished during those two decades, such as Agatha Christie, R. Austin Freeman, Henry Wade, and Freeman Wills Crofts.

Though virtually all major writers were covered in *TAD* articles and checklists, one of the joys of the magazine was the number of obscure—though worthwhile—writers to whom space was given. Such non-household names as Rodrigues Ottolengui, Dennis Wheatley, C. E. Vulliamy, Seeley Regester, and L. T. Meade come to mind.

TAD readers wanted to communicate with other fans, and the letters column quickly became a popular feature. Correspondents corrected and added to what had been written, asked questions, and received answers. Occasionally, some requested assistance, as did William F. Nolan when he did not receive cooperation from Lillian Hellman on the Hammett biography he was writing.

TAD's first issue, October 1967, contained thirty pages. (The cost of a year's subscription then was $2 for four issues.) The lead article was by Sherlockian scholar William S. Baring-Gould, to whom the issue was dedicated because he died three weeks after submitting his article. His article was not about Holmes; it was about Fu Manchu. Considering the popularity of the Holmes canon, *TAD* contained comparatively little Sherlockian material, undoubtedly because *The Baker Street Journal* was available. However, the second issue had a history of Sherlockian fandom by John Bennett Shaw, America's leading scholar of the canon.

Another Sherlockian, James Keddie, Jr., contributed "Rambling Thoughts on a 'Tec Collection," an article about his thirty years of reading and collecting mystery fiction. Especially valuable was Keddie's suggested reading list of twenty-one books *about* mystery fiction and collecting, including one recently published about Agatha Christie by Gordon C. Ramsey. The first issue included "A Teacher Meets Agatha Christie," an article by Ramsey on his interview with Christie for the book. Ramsey described his trep-

Al Hubin (left) and Mike Nevins collating copies of TAD in 1969

idation at the prospect of meeting the great lady.

I had promised, in responding to Hubin's survey, to write for *TAD*. When he announced that he would publish, I was faced with having to write something to keep my promise. I contributed "Religion and Detection: Sunday the Rabbi Met Father Brown," combining a brief survey of authors and detectives who were members of the clergy with a pastiche in which the detectives created by Harry Kemelman and G.K. Chesterton meet.

That first issue was also noteworthy for "The Paperback Revolution," the first of 100 consecutive columns by Charles Shibuk reviewing mysteries in paperback. There were also film notes by William K. Everson, perhaps the leading expert on detective films. *TAD* was also a source of mystery news that eventually included lists of books recently published.

Hubin found that a fellow Minnesotan, Ordean Hagen, was compiling the first bibliography of crime fiction, and in *TAD*'s second issue Hagen wrote about his project. It was published in 1969 as *Who Done It?* but, sadly, Hagen died before it came out. First in the pages of *TAD*, then in a book that was updated three times and became a CD-ROM, Hubin corrected Hagen's work, added thousands of titles, and published his massive *Bibliography of Crime Fiction 1749–2000*.

Though Edgar Wallace, once the bestselling mystery writer of his time, had been dead for thirty-five years, crime writer Nigel Morland was still alive and was able to reminisce about "The Edgar Wallace I Knew" in *TAD*'s third issue. Frank Gruber and Steve Fisher wrote of their early days as pulp writers, with Fisher also recalling the reclusive Cornell Woolrich, about whom there was still much interest. Meanwhile, Francis M. Nevins began his writing about Woolrich that eventually led to an Edgar-winning biography. With the help of Bill Thailing and Hal Knott, he published a Woolrich bibliography. Thailing, the ultimate Woolrich fan, wrote how he first read Woolrich on a troopship going to the South Pacific in World War II, but he let his enthusiasm carry him away when he described Woolrich as "the greatest writer the world has ever known."

Enthusiasm was also apparent in other early work published in *TAD*. Nolan provided the first complete checklist of Hammett's Continental Op stories. Keddie wrote about crime plays, and Frank P. Donovan authored a four-part series on railroad mysteries.

Before *TAD* was born, Robert E. Briney and William J. Clark started a checklist of the works of John Creasey. With Creasey's help, Briney completed the bibliography (521 novels) of the man then considered mystery's most prolific writer. Hubin later discovered and interviewed for *TAD* Lauran Bosworth Paine, who had written over 600 books.

Another Minnesotan, J. Randolph Cox, wrote of a course on the mystery, probably the first for college credit, he taught at St. Olaf's College in January 1971. (Cox also wrote for *TAD* on Nick Carter, A. A. Milne, and George Harmon Coxe, among others.) As the mystery began to achieve academic respectability, that was reflected in the pages of *TAD*, beginning with Joan M. Mooney's Ph.D. dissertation, "Best Selling American Detective Fiction," published in five issues beginning in 1970. Another doctoral dissertation, "The Problem of Moral Vision in Dashiell Hammett's Detective Novels," by George J. Thompson, appeared in seven parts starting in 1973. These articles met with the approval of some *TAD* readers, but there were others who complained that they were dry and lacked the enthusiasm of the fans who had been writing for *TAD* without prospect of academic advancement.

An issue raised early in *TAD*'s history (and still discussed today) is whether it is possible to write intelligent criticism of the mystery without disclosing vital plot elements and/or the ending. Frank McSherry complained that Donald Yates had given away too many solutions and surprises in his 1970 piece on locked rooms. Hubin devised a compromise, warning before Professor Darwin Turner's article on John B. West that it contained plot disclosures.

Because *TAD*'s readers felt strongly about their favorite escape reading, they disagreed with each other in print on other issues as well. They had wildly different opinions about the same book. Shibuk thought Barzun and Taylor's *A Catalogue of Crime* (1971) was "the greatest contribution to the genre in the last thirty years." However, George Wuyek thought Barzun and Taylor "highly biased and selective." Writer Bill Pronzini, also a fan and supporter of *TAD*, responded in two letters. He was critical of *A Catalogue of Crime* for emphasizing classic detective puzzles, calling it "the most exasperating, depressing, and irritating book I've ever come across."

Bruce Monblatt in 1971 criticized "the shenanigans of the Baker Street Irregulars" and "frivolous" attempts to talk of eccentric author Harry Stephen Keeler. He praised efforts to make the mystery "academically respectable and relevant." He thought detective novels were now "preempting the mainstream novel as the mirror of modern society" and told of how moved he was by scenes of violence in the novels of Ed McBain. Nevins replied that there was a surprising amount of social relevance in Keeler, and I pointed out that there was no shortage of descriptions of violence in the various media, but people turned to detective novels for escape.

I applied mock scholarship to Erle Stanley Gardner's creation in my 1971 article "The Secret Life of Perry Mason." I "proved" that Lieutenant Tragg was really Mason's brother and that Mason and Della Street had a love affair. R. Gordon Kelly wrote to punch holes in my theories, missing the point of my perhaps feeble attempt at humor.

Fred Dueren wanted more about Golden Age authors, while Frank Eck and Jon Jackson thought there was too much on early writers. In 1974, Regina Cohen felt Mickey Spillane had been underrated, and James Sandoe, a leading expert on hard-boiled writers, responded by welcoming a debate on Spillane, whom he called a "dreadful fellow" and said about the Mike Hammer novels, "I don't have stomach enough to reread them to speak for the prosecution."

The Daughter of Time by Josephine Tey is often considered one of the ten greatest detective novels, so it was with surprise that *TAD* readers read in 1977 an attack on that book by Guy M. Townsend, a historian who said, "Tey makes a mockery of scholarly research by ignoring and distorting evidence." Many wrote objecting to Townsend's thesis, pointing out he was not distinguishing between historical writing and fiction, and that Tey was writing for mystery readers, not scholars. Strongest in criticizing Townsend was Myrna J. Smith, who he implied was a hysterical female, leading her to reply that he was "snobbish and arrogant."

Despite its considerable scholarship and disagreements, *TAD* was not all seriousness. Jon L. Breen, Veronica Kennedy, Robert Aucott, and R. W. Hays provided quizzes. There were poems from Aucott and Ola Strøm. Ed Lauterbach told Sherlockian jokes. Other articles of mock scholarship, in addition to mine, included Thomas D. Waugh's "The Missing Years of Nero Wolfe" and Eileen Snyder's "Was Watson Jack the Ripper?" Beginning with Vol. 18 No. 1 (Winter 1985), Louis Phillips began a humor column "Dial N for Nonsense."

Though Francis M. Nevins was serious in writing about Harry Stephen Keeler, the wackiness of Keeler's plots (he wrote 700-page mysteries) lent themselves to readers' chuckling at such Nevins articles as "The Worst Legal Mystery in the World," "The Wild and Wooly World of Harry Stephen Keeler," and "Hick Dick from the Sticks: Harry Stephen Keeler's Quiribus Brown." Nevins, calling himself "Hellgate Newlander," a deliberate variation on Newgate Callendar, the pseudonym of the *New York Times* reviewer, wrote humorous reviews, especially of the books of Michael Avallone.

Bill Pronzini contributed funny articles on Phoenix, a publisher known for its poor mysteries, and on his choice as "the *worst* mystery novel of all time," *Decoy*, by the pseudonymous "Michael Morgan." William F. Deeck wrote of James Corbett, another unconsciously funny mystery writer who somehow published over forty books despite prose that included lines such as "Nothing could have surprised the astonishment on his countenance."

For more years than seemed possible, Al Hubin produced *The Armchair Detective* single-handedly, with only help from his five children and the occasional visitor in collating *TAD* for mailing. In addition to his large family, he had a responsible fulltime job and from 1968 through 1971 was mystery critic for the *New York Times Book Review*.

In 1976 Hubin accepted an offer from Publisher's Inc. of Del Mar, California, an adjunct of the University of California at San Diego (UCSD), to publish *TAD*, thus relieving him of the chores of typing copy, addressing, stuffing and mailing over a thousand envelopes, managing subscriptions, and finding sources of revenue through advertising and new subscribers. Hubin retained editorial control.

Publisher's Inc.'s proprietorship of *TAD*, began with Vol. 9, No. 3 (June 1976), and the immediate reaction was favorable, especially because their professional printing permitted double columns that were easier to read than the long lines that Hubin used. Saddle stitching was another improvement over the stapled *TAD* from which the last pages sometimes came loose. Answering Jim Goodrich who worried that he was losing control of *TAD*, Hubin admitted that work on his bibliography prevented his commenting on most letters but that he still had editorial control, though "the selection of the final contents, and their arrangements in the issue, is largely outside my activity." Hubin also said that *TAD* was receiving fewer letters and articles.

Perhaps that was because other magazines had started in the 1970s and had the more personal, fannish quality of early *TAD*.

The short stewardship of *TAD* by Publisher's Inc. lasted only two years. Their ambitions exceeded their resources. As late as their final issue (July 1978), C. David Hellyer, managing editor, promised to make available nationally, through UCSD, a college-level course on the mystery. They also promised mystery lecture tours, seminars, and a volume of the best of *TAD*. Instead, they were having severe financial problems, which also led to the demise of their Mystery Library. They used a mailing service for subscriptions that proved inefficient, and they did not answer letters from subscribers who were not receiving their issues.

By the summer of 1978, *The Armchair Detective* was on the brink of death in California when in New York a rescuer appeared: Otto Penzler, longtime (though he was only thirty-six) mystery fan. Penzler had collaborated on *Detectionary* (1971) and *Encyclopedia of Mystery and Detection* (1976) and had founded a publishing company, Mysterious Press. He took over *TAD* effective with the

Otto Penzler, the fan who became a one-man industry.

October 1978 issue, and though he initially had difficulty getting the material for that issue from Publishers, Inc., Penzler produced it. Despite further problems in receiving subscription information from California, Penzler worked to restore *TAD*'s good reputation. Editorials by Penzler detailed his problems in getting *TAD* back on schedule. By summer 1979, *TAD* had gotten back to normal regarding its contents, with an outstanding issue devoted to Ellery Queen on the fiftieth anniversary of *The Roman Hat Mystery*. Even the covers of *TAD* improved, thanks to artwork by Carolyn Hartman (then Mrs. Penzler). However, there were still delays in mailing, and as Penzler said in the Spring 1980 issue, almost ten percent of copies mailed were never received, the fault, he implied, of the Postal Service. With great personal effort, he eventually kept his promise that "we'll do the best we can to make the magazine appear regularly and that everyone gets all the issues due them."

With the end of Vol. 13 in 1980, Hubin relinquished the editorship of *TAD*, though he continued as consultant and book reviewer. Hubin had edited fifty-two issues (4062 pages) of *TAD*, without any remuneration, but he thanked those who had contributed to *TAD*. He was replaced by Michael Seidman, an editor with Charter Books.

Seidman, writing in *TAD* and elsewhere, had a writer/editor viewpoint regarding fandom, believing that fans needed to support writers by buying books. Of course, he was writing before the genre achieved its boom in the later 1980s. In Vol. 14, No. 3 (Summer 1981), his editorial expressed the opinion that fans were not supporting writers sufficiently, finishing with the admonition "READ AN AMERICAN MYSTERY" (Seidman's emphasis).

Seidman called Bouchercon "a celebration of the writer," ignoring that it had been started by fans. When bookstores reported rising sales of mysteries in 1983, he told *TAD*'s readers, "Obviously, it will now be up to us to make certain we support the bookstores and publishers." On the subject of awards, he closed his editorial in Vol. 17, No. 3 (Summer 1984), by saying, "It is our support for the writers—through book purchases and fan mail—that is the most meaningful recognition."

By the autumn of 1985, Seidman noted the request *TAD* most often received was for more reviews. He offered to send review copies to those who requested them. By the following spring, seventeen of *TAD*'s 110 pages were reviews. Opening the floodgates to reviewers led to some negative reviews. These probably troubled publishers, who were increasingly advertising in *TAD,* more than they bothered fans. Seidman then said that he would like to avoid negative reviews in the future "unless there is some depth to the review and some point is made."

Readers bemoaned the sparsity of letters compared to *TAD*'s early days. Vol. 17, nos. 3 and 4, had only two letters each. Assuming all letters received were published (a generous assumption since several letters I sent never appeared), *TAD*'s readers seemed less interested in writing. Jon L. Breen in Vol. 18, No. 3 (Summer 1985), perceptively questioned whether the shortage of letters wasn't at least partly caused by the time lag between an issue and the publication of letters responding to material in it. For example, the two letters in Vol. 17, No. 4, referred to Vol. 17, No. 1. Still, when *TAD* published something arguable, there was no shortage of comment.

Hubin, not normally a controversial writer, drew flak as a reviewer when he perceived a "tract on leftward feminism" in reviewing an Amanda Cross novel. One reader wrote in Vol. 19, No. 2 (Spring 1986), that she was not renewing her subscription to *TAD* because "almost all the articles are about male mystery writers written by male article writers." Assuming she was referring to Vol. 18, she was ignoring articles about Gladys Mitchell, Martha Grimes, Ellis Peters, and Mary Higgins Clark and several articles written by female authors.

TAD began publishing original short stories in 1990, justifying it as providing another market for writers. This proved unpopular with most *TAD* readers who expressed opinions; they felt the magazine should stick to writing *about* the mystery.

In William L. DeAndrea *TAD* acquired its most contentious contributor, an Edgar-winning novelist whose column "J'Accuse" was either loved or hated by fans, but seldom ignored. His opinions on mysteries as well as the Gulf War and political correctness seldom failed to draw either praise or ire. He was at his angriest reacting to a lengthy *TAD* article by Bill Delaney called "Ross Macdonald's Literary Offenses," calling the article "dreck" and "an attack of alphabetical dysentery." Several letters criticized Delaney, and one reader cancelled his *TAD* subscription because of it.

Vol. 20, No. 4, included comments on the issue of possible discrimination against women. In this *TAD* was reflecting not only American society but also MWA, where there were complaints by Phyllis Whitney and others that women writers had not won a fair share of the Edgars. Members of the 1987 Edgar committees were told to be "gender conscious." In his column, DeAndrea frowned upon another Whitney suggestion, one never adopted by MWA, that there be a separate Edgar for romantic suspense, presumably because women generally wrote in that sub-genre. However, beginning in 2001 MWA has given the Mary Higgins Clark Award, co-sponsored by Simon & Schuster, for the book written most closely in the Clark tradition of romantic suspense.

Not willing to depend only on articles submitted, *TAD* assembled, in addition to DeAndrea, an impressive stable of columnists. Shibuk continued until he had completed twenty-five years. Jacques Barzun and Wendell Hertig Taylor updated their 1971 book. Jon L. Breen's columns, "What About Murder?" and "Novel Verdicts," continued his two Edgar-winning books. The prolific Edward D. Hoch found time to write a short story column, "Minor Offenses." Richard Meyers reviewed television mysteries, Thomas Godfrey reviewed crime films, Chris Steinbrunner reviewed old-time radio mysteries, and Dick Lochte and Tom Nolan reviewed mystery cassettes. Janet A. Rudolph, founder of Mystery Readers International, wrote "Murderous Affairs," which told of mystery conventions, fan magazines, awards, and other activities. There was a Baker Street column by Scott and Sherry Bond and two columns in the form of ongoing newsletters about Rex Stout and Dorothy L. Sayers.

Except for Hubin and Shibuk, I probably wrote more words for *TAD* during its first decade than anyone else. I never stopped reading and caring about *TAD*, and in a letter in 1982, I questioned its current direction, recounting my failure to receive any responses to earlier letters and an article I had sent. Penzler intervened, and soon *TAD* was publishing me again. At the 1986 Baltimore Bouchercon, Kathy Daniel asked me to write a column for *TAD* and beginning in spring 1988 I reviewed first novels in my column "Original Sins." Daniel, as managing editor, helped turn *TAD*'s finances around, even reaching the point, beginning in 1989, where it was able to pay, albeit modestly, contributors for articles and columns. Seidman said he was growing stale as editor of *TAD* and relinquished that job to Daniel effective Vol. 22, No. 1 (Winter 1989). She instituted the practice of guest editorials, though she invariably used professional writers or editors rather than the fans that had supported *TAD*.

Readers said they wanted more reviews, and by the end of Vol. 29, about twenty-five percent of the magazine consisted of reviews of new books. *TAD* also tried to be friendly to booksellers and publishers. It ran a 15-page list of American mystery booksellers in 1992, and the Independent Mystery Booksellers Association's best-seller list starting in 1993.

With Vol. 25, No. 3 (Summer 1992), Kate Stine replaced Daniel, maintaining *TAD*'s standard of quality. In 1995 Judi Vause became managing editor and advertising manager and then bought the magazine from Penzler. *TAD* seemed as strong as ever when in 1996 at Bouchercon it won an Anthony as Best Magazine, while *The Armchair Detective Book of Lists*, edited by Stine, won as Best Critical Work. *TAD* even acquired a new logo that autumn. If *TAD* was in financial trouble, its readers were not aware of it. At the beginning of Vol. 30, almost fifteen percent of the magazine's space consisted of ads. *TAD* had over 6,000 people who bought it either by mail or from dealers. That was far more than any other fan magazine.

TAD's luck suddenly ran out. De Andrea died in October 1996, only forty-four years old, of liver cancer. Elizabeth Foxwell replaced Stine as editor in 1997 for Vol. 30, No. 3, only to find she was boarding a sinking ship. The magazine was suspended after that issue. Foxwell wrote in *Mystery & Detective Monthly* that Judi Vause was having "physical and financial problems." Vause never answered mail, nor did she pay contributors or reimburse subscribers for issues they never received. I'm sorry to include a negative note regarding TAD, especially since I understand how illness and financial problems can befall a publisher. However, I consider it inexcusable for someone not to at least tell her subscribers there are difficulties, and that she will try to reimburse them when she can. Other publishers facing this situation have handled it differently. Rumors circulated that someone else would buy *TAD*, but that never happened, and the magazine that meant the most to mystery fandom died.

TAD's importance to fandom cannot be overstated. It encouraged fans to share their knowledge and enthusiasm with others and helped to create an international fan base, with subscribers from Australia, Belgium, Denmark, Great Britain, Germany, Israel, Italy, Japan, The Netherlands, Norway, Portugal, and Sweden, among other nations. The articles and scholarship that first saw the light in its pages sparked an explosion in the number of books *about* the mystery. Its longevity and professionalism set a standard by which all other fan journals are judged.

3

The Mystery Lover's/Reader's Newsletter (1967–1973)

Coincidentally, a second general-interest fan magazine appeared in the same month as *The Armchair Detective*: October 1967. It actually appeared before *TAD* because a prospectus issue was sent in August to potential subscribers answering a notice in *The Baker Street Journal*. *The Mystery Lover's Newsletter (TMLN)* was the creation of Lianne Carlin of Revere, Massachusetts, then a stay-at-home mother of a two-year old but anxious to use her journalism training. A mystery fan, she wondered why there was no such magazine.

TMLN's first issue had twelve pages. Two articles were reprints: a brief biography of Alfred Hitchcock and the remainder of W. B. Stevenson's chapbook, *Detective Fiction*, the first part of which formed half of the prospectus. Mrs. Carlin's husband, Stanley, using the pseudonym "S. Carl Linn," wrote an article "Detective Fiction and Hemingway," revealing Hemingway as a fan of Raymond Chandler and Georges Simenon. There was also publishing news, queries from readers, and a "Book Mart" page for subscribers to list book wants and those they had for sale or trade.

Gradually, *TMLN* published more original material and attracted most of the same cadre of fan-scholars as *TAD*; Robert Washer, Luther Norris, Robert Sampson, John McAleer, and Bill Crider appeared first in *TMLN*. They wrote articles and checklists about writers, including Ellery Queen, Ernest Bramah, Nick Carter, Anthony Gilbert, Clayton Rawson, and Josephine Tey. Because some checklists contained errors or were incomplete, *TMLN*'s readers used their considerable knowledge for corrections. Charles Shibuk, a movie fan, adapted the annotated checklist, a common practice in film scholarship, to the mystery with his list of Chandler on screen.

TMLN might have been strong on scholarship, but it wasn't all solemn. Nevins published his earliest writing about Harry Stephen Keeler, whom he called "the sublime nutty genius of the crime genre," as well as "Department of Unmitigated Mishmosh" and "Department of Unrelated Miscellanea," two running series about lighter aspects of the mystery. I wrote a parody-pastiche in which the secretaries to famous detectives, e.g., Della Street, Nikki Porter, et al, form a union and go out on strike. It ended with Perry Mason forced to answer his own phone. I also wrote a parody play about Arthur B. Reeve's Craig Kennedy, a detective so popular in the 1910s he was called "The American Sherlock Holmes."

Not having as large a list of subscribers, nor the benefits of a Boucher review, as did *TAD*, *TMLN* began more modestly. It grew larger but only reached twenty-two pages at the end of its second year and never went beyond fifty-one pages. Carlin changed its name to *The Mystery Readers Newsletter (TMRN)* in 1969 because she found that a "smoother, more professional" title. Helped in part by a notice in Hubin's column in the *New York Times Book Review* and an ad in *Ellery Queen's Mystery Magazine*, *TMRN* eventually had about 500 subscribers.

TMRN was strong on interviews, with Mary Stewart, Nicholas Blake, Ira Levin, Joyce Porter, Howard Haycraft, John Ball, and Elizabeth Linington among the subjects. The Linington interview by Ann Waldron drew a heated response from Linington in the next issue because she thought that Waldron over-emphasized her involvement in the John Birch Society, a right-wing organization, making her seem "a very foolish and fanatical person."

It wasn't only about politics that readers of *TMRN* felt strongly. Shibuk and Nevins, who later became good friends after they met in person, came to verbal blows as a result of Shibuk's letter in Vol. 2 No. 1: he disagreed with Nevins calling Hammett's *Red Harvest* "subtle." Nevins defended his point and then, in turn, criticized Shibuk's opinions denigrating Hitchcock's later films, remarking that he couldn't expect to "see eye-to-eye" with someone holding those views.

James Mark Purcell's "All Good Mysteries Are Short Stories" was a self-styled "polemic" which began, "I'd like to start an argument. I think the novel is the wrong length for the straight detective story." He drew an unfortunate analogy to racism to describe what he perceived as prejudice against the short story. He was criticized in the following issue by Bill Crider and Randy Cox. Even I, arguably the biggest fan of short stories, thought he overlooked much, including novel length allowing deeper characterization and more complex plotting. However, I welcomed his infusion of controversy into the pages of *TMRN*.

TMRN published a column by Rona Randall on the mystery scene in the United Kingdom. In 1972 she wrote about the birth and growth of England's Crime Writers Association. Pat Erhardt wrote a report on the first Bouchercon. Professional writers, including Howard Haycraft, Phyllis Whitney, Helen McCloy, and John Creasey sent letters to *TMRN*. In 1970, acting on a suggestion from Lianne Carlin, I started a series, "The American Regional Mystery," in which I described how mysteries captured the distinctive geography, customs, and speech of each US region. I eventually updated it into a book of the same name, published in 2000.

Having fallen behind in *TMRN*'s schedule, Carlin wrote in Vol. 5 No. 6 of her problems as she juggled publishing with raising two small children and holding down a part-time job. Originally bimonthly, *TMRN* became quarterly. A prescient letter writer, William Ruble, wrote in Vol. 6 No. 1, "I hope this is not the first step toward ceasing publication altogether." After the following issue (Autumn 1973), personal problems forced Carlin to terminate publication. When, thirty years later, I interviewed her for this book, she remembered fondly "the newsletter's talented and loyal contributors and readers. They were the true essence of the publication. The newsletter turned out to be an eye-opening enterprise (so much knowledge out there!) as well as fun!"

Mystery Readers' Parties (1969–1976)

Mystery fans began to communicate, but in those days before e-mail it was via letters and the occasional phone call, though after many phone conversations, I met my fellow Bronxite, Charlie Shibuk.

I learned in April 1969 that Al Hubin, Lianne Carlin, and Bob Washer were attending the MWA Edgar Awards banquet in New York City, along with their spouses. Also present would be out-of-town fans Bob Briney, Mike Nevins, Patricia Erhardt, and Hal Knott. I lived in New York then, and looked forward to meeting people I knew only through the written word. With the enthusiastic agreement of Carol, my wife, I sent invitations for Saturday night to what I called "The First Mystery Readers' Party." Because most of the people were staying in Manhattan, I included subway directions to the northern reaches of the Bronx where we resided. Also invited was Shibuk, practically a neighbor.

We lived on the 19th floor of a large apartment building, and, for the first time since we moved there, the elevators went out of commission on the evening of the party. Early arrivals Erhardt and Knott decided to walk up the stairs, an easy job for Hal, a mountain climber. Pat, on the other hand, was a sedentary person and a heavy smoker. She arrived out of breath.

Fortunately, the elevators were quickly repaired because Al and Marilyn Hubin came with a frail, seventyish mystery fan, Estelle Fox of Canada, in tow. She was one of many uninvited people who came as word spread that mystery fans and writers were welcome at the Lachmans. Estelle was proud of her collection of twenty-four scrapbooks containing reviews, articles, correspondence, and autographs of mystery writers. She left those to the Toronto Reference Library in her will. She also had a collection of the first mysteries of over a thousand authors.

The conversations, unfortunately never recorded, were memorable. Hubin quietly became the center. He was knowledgeable and articulate, and it was his founding of *The Armchair Detective* that brought us together. Another highlight of the evening was Nevins describing the wacky plots of Harry Stephen Keeler. Tales of what Nevins called Keeler's "Screwball Circus" had everyone laughing. Carlin called the party "the mystery buff's answer to LSD: habit-forming, heady, but harmless." In a *TAD* editorial, Hubin commented, "What a pleasure to sit among knowledgeable people and talk of things mysterious on into the night!" However, the conversation wasn't only about mystery; some spouses weren't even mystery fans. We learned a great deal about each other's personal lives.

No history of mystery fandom would be complete without some mention of the food Carol prepared. Among her dishes were shrimp in an appetizing cocktail sauce, chicken livers wrapped in bacon, chopped liver, a salami and sweet pickle mixture, and much more. Desserts included a chocolate whipped cream pie.

Two regulars at our parties, beginning in 1971, were Otto Penzler and Chris Stein-

At the first Mystery Reader's Party, in 1969: (l. to r.) Charles Shibuk, Lianne Carlin, Marv Lachman.

brunner, with whom Shibuk and I collaborated on two books about the mystery. I stocked almost every kind of liquor but found that most of our guests preferred soft drinks. Chris was an exception, and one year when he had a great deal to drink and was feeling warm, he decided to get some fresh air. Not seeing the screen door, he pushed it aside, staggering out on to our terrace where only the railing prevented his falling nineteen floors.

Other occasional attendees included Bob Aucott, a Philadelphian who was a poet, a Sherlockian, and an expert on baseball; Randy Cox, the world's leading expert on Nick Carter; Amnon Kabatchnik, book collector and theater director; mystery film expert Norman Nolan; and Richmond Pugh, a friendly Manhattanite who smoked cigars. Many attendees smoked, but, though this was after the Surgeon General's 1964 report, we weren't as health-conscious then and didn't think of asking our guests not to.

Mystery writers attended because they were fans as well as writers. One early guest was Edward D. Hoch, the legendary short story writer. Ed brought another writer, Dan J. Marlowe, who gave up a successful business career to become a writer and became successful in his new field after publishing his outstanding novel, *The Name of the Game Is Death* (1962). Dan told us a fascinating story. That book made fugitive bank robber Al Nussbaum into a fan of Marlowe's work. An admiring phone call Nussbaum placed to Marlowe in Michigan was traced by the FBI and led to his arrest. Marlowe took an interest in Nussbaum, encouraged him to write while he was in prison, where he became a model prisoner. Marlowe was also instrumental in Nussbaum receiving parole. Later, Nussbaum became a successful writer, and in the 1980s, when Marlowe suffered a disabling stroke, Nussbaum became his guardian.

The 1969 party was a huge success, and our parties became an annual event through 1976. The Bronx seemed to become *the* gathering place for mystery fans, which was probably appropriate since Edgar Allan Poe had lived about a mile from where I did. Several times in the 1970s, Otto Penzler invited his collaborators to his Bronx apartment, the place where his publishing house, Mysterious Press, started.

In 1977, Carol and I did not have time to prepare for our usual Saturday party. Friday, we were attending the MWA banquet because Penzler, Shibuk, Steinbrunner, and I were nominated for an Edgar for *Encyclopedia of Mystery and Detection*. Bouchercon was becoming *the* place for fans to meet, and the Mystery Readers' Parties became a pleasant memory.

Other Fan Magazines & Organizations: 1960s

With two general-interest fan magazines established in the United States in 1967, another began in Sweden, and other fans started magazines devoted to favorite authors. It was early days in a publishing revolution that would eventually see over one hundred fan magazines published. Most did not last; the time, effort, and money involved usually defeat even the most enthusiastic fans.

The Rohmer Review (1968–1981)

An early journal devoted to a specific author was *The Rohmer Review*, edited and published for the Sax Rohmer Society by Dr. Douglas A. Rossman, zoology professor at Louisiana State University; it first came out in July 1968. Robert E. Briney, later chairman of the computer sciences department at Salem State University in Massachusetts, was Associate Editor, and a highlight of the first issue was his article "An Informal Survey of the Works of Sax Rohmer."

Rossman and Briney were among those who believed the creator of Dr. Fu Manchu deserved greater fame. Fu Manchu was once one of the most famous characters in crime fiction, and the description of him as "the yellow peril incarnate in one man" is famous, but relatively little was known about Rohmer. By the second issue, *The Rohmer Review* had 134 subscribers. Briney, who started his own Rohmer collection because he couldn't find books by him in public libraries, became editor/publisher with the fifth issue, August 1970. It was published fairly regularly as a semiannual until 1974, and then other pressing matters forced Briney into "irregular" publication. Sometimes a year would go by between issues, and then two would be published within a month. Four years elapsed between #17 and the last issue, #18, dated Spring/Summer 1981. At its peak, about 300 copies of *The Rohmer Review* were distributed, though Briney lost money on it.

Among the material appearing in *The Rohmer Review* was reprints of articles and fiction by Rohmer; bibliographies (generally by Briney); an illustrated article about a forgotten Rohmer play, *The Eye of Siva* (1923); reviews of a 1972 Rohmer biography; John Ball's childhood reminiscences, "My Hero—Fu Manchu"; Ray Stanich's article on Fu Manchu on radio; and a reprint of a Ron Goulart parody, "The Hand of Dr. Insidious." There was even "The Polyglot Mr. Rohmer," the reprint of a lecture by Pulitzer Prize-winning author Jean Stafford.

On several occasions, members of the Rohmer Society met informally in New York City in 1970 when Chris Steinbrunner showed Fu Manchu films as part of his Armchair Detective Cinema. (That film group was founded by Chris Steinbrunner shortly after *TAD* began. It operated out of a machine shop near Times Square called "Joe's Place," whose owner, film fan Joe Judice, frequently showed films.) After 1971, the Society no longer existed as a separate entity, though Briney continued to publish the *Rohmer Review*. The contents of all issues are available on a web site, *The Page of Fu Manchu*.

DAST-Magazine (1968–)

Iwan Hedman-Morelius is the Swedish Al Hubin, a mystery scholar and collector who founded a Swedish-language fan journal, *DAST-Magazine* (its name is short for *Detectives–Agents–Science Fiction–Thrillers*) in September 1968, when he was still unaware of Hubin and *The Armchair Detective*. His collection, about 20,000 books, was almost as large as Hubin's.

Hedman was a professional soldier in the Swedish Army, retiring as a captain at age fifty in 1982. He started *DAST* as a mimeographed publication he sent free to thirty-four friends. After one year he had 100 subscribers, and eventually he had a circulation of over 1,500 and could print in offset thanks to the Swedish government, which partly subsidized it as a "cultural magazine." He had readers in the United States, Japan, and Australia, in addition to those in European countries. Like Hubin, he had the help of his family in assembling his magazine for mailing.

Hedman—he has since adopted the last name of Morelius, his grandfather's original name—gave up publishing *DAST* in 1995 after 143 issues. He moved to Spain for his health in 1986, and, though costs were less, it became increasingly difficult to publish a Swedish magazine from there. His friend Kjell E. Genberg took it over, and *DAST* remains the longest active general-interest mystery fan magazine. However, Morelius was not satisfied with being "idle," so in 1997 he started a Swedish language newsletter, *Läst & Hört I Hängmattan* (*Read & Listened to in the Swingbed*—or *Hammock* in English usage) to recommend mysteries.

Hedman-Morelius's ability to read and write English as a second language made him a prolific contributor to American fan magazines. In 1974, he published the equivalent of Hubin's bibliography, a listing of the crime fiction titles published in Sweden between 1864 and 1973, which he later updated. He also published books and articles about thriller writers, including Leslie Charteris, Dennis Wheatley, Desmond Bagley, and Alistair MacLean.

Morelius entertained writers and fans when they visited Sweden. In 1981, when the Crime Writers International Congress was held in Stockholm, seventy miles from his home in Strängnäs, he invited half of the delegates to a party, with buses to bring 150 people there.

The Queen's Canon Bibliophile (1968–1971)

Though many current readers have never read an Ellery Queen mystery, Anthony Boucher said in 1961, "Ellery Queen *is* the American detective story," recognizing Queen's preeminent roles as detective, author, and editor. In October 1968, the Reverend Robert E. Washer, a Baptist minister, from Oneida Castle, New York, published the first issue of this fan journal devoted to all aspects of the work of Frederic Dannay and Manfred B. Lee, who wrote as Queen. So popular was Queen then that soon leading fan-scholars were submitting articles, checklists, and letters. Francis M. Nevins began *Royal Bloodline*, his Edgar-winning book about Queen, in the pages of *TQCB*. Joe R. Christopher interrupted his doctoral dissertation to write an article

"The Retirement of Richard Queen."

My first regional writing was an article about Ellery's New York City, and then I wrote a history of *Ellery Queen's Mystery Magazine*. *TQCB* led to one of the earliest meetings of mystery fans. In November 1968 Washer and his wife came to the New York area to visit Dannay and Lee, stopping first in the Bronx to visit the Lachmans. It gave me the idea for the first "Mystery Readers of America" party the following spring.

TQCB acquired a new—and better—title, *The Ellery Queen Review,* in October 1971, but unfortunately that issue was the last as illness and family matters caused Washer to suspend publication.

The First Bouchercon: 1970

Bouchercon began in a bar. Writing about its origins in the 1991 Bouchercon program, Len and June Moffatt recalled that in a bar, at the close of a July 1969 science fiction convention in Santa Monica, California, they were reminiscing with the late Bruce Pelz about Anthony Boucher and his enthusiasm for both science fiction and mysteries. Pelz said, "I wonder if it is time to put on a mystery convention." There had never been one.

Pelz asked Phyllis White, Boucher's widow, for permission to use his name. She readily agreed, writing, "The only misgiving I have is that calling a convention a memorial—to anyone—sounds rather anti-festive. Tony would never want to turn up as a wet blanket at a convention. If the committee thinks that there is no danger of anyone being downhearted, I am very much in favor of the idea." Phyllis White was given membership number 000, an honor continued until her number was retired after her death.

Pelz and Chuck Crayne were co-chairmen, but in the first Anthony Boucher Memorial Mystery Convention program Pelz said that the Moffatts, who originally agreed to be liaison with MWA, were far more active and that there might never have been what has become known as Bouchercon without them. He referred to the convention as "this experiment, which could not guarantee any particular results."

During Memorial Day weekend 1970, eighty-two fans gathered at the Royal Inn in Santa Monica. Most were from California, but some from far afield, for example, Pat Erhardt and her father from Utica, NY, and editor Donald A. Wollheim from New York City.

Bouchercon began May 29th with a Friday evening opening reception. This became a tradition, though future receptions became elaborate, with food served and awards presented. The reception was followed by several room parties, which, because of the relatively small attendance, almost everyone who wanted to could attend.

The official opening was at 1 PM on Saturday, and Poul and Karen Anderson, writers who had known Boucher, spoke about his work and varied interests. (This was a time of single-track programming, so attendees did not have to choose which panel to attend.) They were followed by a panel called "Mysteries in the Old Pulps," moderated by Len Moffatt, that included writers and editors Howard Browne, William P. McGovern, Larry Shaw, and Robert Turner, as well as bibliographer Bill Clark. It was so successful, with so much audience participation, that Moffatt finally had to stop it so the rest of the day's program could continue. Enthusiasm was so great that fans were asking, "Why haven't we done this before?"

Next came an auction to raise money to help pay the costs of the convention; advance registration was only $4 for the weekend. Auctions later became a regular Bouchercon event, but they would raise funds for charities, often those promoting literacy.

The next panel, called "The State of the Art," moderated by Pelz, included three people primarily for their science fiction writing and/or editing: Larry Niven, Jerry Pournelle, and Wollheim. There were also mystery writers Bill S. Ballinger and Clayton Matthews. A question by Pournelle to the audience, asking what readers want in the way of crime fiction, led to the creation of an unscheduled panel to be held that evening to discuss that topic.

Because this convention had its roots in science fiction, there was a masquerade, a frequent event at science fiction meetings. One teenager came as a vampire, but other costumes were mystery-related. Pelz was Dr. Gideon Fell and challenged people to spot the deliberate mistakes in his costume. Niven was "Flavius Maximus," Roman private eye investigating the murder of Julius Caesar.

An unfortunate tradition was started at Sunday's banquet-luncheon with food that was generally described as "mediocre," a word applied to most Bouchercon meals thereafter. Guest of Honor Robert Bloch spoke, talking of Boucher and of how they met at a science fiction convention. Bloch joked, "We met, we fell in love,

Robert Bloch, author of *Psycho*, Guest of Honor at the first Bouchercon in 1970.

got married and lived happily ever after." He also spoke of the mystery in general and said that literary critics did not take it seriously enough. He predicted that in 1990 historians would read John D. MacDonald to find out what life in the US was like, rather than the works of mainstream writers.

The convention closed with a business meeting to discuss the future of Bouchercon. There was agreement that it would become an annual event, although it should be held in October to avoid conflicts with MWA's spring meeting and summertime science fiction conventions. However, one person said he thought Bouchercon was a meeting for writers and would-be writers and that fans should not be included. There was a roar of disapproval, and Clayton Matthews said that it was beneficial for writers to meet readers in relaxed settings so they could find out what they were doing right—or wrong.

Another unpopular suggestion, rejected by the organizers, was that the name of the convention should be changed each year to honor others in the mystery. It was decided that the convention would continue to honor Boucher. Because Boucher was known to love gatherings of fans and writers, a sentence heard often during the weekend was, "It's too bad Tony can't be here to enjoy this."

7 Bouchercon: 1970s

1971: Los Angeles

Bouchercon moved to Columbus Day weekend (October 8–11) at the International Hotel in Los Angeles. Bruce Pelz was the chairman, aided by the Moffatts, Gail Knuth, and Drew Sanders. Official attendance was only seventy-six, down from the prior year, apparently due to insufficient advance publicity. It was not the cost; registration was still only $4, and a single room at the hotel was $14 per night. Because of the low attendance, it was decided to end the convention on Sunday, rather than Monday as scheduled.

Phyllis White was there, along with Boucher's sons, James White and Larry White, and their wives. Bill S. Ballinger was the Guest of Honor, but he had to leave the opening reception to finish a teleplay he was writing for the *Cannon* series. This was only one of several problems. The opening session was delayed because one speaker, Joe Gores, was late, his plane from San Francisco delayed by fog. Pelz had to leave to pick up another speaker, Howard Browne, who was without transportation. William P. McGivern was unable to appear because he had the flu.

Edward D. Hoch of Rochester, NY, attended and appeared on a panel devoted to "The State of the Art, 1971." The popular 1970 pulp panel was repeated, with Richard Deming and Robert Bloch added. According to Leo Rand's Bouchercon report in *JDMB*, beer was served to the panelists, and Bloch spoke from the podium rather than his seat, joking that since he had been the only one not to imbibe, he was the only panelist capable of standing.

Crime movies, an important part of early Bouchercons, were shown on Saturday and Sunday nights. There was also a poker game, a tradition that has lasted into the 21st century.

Pelz and the Moffatts had suggested in flyers that awards, using Boucher's pseudonym, "H. H. Holmes," be awarded, but there was little positive response, so it was not until 1986 that the first award hon-

Bruce Pelz (r.) who first had the idea for Bouchercon, with 1971 Guest of Honor Bill S. Ballinger.

oring Boucher, the Anthony, was given.

Assessing the convention, Rand called it a success. He also blamed low attendance on fans and writers not being "used to the idea of an annual convention. They may see a notice about it but still not really know what it is all about." Then, trying to explain the pleasures of such a convention to someone who had never attended one, he used words many were to use in the future, "You had to be there to truly appreciate it."

1972: Los Angeles

Bouchercon returned to L.A.'s International Hotel for the weekend of October 20–22, and attendance (ninety-three) was larger. Rand reported that some attendees remarked that smaller conventions were more fun! The Moffatts co-chaired Bouchercon III, with Pelz as treasurer.

Frederic Dannay, the surviving half of the Ellery Queen team, was scheduled to be Guest of Honor but was unable to attend due to illness. Robert Washer spoke on his behalf at Sunday's luncheon, citing the importance of Boucher and Queen in his own life. Before his talk, a tape of Boucher giving one of his mystery reviews on radio was played.

There were more panels than before, and more varied speakers. Rand said, "Programs ran overtime both days, as the question-and-answer sessions with the audience were longer than anticipated and quite lively." Panelists included Mike Nevins of New Jersey and Bob Briney of Massachusetts. Also present was John Nieminski of Illinois, who attended every subsequent Bouchercon until his death in 1986. It was obvious that Bouchercon, despite its California roots, was becoming national. Emphasizing this was the announcement that the fourth Bouchercon would take place in Boston.

1973: Boston

The idea of an East-Coast Bouchercon came from Stewart Brownstein, another person experienced at putting on science fiction conventions but also a mystery fan. Those in charge of Bouchercon III gave their blessing. Briney and Brownstein were co-chairmen, with Washer and Lianne Carlin completing the committee.

Bouchercon IV was held Columbus Day weekend (October 5–7) at the Sheraton-Boston Hotel. Illness and accidents continued to plague Bouchercon, as Washer, who spoke for Dannay in 1972, was unable to attend because of illness, while car trouble forced Carlin to miss much of the event. There was no Guest of Honor, but the leading American expert on detective stories in Spanish, Professor Donald A. Yates, was featured speaker, delivering an outstanding talk on Jorge Luis Borges and Anthony Boucher. A Boucher translation in *EQMM* was the first appearance of Borges in English. Briney had a moment of panic Friday night when he learned that the printer had closed early, and he was not able to pick up the programs. Fortunately, the shop opened early Saturday.

One hundred and five people registered. Columbus Day weekend coincided with Yom Kippur that year, reducing attendance. Still, many Easterners got to attend their first Bouchercon, including *EQMM* editor Eleanor Sullivan, Ron Goulart, and

Charles Shibuk. Friday night's only activity was a get-acquainted party where the conversation was so enjoyable it lasted four hours.

For the first time a book was published in conjunction with Bouchercon: *Multiplying Villainies: Selected Mystery Criticism 1942–1968* by Anthony Boucher. It was edited by Briney and Nevins and contained a foreword, "Tony Boucher As I Knew Him," by Helen McCloy. Published in a limited edition of 500 copies, it took three years to sell out, but is now highly collectible, with prices up to $400 in catalogues and on the Web.

The formal program included Nevins talking about Cleve F. Adams and Randy Cox on Nick Carter. Charlotte MacLeod spoke on "The Occult in Mystery Fiction." There was an especially good "Science Fiction and Mystery Fiction" panel with Edward D. Hoch, Goulart, and Briney. A last-minute panel on Cornell Woolrich, with Nevins, Yates, and Hal Knott went as smoothly as if it had been planned months before.

This was my first Bouchercon, and I was drafted for another impromptu panel, "Mystery in Films," though I wasn't sure why since film experts Shibuk and Chris Steinbrunner were panelists. For the first of many Bouchercons, Steinbrunner was responsible for the film program, and it was varied, including *The Laurel and Hardy Murder Case*, *And Then There Were None*, and the first chapter of the *Drums of Fu Manchu* serial.

This Bouchercon received media attention. An interviewer and camera crew from Boston's WBZ-TV, at the Sheraton to interview Liza Minnelli, filmed part of it and an interview with Yates, both of which were aired. There was also coverage by *Boston Globe* columnist Bill Fripp, who called it MWA's fourth annual convention, though the local chapter of MWA had not been helpful. It would not be the last time that credit for Bouchercon would mistakenly go to professional writers instead of the fans who put it on. The editor of a book using Boucher's Sherlock Holmes radio scripts said, "After his death, the Mystery Writers of America named their annual convention after him."

1974: Oakland

Bouchercon returned to California October 4-6 at the Royal Oak Inn at Oakland's Airport, with science fiction writer/editor Adrienne Martine-Barnes as chairwoman. Because of a lack of publicity, attendance dipped to about fifty, and almost all who came were from Northern California. However, John Nieminski and I traveled there with our wives, from Chicago and New York respectively, and the Moffatts came up from Southern California.

The convention began Friday night with the now traditional reception, this time a wine-and-cheese affair held in the bridal suite, of all places. The formal program on Saturday and Sunday heavily involved Boucher, but that was appropriate since he had lived in nearby Berkeley. Phyllis White gave personal reminiscences, as did colleagues Karen and Poul Anderson, Shirley Dickensheet, and Lenore Glen Offord. Guest of Honor Reginald Bretnor spoke about his friendship with Boucher, describing the latter's many talents, from gourmet cooking to poker playing.

Among other panelists were Joe Gores, Bill Pronzini, and Frank McAuliffe. On

Sunday morning, I spoke about "The American Regional Mystery." It was early, and barely a half-dozen people were there at the start, but others drifted in. Oakland was an enjoyable Bouchercon, albeit the smallest, and one forgotten because so few "regulars" attended.

Nieminski asked Len Moffatt how one went about bidding for Bouchercon. Moffatt recalled, "I told him he had just won the bid (knowing of no others), and so the sixth Bouchercon went to Chicago."

1975: Chicago

Bouchercon not only moved to Chicago, but it moved to summer (July 18–20) to avoid a conflict with the first International Crime Writers Congress scheduled for October. (The Congress had no connection with the International Association of Crime Writers, which was founded in 1986.) Nieminski and Robert Hahn were chairmen, and the site was the Midland Hotel, near Chicago's Loop. On arriving, I spotted a sign on the hotel marquee announcing "Boucheron." It was the first, but not the last, time for that misspelling. (Boucheron is the name of a French perfume and also a French winery.) The Midwest location allowed people from the area, including Max Allan Collins, Allen J. Hubin, and Dan J. Marlowe, to attend their first Bouchercons. Attendance was 110, highest yet at Bouchercon.

Programming was still single-track, with a total of eight panels. Don Yates chaired a panel on reviewing which included Hubin and Alice Cromie of the *Chicago Tribune*. With Nicholas Meyer's *The Seven-Percent-Solution* on the bestseller list, a Sherlockian panel was logical, and one on Saturday drew four experts: Otto Penzler, Jon Lellenberg, Robert L. Fish, and Nieminski. Another Saturday panel asked, "Who is the Big Mac?" in considering John D. MacDonald, Ross Macdonald, and Philip MacDonald. Saturday night's banquet had a witty speech by Fish, the Guest of Honor.

On Sunday, along with Hal Knott, Hubin, and Woolrich-expert William Thailing, I was on a "collecting mysteries" panel. I recall Otto Penzler being miffed that he hadn't been selected since he had an outstanding *collection* of first editions, while my *accumulation* then consisted mainly of old paperbacks and a complete run of *EQMM*. The last panel had lawyer Mike Nevins on the subject of Perry Mason, about whom no one is more knowledgeable.

1976: Culver City, CA

A projected geographical rotation system (East Coast, Midwest, and Pacific Coast) did not materialize as Bouchercon returned to California and the Pacifica Hotel in Culver City, October 1–3. The Moffatts chaired their second Bouchercon; John Ball was Guest of Honor. This Bouchercon broke all attendance records with 157 people registered in advance, and a few showing up as daily registrants. The registration fee was only $6, with another $6.50 to attend the Sunday luncheon, which 114 people did.

Ball was an author of police procedurals so he was a logical choice to moderate a panel that included three investigators from the Los Angeles Police Department. They commented on the accuracy of police work shown in novels and television. One panelist called *The Rookies* the worst of the current "cop" shows on TV. To the panelist's embarrassment, the creator of that series was in the audience. She defended herself, blaming its producer for changing her scripts. This Bouchercon had more law enforcement procedural panels—five—than previous Bouchercons. One was a talk on "Nitrobenzene and Other Horrors" by James White, Boucher's criminalist son.

Fiction-related panels included "Clergyperson-Detectives" and one on the late Fredric Brown, who always complained when his name was misspelled "Frederic," as it was in the convention program.

The most enjoyable event was a talk by British mystery writer Christianna Brand. As Bob Briney wrote in his report for *TAD*, "Miss Brand is a warm, funny, and utterly delightful woman, and she captivated the audience instantly and completely with her anecdotes about herself, the Detection Club, the peculiar behavior of Dorothy Sayers (mimicked hilariously), John Dickson Carr, and others."

Bouchercon had its first bookdealers, Ruth and Al Winfeldt of the Scene of the Crime bookstore in Sherman Oaks, California. They sold books at the back of the room in which panels were held. The noise of their selling sometimes interfered with panels.

The program ran long on Sunday so the business meeting, at which the site of the next Bouchercon was to be announced, was cancelled. However, the "Dead Dog Party," a science-fiction convention custom, was on its way to becoming a Bouchercon tradition too: Those who did not have to leave early gathered for more good talk, including discussion of 1977's location: New York City.

1977: New York City

Bouchercon came to its most prestigious locale thus far, the Empire Room of New York's Waldorf-Astoria Hotel, during Columbus Day weekend, October 7–9. Otto Penzler and Chris Steinbrunner were co-chairmen, and they selected Stanley Ellin as Guest of Honor. Past complaints of lack of publicity for Bouchercons did not apply here. There was even a humorous article by Eric Pace in the *New York Times* commenting, "Admission to all these events is a steal at $20." Of the 351 people registered, 331 showed up. Over one-third (119) attended the banquet for another $20.

There was a separate room where Carol Brener, of Murder Ink, sold new and old books. There were also autographing sessions for attending authors. Nearby was the Bouchercon Mystery Art Exhibit, with works by William Teason and Frank McSherry among others.

On Friday evening, before the official opening, Carol and I went with John Nieminski and Pat Erhardt to our favorite French restaurant for dinner and enjoyable conversation. We returned to hear Phyllis White speak of Boucher's personal life and interests outside of mystery and science fiction.

This well-organized convention included imaginative panels and talks. There was one in which John M. Linsenmeyer, editor of *The Baker Street Journal*, portrayed Sherlock Holmes and was questioned by a panel of Sherlockians. Individual speakers included Al Nussbaum, the bank-robber-turned-crimewriter, who talked about his first "career"; Walter Gibson, who spoke about The Shadow and did magic tricks for an encore; and Brian Garfield, author of *Death Wish*. He expressed his unhappiness with the Charles Bronson film version because it appeared to advocate vigilantism. There were also talks by Phyllis Whitney on romantic suspense, by Himan Brown on old-time radio mysteries, and by Robert L. Fish, who appeared with a US Coast Guard lieutenant and discussed smuggling.

On Saturday night, there was the American premiere of Sax Rohmer's 1923 play, *The Eye of Siva*, in a condensed version by Bob Briney. Christianna Brand was in America again and, with anecdotes, delightfully introduced the film version of her *Green for Danger*.

At Sunday's luncheon, Stanley Ellin was "roasted" by fellow writers, editors, and even his wife. Garfield said that when Ellin, author of a famous story about cannibalism, was asked by the steward on a Cunard ship if he would like to see the menu, he replied, "No, bring me the passenger list." During the speeches, Isaac Asimov, busy perfecting his image as a dirty old man, "goosed" Eleanor Sullivan, much to her embarrassment, as he passed behind her. When Ellin got his chance to talk, he thanked Frederic Dannay, in attendance, for accepting his story when he was an unpublished author, but then he took his revenge on his roasters, turning their words against them.

Phyllis White, Anthony Boucher's widow, at one of the many panels she attended for 30 years.

1978: Chicago

I missed my first Bouchercon in five years when, in a neck brace due to a herniated cervical disk, I couldn't attend October 6–8 at the Bismarck Hotel in Chicago's Loop. Robert Hahn and John Nieminski, who co-chaired the 1975 Chicago Bouchercon, were joined by Professor Ely Liebow in putting on a successful meeting with about 150 people in attendance. All Sherlockians, they proved that not only science fiction fans could put on a mystery convention. In writing about it for *The Mystery Fancier*, Don Yates lauded the intimacy of the gathering and made an observation that seemed reasonable at the time: "Indeed, there may not be more than two hundred hard-core mystery fans to be convened anywhere at any one time—outside New York City—and, in any case, ever larger numbers are clearly not necessary to assure success."

Walter Gibson was, at eighty-one, the oldest Bouchercon Guest of Honor, and in addition to speaking wittily at the banquet, he again performed magic tricks. There was a panel on Chicago writers, and Mike Nevins spoke on Harry Stephen Keeler, painting so intriguing a picture of the eccentric writer that all Keeler books in the book room were quickly sold. Another panel discussed "new" writers such as Ruth Rendell and P. D. James, who obviously had not then achieved their present fame.

Bob Briney spoke about Anthony Boucher, Yates spoke of Agatha Christie, and John McAleer spoke of Rex Stout, subject of his Edgar-winning biography. The Chicago Sherlockian scion, Hugo's Companions, held one of their monthly meetings at the banquet, in the words of Sherlockian Yates, "to perpetrate their arcane rites and ceremonies" while initiating two new members. When a Sunday morning panel was about to be cancelled due to the non-appearance of a speaker, a lively ad-lib panel of editors of fan journals was substituted.

A notable part of the 1978 Bouchercon was the gatherings of fans that, after the formal sessions, went on into the early hours of each morning. Most party-friendly were the *DAPA-EM*ers, a group discussed elsewhere in this book. Hal Rice joined the *DAPA-EM* crowd by accident when in a darkened film room Nieminski mistook him for Bob Briney, another big, bearded gent, and invited him to a room party.

1979: Universal City, CA

The tenth Bouchercon at the Sheraton-Universal in Universal City, California, October 5–7, was especially sweet to me, having missed the previous year and arriving at it following a depressing week's visit in Los Angeles with my mother, who was ill. It provided a lift almost from the beginning: a dinner at which fans kicked around such arcane topics as the music referred to in Cornell Woolrich mysteries. Later that Friday evening was the first of many parties held over the years in Hal Rice's suite at Bouchercons.

Noreen Shaw was listed on the program as "Chairman" of this Bouchercon; her husband Larry edited the program. Attendance was again about 150. Saturday started for me with a private discussion about opera with Phyllis White, as knowledgeable on that subject as was her husband. There was a good panel on old-time radio and in the afternoon a funny, angry talk by Harlan Ellison, the science fiction writer who has written enough mysteries to have earned two Edgars. His targets: television executives and publishers.

The feature at Saturday night's banquet was the speech generally conceded to be the funniest ever presented at Bouchercon. Guest of Honor Tony Hillerman spoke about the inept bank robbers of Taos, New Mexico. There were gales of laughter, and Ellison laughed so hard he literally fell off his chair.

On Sunday, reformed bank robber Al Nussbaum discussed his fourteen years in prison. I moderated a panel on reviewing at which it was agreed that it is easier to pan a book than to praise it. Jon L. Breen spoke about the sports mysteries of Cortland Fitzsimmons, once popular but now forgotten. They are fun to hear about (and read), partly for their corniness. Sunday also had a great "Dead Dog" party, at which I finally agreed to join *DAPA-EM*, members Nieminski and Ellen Nehr having made it sound too appealing to miss.

8 DAPA-EM (1973–)

"What is a *DAPA-EM?*" is a question its members are often asked. *DAPA-EM* is short for Elementary, My Dear APA and is the only APA (Amateur Press Association) devoted to the mystery. *DAPA-EM* has become the core group of mystery fandom. Its members have chaired more than a dozen Bouchercons and been active in many more, as well as in regional conventions. In addition to producing their APA magazines, they write widely in the field, producing books and articles, usually for little or no remuneration. Because of their activities, eighteen of the twenty-five people honored as Fan Guests of Honor at Bouchercons through 2005 have been *DAPA-EM*ers. Many have been similarly honored at regional conventions.

DAPA-EM was founded in 1973, as a quarterly, by Donna Balopole of Floral Park, New York. There were six members then, one of whom, Jeff Smith, continues as of this writing. APAs are limited-membership groups whose members produce copies of their magazines, which they send to an Official Editor. He or she collates and mails them to members as well as keeping track of finances, a waitlist, and whether members meet the requirements of minimum activity ("minac"). Balopole, editor for the first twelve mailings, was replaced by Art Scott of California, a research chemist, in mailing #13. He had campaigned on a platform including a switch to bimonthly status and stronger recruitment efforts. He remains Official Editor. By 1980, the membership reached its current limit of thirty-five, and the total pages of each mailing were often more than 300; the first mailing had 27 pages.

To satisfy "minac," each member must submit at least four pages, three of which must be original material, every four months. The other requirements are minimal, mainly paying dues to cover mailing costs. The magazines members produce are as diverse as the individuals. The titles are also varied and often humorous. Among the titles in 2004 were Bill Crider's *Macavity*, named after T. S. Eliot's mystery cat, and Bob Briney's *'Contact' Is Not a Verb*, using a rule of grammar on which Nero Wolfe insisted.

Most members consider their mailing comments to other members the most important part of their magazine. In addition, members write about their personal lives, including travels and attendance at mystery conventions. Since many are collectors, they write of their "booking" experiences. For example, Crider told of finding $270 inside a used book he bought. Scott, a collector of old

Art Scott, "The Emperor," Official Editor of DAPA-EM for over 30 years.

paperbacks, was ejected from a bookstore in Buffalo, where he was booking with George Kelley, by a less-than-rational owner. Graeme Flanagan of Australia went booking in the only second-hand bookstore in Port Moresby, Papua, New Guinea.

Many members put considerable effort into their magazines Some write book reviews and articles. Scott (and others) include photographs taken at Bouchercons. Former member Dave Lewis did considerable research in writing about Frederick Nebel. I have written parodies and in an attempt at humor, I wrote "If I Were Official Editor," imagining the platform on which each member would run against Scott for that position. Obviously what I was writing was fantasy, since during my twenty-five years of membership no one has been willing to seek the office and do the work that he does.

*DAPA-EM*ers are interested in their history. For several years, Jeff Smith wrote "50 Mailings Ago," describing each mailing since the first. In May 1989, picking up with the 30th mailing, I began a column that I first called "A Touch of the Past," then "Down Memory Lane," but renamed with its present title, "Remembrances of Mailings Past," in July 1990.

Members have generally been American, though several lived in Canada, another in Australia, and two in England. Every region of the United States has been represented at one time or another. Backgrounds vary, with librarians, teachers, and government workers predominating. There have also been lawyers, policemen, a fireman, and a pharmacist. With 125 people having been members in the past or at present, space does not permit me to describe each, but some stand out and define *DAPA-EM*.

When Ellen Nehr died in 1995, she was called the "heart and soul of *DAPA-EM*." One year she came to Bouchercon wearing a t-shirt proclaiming her "*DAPA-EM* Den Mother." She enjoyed Bouchercons and *DAPA-EM* room parties so much that she complained loudly if World Series games were played on television, calling them distractions from the yearly conventions she so anticipated.

Ellen had been an officer in the US Air Force, and few were surprised to learn that, considering her strong opinions and personality. For dinner during the 1980 Bouchercon, thirty-one people, members of *DAPA-EM*, their spouses and friends, went to a restaurant where Nehr announced to the waiters, after everyone had been seated, "Separate checks." Yet, despite her hard-boiled exterior (which masked a soul of great generosity), she insisted on calling herself "a typical American housewife," and her reading tastes ran to the coziest of mysteries.

Ellen felt strongly about the authors she disliked, especially Robert B. Parker, creator of Spenser. She read one of his books only because she lost a bet. When I started my book on regional mysteries, she wrote me, "If you promise to leave Parker out of your New England listing, I promise to answer both the letters of complaint you get when the book is published." I decided Parker's Boston mysteries were too important to take advantage of her offer.

While Nehr disliked hardboiled crime fiction, she felt equally strongly about other types, opining, "You will never convince me that Sherlock Holmes is either readable or viewable." She recommended that people not read an Edgar-winning biography of S. S. Van Dine because he was "a nasty man." Yet, she loved scholarship

George Kelley, center, proves to Frank Denton, left, and Jeff Meyerson, right, that he's attending a Bouchercon.

and discovered a previously unknown pseudonym for Phoebe Atwood Taylor. Her book about the Doubleday Crime Club received an Edgar nomination and won an Anthony. Her *DAPA-EM* magazine, *The Apron String Affair*, was replete with "typos" and spelling errors, about which fellow members kidded her. She responded by asking for a moratorium on commenting on these, typically making a mistake when she wrote, "Typo's can happen to anyone."

At the1980 Bouchercon, when Jon Lellenberg chided John Nieminski for not wearing his convention badge, Nieminski immediately echoed the bandit chief in *The Treasure of the Sierra Madre*, saying, "Bahdgis? We doan need no steenking bahdgis." Behind Nieminski's scholarly exterior was a sense of humor that delighted his friends and those who read his magazine, *Somewhere a Roscoe*, whose title came from S. J. Perelman's parody of private eyes. Though he was not a professional writer, Nieminski's writing was often compared to Perelman's. He was also a serious bibliographer. Without a computer database system, Nieminski lovingly, using thousands of 3x5 cards, prepared indexes to *Ellery Queen's Mystery Magazine* and *Saint Mystery Magazine*.

George Kelley's "non-appearance" at Bouchercons became legendary. He had cancelled several times, but though he often attended and was seen by most of the membership, the joke continued to circulate that he had disappeared again. Kelley, a professor at the State University of New York at Buffalo, had one of the largest collections of paperback books in the world and donated 25,000 to his school's library. Andy Jaysnovitch's compulsive collecting of books, magazines, videotapes, and almost everything else has also become legendary.

Bill Crider wrote that he liked books about alligators in the sewers, and he even wrote an article about them. This became an in-joke in *DAPA-EM*, and at one Bouchercon, Criderwas presented with a hand puppet in the form of an alligator that was promptly named "Bill, Jr." Now retired chairman of the English department at Alvin

State College in Texas, Crider is also a prolific writer of crime fiction, in which he usually mentions his favorite soft drink, Dr Pepper.

Another Texan, Barry Gardner, joined *DAPA-EM* in 1992 after thirty-one years in the Dallas Fire Department, having risen to second in command. Jeff and Ann Smith expressed the feeling of most members when they said he "fit in so smoothly it was like he'd been there all along." Unfortunately, he wasn't there for long because he died suddenly of a heart attack in July 1996.

Steve Stilwell has been the leading exponent of what editor Scott has called "The Ferris Wheel theory of APA-ship," dropping off the roster and rejoining more times than anyone wants to count. When he is on the roster and writes, he is invariably worth reading. At Bouchercons, without obviously taking notes, he captures the best lines at parties. He represented *DAPA-EM* at the funerals of Gardner and Hal Rice. Though long married, with two grown daughters, Stilwell promotes the idea of himself as a ladies' man. Able to joke about his reputation, he once reported asking attractive mystery writer Deborah Crombie for a date, and being told she agreed if she could bring her husband along.

More untoward things happen to Richard Moore than to any other member. He has had multiple bouts of surgery, once for a broken shoulder when his dogs tripped him. His former boss was killed by a letter bomb from the Unabomber, and a friend was murdered in Washington, DC. Richard is *DAPA-EM*'s prime raconteur, captivating audiences at parties with tales of his Uncle Buren in Georgia and also the strange, uninsured motorist, known only as "Mr. Darko," who crashed into Moore's car. During a 2003 hurricane, a tree fell on Richard's car. Richard is another of *DAPA-EM*'s published mystery writers, with three novels and several short stories to his credit.

Richard Moore in his role of DAPA-EM raconteur.

Len and June Moffatt are considered the founding parents of Bouchercon. Their *DAPA-EM* magazine is called *A Flash of Blue*, a tribute to John D. MacDonald, who used a color in each Travis McGee title. They have long been active in science-fiction fandom too, and in 1951 Len was "Tuckerized" by Wilson Tucker, whose name is now used for the practice of including real people as fictional characters in books.

Though usually only seeing each other once a year, *DAPA-EM*ers consider themselves part of a family. Typically, two-thirds of the membership attends a Boucher-con, and for many of them the *DAPA-EM* room parties are convention highlights. For many years Hal and Sonya Rice would take a suite and generously host these parties. A smoker himself, Hal would leave his own room to have a cigarette rather than subject people to second-hand smoke. Though little alcohol is consumed, these parties are scenes of considerable mirth, especially when Richard Moore has the floor.

*DAPA-EM*ers care for fellow members. When newcomer Sandra Scoppettone was nervous about attending her first Bouchercon, Ellen Nehr took her under her wing and introduced Sandra around. When Ellen moved, fellow Ohio member Jo Ann Vicarel helped her. Leslie Slaasted, then the youngest female member of *DAPA-EM*, was bothered by a stalker at one Malice Domestic conference until Richard Moore threatened him.

Members have felt they could share the good and bad in life with each other, telling of marriage problems and illnesses (even alcoholism), and deaths in the family. Earthquakes, fires, and riots in California led to phone calls to members there, inquiring about their safety. Learning that Bob Briney was hospitalized, members of *DAPA-EM* telephoned him from the Omaha convention in 1990 to wish him well. When members Larry French, Jud Sapp, Trevor Cotton, John Nieminski, Ellen Nehr, Barry Gardner, Don Sandstrom, Hal Rice, and David Rose died, one could sense genuine sadness in the tributes paid them. During Sandstrom's terminal illness, members came from California, New Mexico, New York, and Wisconsin to visit him in Indianapolis. Two months after Hal Rice's death, his wife Sonya and son, Hal Jr., came to the Austin Bouchercon Hal had been planning to attend. They said they felt they were with friends. Cotton was the first English member; his magazine was called *My Body Lies Over the Ocean*. When he learned that Jeff Meyerson and his wife, whom he had never met, would be in England at the time of his daughter's wedding, he invited them. In 1986, the Meyersons threw one of their parties in Brooklyn to celebrate a Special Edgar won by Walter Albert.

When the mystery writer Michael Dibdin labeled mystery fans "nerds," *DAPA-EM* was quick to respond, pointing out how little he knew of fandom. Another writer, Robert J. Randisi, took what they considered a "cheap shot" at *DAPA-EM* in the Spring, 1983, issue of *The Armchair Detective* when he complained about that magazine's Rex Stout and Dorothy L. Sayers newsletters, claiming *TAD* was turning into "another *DAPA-EM*." There was no comparison, and it seemed unlikely Randisi had ever seen a mailing. However, his animus toward *DAPA-EM* may have been caused by his experience at the 1981 Milwaukee Bouchercon when he "crashed" a *DAPA-EM* party. His gratuitously foul language (*DAPA-EM*ers are not prudes) brought silence, and he left, realizing he was not welcome.

If *DAPA-EM* is a family, it is occasionally a dysfunctional one. Guy Townsend, whose writing in *TAD* and editorship of *The Mystery Fancier* was controversial, proved equally so during his *DAPA-EM* stay. He complained when he was dropped because he had been two pages short of "minac." He felt his past contributions warranted an exception. However, Scott, better known as "the Emperor," said that with people on the waitlist, and without a substantive reason, it was not fair to make an exception. However, Scott has always been willing to excuse members when they have reasons such as illness, death in the family, or moving.

Townsend accepted "demotion" to the waitlist and continued to contribute, eventually coming back to the roster. During this period he engaged in feuds and accused members of conformity and lack of courage, dubbing the membership "old maids" and "a knitting circle." He proposed that annually the membership cast ballots for the five least productive members, who would be then be dropped to the waitlist. While a few thought there was merit in encouraging some members to submit more substantive magazines, the majority were against Townsend's proposal. Frank Denton said he would not remain a member if this went into effect, and David Doerrer asked, "Do we really want performance evaluations as part of *DAPA-EM* membership?" Townsend's plan was voted down, and Guy sarcastically apologized for "overestimating" the membership and soon resigned.

Walter and Jean Shine were members for only a few years. After quitting, they sent a missive, only signed "Erstwhile Member," that a current member allowed to be franked into the mailing with his magazine. In their letter they complained about those "who regard their daily activities however pedestrian as worthy of perpetuity" in the mailings. They singled out people who wrote about their pets. Members pointed out that no one had forced the Shines to read anyone's magazine in its entirety, and it was personal touches that made *DAPA-EM* unique.

When David George of Vancouver joined he, as do most new members, included a brief biography. He said he had gone from the United States to live in Canada because he did not believe in the Vietnam War. Bob Napier, who had served in Vietnam, expressed his displeasure with this viewpoint because it meant that someone else had to be drafted while George avoided service. However, David George's biggest contretemps proved to be with another member, Bill Trojan.

Trojan brought up the issue of unpaid bookstore debts allegedly owed by George to friends of Trojan who resided in the US. George denied the debt, claiming Trojan had raised the issue "because I know about his relationship with my ex-wife." He variously asked that Trojan be expelled, censured, or required to apologize.

Most members wisely said they did not have the facts to make a judgment as to who was right. Trojan apologized—though not to George—to the membership for having raised the issue in *DAPA-EM*. However, the matter still was not over.

George asked Scott, "Will you please, as Official Editor, request that he [Trojan] cease and desist from mentioning the matter any further." The Emperor blew his editorial top and told George, "NO, I will not tell Bill Trojan—or anybody else—what he may or may not discuss in his zines.… I am not a Censor, I am not an Ayatollah, I am not your Mommy, David. Fight your own goddamn battles." As an aside, Scott said, "Revealing the ending to a murder mystery without a warning is 'conduct unbecoming a member of *DAPA-EM*,' and that's about the only action that qualifies." George then accused Scott of "offensive statements about him" and asked for an apology—which he did not get. David George soon left *DAPA-EM*.

There were other disagreements in *DAPA-EM*, but they were resolved more amicably, or at least did not go on as long as the George-Trojan War. Dan Stumpf and Bob Napier disagreed rather heatedly about the film *High Noon*, which the latter liked. Stumpf complained about my puns, and I was amused by his remarks, even

Sonya and Hal Rice, hosts to many DAPA-EM parties at Bouchercon.

more so when one year in the annual Prestige Poll I received two votes as best *DAPA-EM* humorist, while there were three votes for "anybody but Lachman."

In his fanzine, Walter Albert's wife, Peggy, favorably reviewed mysteries by three black females, including BarbaraNeely, alleging they had been discriminated against. When some members questioned how good Neely's books were and wondered if there was proof of discrimination, Peggy Albert claimed that *DAPA-EM* males "hate" Neely. Tom Robinson, who was briefly a member, left after others remarked that what he was writing in his magazine had more to do with issues of gay rights than mystery fiction.

By 2005, it was quite common to have fewer than thiry-five people on the roster, with no one on the waitlist. Those remaining seemed as enthusiastic as ever; half had produced at least one hundred issues of their magazines. They generally responded to others via mailing comments, even if family and writing commitments reduced the size and amount of original material in their fanzines. An exception was new-comer Steve Steinbock, whose magazines were well-illustrated and imaginative. One issue was devoted entirely to mysteries connected with Lewis Carroll.

The biggest long-range problem for DAPA-EM is that it has an aging roster; the average age is about fifty-five, and few members are as young as forty. Younger fans, with whom DAPA-EMers talk at mystery conventions, do not seem interested in the amount of work and commitment needed to produce even a small bimonthly magazine, especially in a world in which one can communicate with other fans via cyberspace.

9   Mystery∗File (1974–)

No other fan magazine has risen, phoenix-like, from self-imposed ashes more often than Steve Lewis's *Mystery∗File*. Lewis, a mathematics professor at Central Connecticut State College, started it in the spring of 1974 as "a combination fanzine and sales list." After seven issues, it had its first hiatus but soon reappeared, though not always as an independent magazine. It was part of Don Miller's *Mystery Nook*, where Lewis was briefly Associate Editor, and then in *The Mystery Fancier's* preview issue of November1976, continuing for *TMF's* first six years. Sporadically, it was Lewis's magazine in *DAPA-EM*. Sometimes his magazine would be called *Fatal Kiss,* and occasionally *Fatal Kiss* would be the title of the review portion of his magazine.

Lewis resumed publishing *Mystery∗File* as his own magazine with issue #26 in December 1990. Ten of twenty-four pages consisted of Lewis's mystery and movie reviews. Another five of the pages were "Fatal Kiss: A Letter Column." However, he also had reviews by Dorothy Nathan, Kathi Maio, and Sue Feder, plus Ellen Nehr's column "Murder Ad Lib," consisting of reviews and interviews. Beginning with #29, Maryell Cleary wrote a column "Vintage Crime" in which she discussed classic writers such as Mary Roberts Rinehart, and H. C. Bailey.

There was another hiatus after issue #34 in 1991, but when *Deadly Pleasures* began in 1993, Lewis was part of it, suspending his own magazine again, with a review column under the punny title "Fatal Quiche" in the second and third issues. The latter column was numbered *Mystery∗File* #35. Lewis then did reviews as *Mystery∗File* #36–38 in the next three issues and again in the twelfth issue with what was apparently intended as #39, though it was not numbered.

In December 2003 Lewis began his most ambitious incarnation of *Mystery∗File* with issue #40. He said it was "not to be an up-to-date newsletter for the field, but a place where old

Steve Lewis, founder of *Mystery∗File,* and one of his columnists, DAPA-EM "den mother" Ellen Nehr.

and new works co-exist, where older mysteries can be brought up and discussed as well as those by the most recent hot authors, and where the careers of writers can be looked at in perspective. *Mystery*File* will be for those fans who love to read and talk about mysteries and series characters, and those who love to make checklists and those who love to have them, and if you can assist in accomplishing any of these goals, then so much the better."

Lewis attracted knowledgeable fans who liked writing about mystery's past because the other current American fan magazines were specializing in reviews of new books. Al Hubin wrote "Addenda to Crime Fiction IV," correcting and updating his bibliography which had gone through the year 2000 in its final edition. Bill Crider wrote about (and reviewed) legendary paperback originals in "The Gold Medal Corner." Mike Nevins had a column of autobiographical mystery commentary called "First You Read, Then You Write." I had a column of reviews and miscellanea called "The Crime of My Life." Lewis encouraged my penchant for puns by naming his letters column, at my suggestion, "Scarlet Letters," and not complaining when I called my film review section "Déjà View."

In line with Lewis's plan to cover past writers in depth, much of *Mystery*File* #42 was devoted to Robert Wade, best known as co-author of the Wade Miller mysteries of the 1940s and 1950s. There were five articles about him and an interview with him. #45 had Ed Lynskey's article on Ed Lacy, probably the best writing ever on that almost forgotten writer. #46 had an article, interview, and bibliography of Jonathan Latimer (1906–1983). In February 2005 Lewis added *The Crime Fiction Research Journal* to *Mystery*File*'s title to reflect the direction in which his readers had taken it.

10 The Mystery FANcier (1976–1992)

Because of its editor, Guy M. Townsend, *The Mystery FANcier* was not only one of the earliest but one of the best-remembered fan journals. It started with a preview issue in November 1976, in which Townsend set forth his reason for launching this bi-monthly magazine: his belief that there was room for another general fan magazine. What he wanted in *TMF* was "a balance of articles, reviews, and letters," but the third category gave *TMF* its special flavor. Townsend noted a lack of disputation in the letters to *The Armchair Detective* then. He hoped to see in *TMF* "a lively letter column with, perhaps, a healthy mixture of back-patting and back-stabbing.... The letter column will be open to all opinions, provided they are literately expressed and not libelous." He planned to give contributors of "articles, reviews, or substantial letters of comment" credit against the subscription price, one issue for each submission.

Townsend achieved his aim of producing a frequently impassioned magazine because of his own persona and strong opinions. At the time he launched the magazine, he was living in Memphis, Tennessee, and teaching history in college. He eventually became peripatetic, residing at four different Memphis addresses during the first two years of *TMF* and then moving to Arkansas, Indiana, Pennsylvania, and back to Indiana.

TMF was greeted with the same enthusiasm shown early *TAD*. People wrote of "devouring" each issue on the day it arrived. In March 1978 Jo Ann Vicarel contrasted it with *TAD*, which she said now had "too many Ph.D.s, too many scholarly works, too much name dropping." She gave praise to *TMF* that was unique in mystery fandom. "When I went to the hospital to give birth to my daughter at the end of September, my husband noted that I was clutching the latest issue of *TMF* to read between contractions and Lamaze breathing." Another reader, Sandy Sandulo, sent a picture of herself reading *TMF* while she donated blood. Nurse Linda Toole wrote of discovering a stack of unread *TMF*s at 1:00 AM. "I succumbed, and the next thing I knew the birds were singing, the sun was rising, and it was 5:00 AM! A bit tough when you have to go to work that day. It was, however, time well spent."

By the second volume Townsend was engaging in some of the feuds that kept *TMF* interesting. While printing reviews by Martin Morse Wooster, he questioned Wooster's opinions and expressed his anger at having to correct his copy, which used British spelling—Townsend regarded this as an affectation because Wooster is American.

A feature of *TMF* editorials was Townsend's explanations of why issues were late. Most often the post office or his printer was at fault, though he was also willing to blame himself and his hectic life. In 1978, when he announced a price increase from $7.50 for six issues to $9, Townsend took an approach that was direct, but not likely to win popularity contests, when he said, "frankly, I don't care to hear any negative comments about the increase. If any of *TMF*'s current subscribers feel that the increase is unjustified, kindly send me an SASE and I will send you explicit instructions as to what you can do with your cheapskate opinions."

The contents of *TMF* were not terribly different from early *TAD*. They included checklists of collectible paperbacks; Bouchercon reports; chapters from Michael Avallone's biography-in-progress, *Death of a .300 Hitter;* and a book-by-book analysis of the Nero Wolfe saga by Townsend. Robert Sampson wrote about detectives in pulp magazines, and Jeff Banks became *TMF*'s resident expert on nostalgia, with articles about old radio, movie serials, "B" films, and comic books.

There was room for humor. William F. Deeck's "Further Gems from the Literature" was a running compendium of inadvertently funny lines from mysteries. Using the mock scholarship beloved of Sherlockians, I provided a chronology of the life of Gideon Fell, one that suggested he had murdered his wife.

Larry French, a leading expert on the works of John Dickson Carr, had already written a serious article on Carr for *TMF* and was kind to my effort. Then the cover of Vol. 3 (1979), No. 1, carried an obituary for French who was killed in an auto accident on an icy road. He was the first of the new breed of mystery fans to die.

In July 1978 I began "It's About Crime," the column I would write for *TMF*'s remaining fourteen years. It included various features, besides reviews, that I still write for fan magazines: "Death of a Mystery Writer" (obituaries), "Doom with a View" (reviews of mystery movies and television), and "The Short Stop" (reviews of short stories). Al Hubin, Sue Feder, and Deeck were among *TMF*'s other reviewers.

TMF drew arguments as a flame draws moths. Bill Loeser boasted of "my new campaign to have my say, speak my mind, and thereby make myself obnoxious to everyone else." He was so critical of a Jane Bakerman article that Townsend joked that Loeser was "wise to use a post office box number instead of a street address." Loeser called himself "The Curmudgeon in the Corner" and claimed that real criticism of mystery fiction was not possible without giving away the solution or important plot elements of books. He proceeded to do this with Christie's *The Murder of Roger Ackroyd* and Carr's *Death Turns the Tables*. In the next issue, I disputed him and wondered if Loeser (or Townsend) had considered giving readers advance warning there would be plot disclosures. Eventually, Loeser claimed he was retiring from writing to *TMF* and its "fannish bleat" and had given up reading mysteries. In the same issue, Carl Larsen praised *TMF*'s letters column, "The Documents in the Case," as "a form of New England town meeting with everyone demonstrating his belief in equality through open discussion."

In his Vol. 4 (1980), No. 5 , editorial, Townsend wrote of the time and labor *TMF* entailed, which he wouldn't mind if he weren't also losing money. He gave readers a choice as he contemplated raising the subscription price of Vol. 5 to $12 for six issues, asking them to commit to that price. "If I get at least 100 commitments, *TMF* will continue; if I get 99 or fewer, volume 4, number 6, will be the last issue of *TMF* ever printed." More than one hundred agreed. John Nieminski was glad though he said he would have taken over *TMF* if Townsend ceased publication.

The early 1980s was a period of relative growth for *TMF*, with its paid circulation more than doubling from 214 in September 1981 to 445 in November 1982, as a result of an advertising "blitz" that including giving out a thousand free issues to prospec-

Bibliographer John Nieminski (l.) and Guy Townsend, controversial editor-publisher of *The Mystery Fancier*..

tive subscribers. Townsend was embarked on what he termed a "publishing empire" known as Brownstone Books, its name taken from the West 35th Street brownstone in which his favorite detective, Nero Wolfe, resided. Townsend had moved to his wife's hometown, Madison, Indiana, ending his travels temporarily. Brownstone achieved notable successes, if not a great deal of money. It began with a facsimile edition of the first volume of *TAD*. It also published Walter Albert's Edgar-winning bibliography of secondary sources, and about a dozen chapbooks.

Strong opinions were frequent in *TMF*. In Melinda Reynolds's "Women Mystery Writers: Thanks, But No Thanks," she said she was unable to enjoy (or in some cases even finish) such highly regarded authors as Dorothy L. Sayers, Ngaio Marsh, P. D. James, Margery Allingham, and Josephine Tey. Teri White, a hard-boiled novelist, agreed with Reynolds, though recommending the work of new female authors such as Marcia Muller. Linda Toole also agreed with Reynolds, though she did recommend Lucille Kallen.

Whatever stability Townsend achieved was vanishing in 1983. Half of his new subscribers failed to renew, so he was left with a circulation of about 300. He made the decision, announced in the Nov.–Dec. 1983 issue, to go to law school, while keeping a full-time job. Furthermore, he would be commuting from Madison, Indiana, to law school in northern Kentucky, a round-trip of 150 miles. Because of other commitments, Nieminski couldn't take over the magazine, but Steve Stilwell of Minneapolis agreed to assume all editorial duties while Townsend was in law school, with the latter handling publishing, mailing, and subscriptions. In announcing the transition, Townsend said, "Some of you may be leery about continuing your subscriptions, or submitting contributions, under an as yet unknown editorship—although, God knows, if you've put up with my editorial capriciousness over the past seven years the unknown should hold no terrors for you." He then listed Stilwell's credentials, concluding, "He is brash, opinionated, obstinate, ornery, and obnoxious—in other words, you probably won't notice any difference when I'm gone."

After the March/April 1984 issue, it became apparent that Stilwell's understanding of the arrangement by which he had become interim editor differed substantially from Townsend's. Matters came to a head when Stilwell cut part of a Townsend letter regarding Jon L. Breen's novel, *The Gathering Place*. The deleted portion, not a large one, concerned a character in the book who had a typing speed of 200 words per minute (a speed I, too, had questioned in my review of that book). When Townsend protested, Stilwell replied that his cutting of the material was within his purview as editor. He then told Townsend to fire him if he were dissatisfied with the job he was doing. Townsend did so and suspended the magazine, bringing it back in July/August 1986, after finishing law school.

Townsend resumed *TMF* with wrangling, of course. Not having much material for his return issue, due to the hiatus, he allowed himself eight pages for his editorial. After recounting some of his law school experiences, he devoted his attention to *Mystery & Detection Monthly* and Bob Napier's ban on mention of L. A. Morse. (See the chapter on *MDM*.) Townsend accused Napier of being a censor rather than an editor by not publishing letters about Morse that disagreed with him. Some letter writers agreed with Townsend, while others felt Napier, as editor, had the right to decide what went into his magazine. In Vol. 8 (1986), No. 6, Townsend used his editorial to summarize his disagreement with Napier. Otto Penzler, referring to what he called Townsend's "one-dimensional political harangues," said, "Stuff it. If you want to publish a politically oriented fanzine, go ahead. But don't call it a mystery fiction fanzine."

The argument with Napier was largely over in Vol. 9. Townsend was assessing his problems of time and finances and said he would have to publish quarterly instead of bimonthly. Also, he would increase the price from $15 to $25. Furthermore, that rate was predicated on his having at least 200 subscribers. In another ultimatum, he said he would have to cease publication at the end of Vol. 9 if he didn't.

In Vol. 9 (1987), No. 4, Townsend announced that *TMF* would continue because 114 of 130 readers who responded were willing to pay the higher rate and, furthermore, he had received a check for $1,000 from an anonymous benefactor to help keep the magazine alive. My own attempts at detecting the identity of this patron were unsuccessful. I suspected Bill Deeck because at about this time he was especially active in *TMF*, contributing many articles and reviews and volunteering to type several long articles by others. Townsend rightly called him "a prince among princes." However, when I asked Deeck, near the end of his life, he denied being the donor, so I must leave that generous person nameless.

Most of Vol. 9, No. 6, was devoted to Mike Nevins's article covering the last years of Cornell Woolrich. Townsend had ended his brief experiment in paying his contributors and then announced that he would only accept contributions from subscribers so, in essence, one had to pay to have one's writing published in *TMF*. In that issue, Townsend explained his reasons. He said his goal was not to increase subscribers and, in fact, he might have lost some by his policy. However, he wanted *TMF* to be a forum for mystery fans and thought that people who wrote for it should be willing to pay for and read it regularly. "There's something vaguely dishonest about expressing an opinion to an audience and then refusing to listen to the audience's response."

The quarterly *TMF* in Vol. 10 (1988) had a slightly changed, more attractive format, and each issue was larger at 104 pages. It also had *TMF*'s first Associate Editor, Bill Deeck, beginning with No. 2. Besides spending many hours putting *TMF*'s contents on disk, Deeck was preparing an index for *TMF* and wrote a column, "The Backward Reviewer," in which he reviewed older mysteries.

Unable (or unwilling) to avoid provocation, Townsend in Vol. 10, No. 3, went back to bashing Tey's *The Daughter of Time*, accusing her of intellectual dishonesty and saying she had maligned the profession of historian. However, in Vol. 8, No. 5, Townsend had used his editorial column to take umbrage at *The Drood Review*'s criticism of his own novel, *To Prove a Villain*, in which he supported the belief that Richard III was guilty of the murder of "The Princes in the Tower." As a historian, Townsend objected to the *Drood* reviewer questioning his accuracy.

Vol. 10, No. 4 saw a new review column, one that would stay with *TMF* until its demise. "The Armchair Reviewer" was Allen J. Hubin, the man with the best claim to using that title. Townsend had complained in the previous issue that he needed more material. Of the 104 pages in this issue, 45 consisted of Deeck's Index to Vols. 6 and 7, and another 40 of William A. S. Sarjeant's article on Sara Woods.

The unknown sponsor donated $500 to help *TMF* into its 11th volume (1989). Vol. 11, No. 2, was mailed *before* Vol. 11, No. 1, with Townsend blaming the delay on its printer. Naturally, there were no letters in No. 2 because readers had not received the prior issue. However, Vol. 11, No. 3, had twenty pages of letters.

The anonymous *TMF* backer struck again with $500 to begin Vol. 12 (1990). Townsend announced that he was running for District Attorney of Jefferson County, Indiana. (He was elected and served in that job until 1994.) Sarjeant began an interesting new column in that issue, "Crime Novelists as Writers of Children's Fiction," with a piece on Manning Coles. Townsend's eccentric mailing continued, and that issue was mailed only a week before No. 2.

The 13th volume of *TMF* began with announcement of receipt of another $500 from its unnamed friend. In Vol. 13, No. 2 (Spring 1991), Townsend announced that *TMF* would cease publication after the final issue in that volume. He was down to about 100 subscribers, and the magazine took a great deal of his time, though Deeck was doing much of the work.

Townsend graciously said goodbye in Vol. 13 No. 4 (Fall 1992), noting how much richer *TMF* had made him, not financially but in terms of contacts with other mystery fans. "So to all of you who have subscribed to *TMF* over the years, I thank you for giving me the privilege of doing this. To all of you who have written articles and letters and reviews, I thank you for giving me, free, things of such great value."

Townsend did not leave crime and the mystery entirely. He continued to publish books about the mystery. With Joe L. Hensley he published a crime novel, *Loose Coins*. As District Attorney of Jefferson County he received national coverage when he prosecuted the perpetrators of a horrific crime in which four teen-age girls killed a 12-year-old schoolmate. In a 1995 interview in the *Indianapolis Star*, Townsend said, "The entire case was gruesome and depressing and I needed something to take my mind off the case once in a while." He turned to an old hobby as an amateur magician and eventually opened a magic store in Jeffersonville, Indiana. He is now a prosecuting attorney in Indiana.

11 The Poisoned Pen (1978–1987)

Jeff Meyerson began *The Poisoned Pen* (*TPP*), his mimeographed magazine for *DAPA-EM*, in February 1977. The first issue was only six pages, but by the second, the page count increased to sixteen, and Meyerson, sending copies to a wider audience than *DAPA-EM*, received letters from non-members such as Al Hubin, Mike Nevins, and Bill Pronzini. He even received articles and checklists.

The Poisoned Pen became a bimonthly, general-circulation fan magazine in January 1978 and eventually reached a circulation of about 250. In his first editorial, "The Pen Rambles," Meyerson said the direction of the magazine was in the hands of its readers, depending on what they submitted to be published. He did not want *TPP* to be merely a forum for the current mystery scene, saying, "Reviews can be of any mystery, new or old, though I'd especially like the older, out-of-print titles, obscure or otherwise." The contents of *TPP* were similar to its contemporary *The Mystery Fancier*, though the editorial voice of Meyerson was more relaxed and less contentious than Guy Townsend's.

The first issue contained "All Too True" by Mary Groff, starting her long series about fiction that was suggested by true crime. Mary Ann Grochowski contributed a Sherlockian parody, set in Poland. Also in the first issue was Neville Wood's article on "The Golden Age," based on a speech he gave to the Cambridge Old Boys Book Club. R. Jeff Banks began "Mystery Plus," his series on books with a crime element that are "not labeled so that they will appeal to mystery fans" (usually Westerns, science fiction, or horror).

In the second issue I began a series called "Department of Unknown Mystery Writers" about those who "have written at least one good mystery and yet have either received little attention or else are almost forgotten now." I started with an article on William Krasner, who had not published a mystery in twenty years. A couple of years after my article, he published two new novels, though I'm sure there was no connection.

Sometimes, material in *TPP* took on a life of its own. I included South African writer Peter Godfrey as one of my "Unknown Writers." Bob Adey, searching for a possible Godfrey short story collection published in South Africa, wrote to him and received three letters (reprinted in *TPP)* that provided considerable additional information about him. In 2001, Godfrey was no longer unknown when Crippen & Landru published the first American collection of his stories.

Other articles in the early issues included Howard Waterhouse on Roy Vickers, Maryell Cleary on Elizabeth Daly, Steve Lewis on old-time radio programs, and Barry Pike regarding David Williams. There were checklists of the Mercury, Bestseller, and Jonathan Press digest-sized books, the short stories of John Lutz, and the contents of *Mystery League*.

It wasn't all solemn. Philip Asdell wrote about E. C. Bentley's humorous poetry, the clerihews. After giving some examples, Asdell contributed his own. Ola Strøm of Norway also included a few, saying "Too many people are taking mystery fiction much too seriously these days—a more balanced view is sorely needed." Gary Crew, punning that he was "fairly well-versed in crime," submitted some, and Jane Gottschalk provided ten.

I wrote one of my speculative articles, "The Detective Who Would Be King," in which I drew "evidence" from Margery Allingham's Albert Campion series "proving" that Campion was really a fictionalized version of British King Edward VIII, who abdicated the throne in 1936. I received three letters disagreeing, including one from Barry Pike of England in which he said George VI was Campion's more likely source.

The dissents regarding Campion were in good humor, unlike what greeted the article I wrote regarding Elizabeth Linington's Luis Mendoza. I said that her intrusive right-wing politics was spoiling the series. I gave examples of her reactionary views, including her saying that women who wear miniskirts invite rape. Rinehart Potts, who published the *Linington Lineup*, asserted that I was against freedom of speech for Linington. Jon L. Breen and Bob Briney, in letters to *TPP*, defended me. Breen was unable to understand how Potts could consider me "some kind of a wild-eyed left-wing revolutionary," since I am generally considered rather conservative (I usually wear a tie).

Another series was Pike's "Pen Profiles," brief biographies and bibliographies of English writers. He eventually published thirty-four of these in *TPP*. In "First Appearances," Cleary wrote of the first mysteries in which well-known series characters appear. Waterhouse, one of the earliest contributors, died of a heart attack early in 1980. Ironically, he had just purchased the mystery collection of Don Miller of *Mystery Nook*, when the latter was seriously ill with cancer. Miller outlived Waterhouse by two years.

The contents of *TPP* were lively, and Joe R. Lansdale favorably compared it to *TAD*, which he considered "stuffy." Jim McCahery said *TPP* "exemplifies the best in serious scholarship without undue erudition; it is clearly a vehicle *by* mystery lovers *for* mystery lovers." Reviews were often negative, warning people away from books. Two decades later, almost all reviews in US fan magazines are favorable.

By the start of Vol. 5, dated July 1982, *TPP* became a quarterly. The pressures of putting out a regular fanzine had led to a six-month delay between the last issue of Vol. 4 and the first of Vol. 5. Other delays followed, and Meyerson announced in Vol. 6, No. 3 (Fall 1985), that *TPP* would be "irregularly published," something already apparent. Letters were fewer due to irregular publication, and *TPP* was suspended indefinitely after Vol. 7, No. 1 (Fall/Winter 1987), finally appeared—one year following the previous issue. Meyerson announced that he was no longer accepting subscriptions but would publish on an issue-by-issue basis. To date, it has not reappeared.

12 Other Fan Magazines, Organizations, & Conventions: 1970s

Pulp (1970–1981)

Interest in pulp magazines continued in the 1970s, partly due to a new generation of fans, too young to have read them when they were originally published. *The Pulps* (1970), edited by Tony Goodstone, was a survey of pulp magazines. It included fifty stories and one hundred full-color cover illustrations, capturing the essence of the pulps for a new generation. That same year the first issue of *Pulp*, a magazine edited by Robert Weinberg, one of the younger fans, was published. The emphasis from the start was on heroes, including those whose adventures were crime-related. There were interviews with Walter Gibson, creator of The Shadow, and Frederick C. Davis, a prolific writer of pulp stories and crime novels. Files from Popular Publications provided bibliographic material, allowing fans to identify some of those who wrote pulp stories under "house names." *Pulp*'s publication schedule was erratic; it seldom published more than one issue a year before ceasing in 1981.

The Mystery Trader (1971–1980)

Long active in science fiction fandom, Ethel Lindsay, a retired Scottish nursing officer, started *The Mystery Trader* in June 1971. As its title indicates, it was a magazine for selling and trading mysteries and included fans' want-lists. By the third issue in 1972, it became a general fanzine, with a subscription base extending beyond Great Britain. Bob Adey wrote articles about impossible crimes. John A. Hogan wrote about Edgar Wallace. Francis M. Nevins, Mary Groff, and Derek J. Adley were other contributors. There were also reviews, news, and letters. After twenty-one issues, the last July 1980, Lindsay retired from publishing, though she continued writing letters to other fan magazines.

Jury (1971–)

Also in 1971, Bertil Widerberg started *Jury*, a quarterly journal that, though in Swedish, attempts to be international in scope and is still published. It includes articles, interviews, reviews, and occasionally short stories.

Pulpcon, Paperbacks and Other Media Conventions (1972–)

Pulpcon, a conference for fans of pulp magazines, started in 1972. The most popular magazines during the pulps' Golden Age (1925–1945) included *Black Mask*, *Dime Detective*, and *Spicy Mystery*. Though generally held in Ohio (most recently in Dayton), Pulpcon has been held in New Jersey, Arizona, and California. Pulpcon has honored mystery writers Hugh Cave, Michael Avallone, and Francis M. Nevins, among others, as Guests of Honor.

Following the successful paperback reprints of Mickey Spillane's Mike Hammer books, paperback originals became very popular, eventually dealing a death blow to pulp magazines already in poor financial shape. These books, especially those in Fawcett's Gold Medal line, are collectible, especially

Pulpcon regulars (l. to r.) Walter Albert, Randy Cox, and Bob Briney.

by those who are also mystery fans. Part of the reason is the quality of writing, since writers as good as John D. MacDonald had their first successes in paperback originals. The cover art work, often of attractive women in various states of undress, has been the subject of slide shows at Bouchercons, and some fans are frank enough to say they collect mysteries as much for the covers as for any reason, using "GGA" (Good Girl Art) as their politically incorrect abbreviation. The late Lance Casebeer, called the Godfather of paperback collecting, put on a small annual convention, **Lancecon**, at his Oregon home for friends and diehard collectors. On a larger scale are **Lessercon**, the paperback show in the Los Angeles area organized by Tom Lesser; the **NYC Collectible Paperback & Pulp Fiction Expo** in Manhattan, organized by Gary Lovisi; and several London paperback shows. Doug Ellis sponsored the 2004 **Windy City Pulp & Paperback Convention** in Chicago.

Fans of "**old-time radio**" (OTR) are often mystery fans because some of the great fictional sleuths, including Ellery Queen, Nero Wolfe, Mr. and Mrs. North, and Sam Spade, had their own programs. There were such popular non-detective shows as *Suspense* and *Escape*. There are various regional old-time radio groups, with conferences in Seattle, Newark, New Jersey, and Los Angeles, among other locations.

Fans of mysteries seem, more often than not, to be fans of mystery films. **Cinefest** is held each winter near Syracuse, New York. There is also **Cinevent**, held for over thirty years in Columbus, Ohio, and **Cinecon**, a Labor Day Weekend film festival held for the last forty years in Hollywood. All show obscure mysteries, for example the silent film *The Cat and the Canary*, seldom seen elsewhere. Especially mystery-related are *film noir* festivals. The oldest of these is probably the one held at the Seattle Art Museum since 1977. Similar events have been held in the last decade in New York, Palm Springs, Los Angeles, San Francisco, and Santa Fe, New Mexico.

James Bond Clubs (1972–)

The popularity of Ian Fleming's character led in 1972 to the **James Bond 007 Fan Club**, founded by two high-school students, Richard Schenkman and Bob Forlini of Yonkers, NY. Forlini dropped out, leaving Schenkman to run the club, which grew in the 1980s to 1,600 members, mostly males in their twenties. An article about the club in *Playboy* helped swell the membership. In the summer of 1974, it began to publish *Bondage*, a semiannual journal which emphasized interviews with those connected with Bond films. The magazine, no longer printed, carried considerable advertising of movie posters, pins, tee-shirts, etc.

The **James Bond International Fan Club**, founded in 1979, is still healthy as of 2005, with members in forty countries and operating many websites, including such unusual web locations as "Roger Moore, a Polish Fan Site." JBIFC publishes *007 (Double-O-Seven) Magazine*. Like its predecessor, the emphasis is on the screen versions of Fleming's work. Special events are held at Pinewood Studios, London's Odeon Theatre, and Planet Hollywood.

Other Doc Savage Magazines (1973–1991)

The success of Bantam's Doc Savage reprints led to *The Doc Savage Reader*, a mimeographed magazine whose first issue (January 1973) was published by John Cosgriff of Illinois, and Mark J. Golden of Virginia. Golden published the remaining three issues. Other commitments forced this magazine to be discontinued after October 1973; its circulation then was 125. *The Doc Savage Reader* was notable for the earliest fan writing of Will Murray, later a prolific writer of action novels, and the appearance in all issues of Dave McDonnell's satire "Doc Garbage."

Murray was also a contributor to the similarly titled *The Doc Savage Club Reader*, begun by Frank Lewandowski of Berwyn, Illinois, as an outgrowth of the Doc Savage fan club, started by paperback cover artist Jim Steranko. Like Sherlockians, Doc Savage fans formed local chapters; Lewandowski formed two in the Chicago area. When Bantam suspended reprints of the Doc Savage series, Lewandowski led a letter campaign that led to their resumption. Because of non-Savage material he was receiving, in 1981 Lewandowski changed the magazine's name to *Nemesis, Inc.* It continued until 1991.

Also devoted to the most popular pulp hero was *Doc Savage Quarterly*, started in January 1980 by Bill Laidlaw of San Luis Obispo, California. Despite its title, it also offered articles and reviews on non-Savage subjects, for example one on Richard Benson, the pulp hero known as "The Avenger." It published a total of fourteen issues.

Xenophile (1974–1980)

Nils Hardin of St. Louis started *Xenophile* in March 1974 as "a monthly advertiser and journal devoted to fantastic and imaginative literature." The advertising was especially important because for much of the time *Xenophile* was a full-time job for Hardin. In 1978 he reported he had only earned $324 the previous year. Though some issues consisted primarily of ads, and others were mainly about science fiction, Hardin also published outstanding mystery-related issues, including one in June 1975 devoted to Ellery Queen. Several other issues were devoted to pulp detectives and included bibliographies. *Xenophile* lasted forty-five issues, until March 1980.

Baker Street Miscellanea (1975–1995)

Interest in Sherlock Holmes has never flagged, but it increased in the mid-1970s when this journal, whose first issue was April 1975, was founded in Chicago by long-

time Sherlockians, John Nieminski and William D. Goodrich. It was probably the best magazine in that subgenre except for *The Baker Street Journal* and *The Sherlock Holmes Journal*. In the first issue Nieminski stated that the motivation of the founders of this quarterly was "an abiding interest in the great detective and his life and works; a desire to share our enthusiasm through the medium of a self-wrought amateur publication which, hopefully, will open yet another channel for speculation and creative expression for ourselves and others; and not the least, the making of a few new friends along the way."

Beginning with the fourth issue in December 1975, the magazine obtained the sponsorship of Northeastern Illinois University, thanks to another noted Sherlockian, Professor Ely Liebow, chairman of its English Department. This helped its finances and permitted it to reach

Prof. Ely Liebow, co-publisher of *Baker Street Miscellanea*

a circulation of 430 by 1981. Among its features were Goodrich's lengthy series "The Sherlock Holmes Reference Guide," Sherlockian parodies, comments by Dame Jean Conan Doyle regarding Charles Higham's biography of her father, and an article on Sherlock Holmes and Tarzan by science fiction writer Philip José Farmer.

Baker Street Miscellanea survived the premature death of Nieminski in 1986 and, under the stewardship of Goodrich and Liebow, published until the first issue of 1995 when, after twenty years, they ceased publication.

The Mystery Nook (1975–1981)

Don Miller of Wheaton, Maryland, a longtime science fiction fan, founded *The Mystery Nook* in July 1975; it was designed to give mystery fans a forum similar to that which science fiction fans had. The first two issues consisted mainly of comments by the editor, along with reviews and sales lists. However, by the third issue mystery fans were sending letters and articles, and *The Mystery Nook* had several outstanding issues during its relatively short life.

Though *The Mystery Nook* came out fairly regularly in 1975, thereafter Miller's ill health (he had two bouts of cancer) caused long delays between issues. For example, there were eight months between #8 and #9 and nine months between #9 and #10. Nos. 10 and 11 appeared only a month apart, but then there was another eight months before #12, and over three years before the final issue in July 1981. Guy Townsend joked that *The Mystery Nook* was "the only quarterly in the business that comes out every other year." Its subscribers knew about Miller's health problems and were forgiving. Early in 1982 Townsend learned of Miller's death when Miller's copy of *The Mystery Fancier* was returned by the Postal Service marked "deceased." The May/June 1982 issue of *TMF* was dedicated to Miller.

Most of those involved in other fan magazines of the 1970s also wrote articles for

Miller and letters for the section he called "Things That Go Bump in the Night." A Rex Stout memorial issue in August 1976 drew outstanding articles from the leading Nero Wolfe scholars, including Townsend, John J. McAleer, Judson C. Sapp, and Art Scott. A Ruth Rendell issue in 1977 contained eleven items about her, including a bibliography. The final issue of *The Mystery Nook* had a dozen pieces about Georgette Heyer, a writer usually ignored in mystery fan magazines.

Nero Wolfe Fandom (1975–)

So popular is Nero Wolfe that Rex Stout is one of the few Golden Age authors whose work remains available in reprint. A brief start in Wolfean fandom was the *Nero Wolfe and Archie Goodwin Fans Newsletter*, edited and published by Lee E. Poleske of Seward, Alaska, beginning in 1975. After three issues, its title changed to *Lone Wolfe*. It discontinued publication after its sixth issue, January 1976. It contained reviews, quizzes, biographies of Wolfe's favorite chefs, and even a diagram of the structure of a *cattleya* orchid.

In 1978, inspired by Carol Brener, owner of Murder Ink, Ellen Krieger founded **The Wolfe Pack**, and it soon had over a thousand members. Its quarterly publication, *The Gazette*, commenced with the Winter 1979 issue. The consulting editor was John McAleer, Stout's biographer. *The Gazette* includes a variety of scholarly articles about the Wolfe canon, including such perennially popular topics as Wolfe's parentage, early life, and the actual address of the brownstone on West 35th Street. Now semi-annual, *The Gazette* lists as editor "Lon Cohen," the name of the reporter on the fictional newspaper, *The Gazette*, who often helped Wolfe and Archie.

The Pack has held an annual Black Orchid dinner in New York on the first weekend in December—to correspond with Stout's birthday—since December 2, 1978, when 127 persons gathered at the Gramercy Park Hotel. It was an evening of food (prepared by a European chef following recipes in *The Nero Wolfe Cook Book*), songs, speeches, quizzes, and even a fake murder. At this dinner in 1979, the Pack first awarded the Nero Wolfe Award to a mystery novel "Meeting Stout's Criteria for Excellence." At the Nero Wolfe Assembly, a symposium first held in New York on December 1, 1979, scholars read papers concerning Wolfe, and these are often reprinted in *The Gazette*. In addition, since 1979 the Pack has held a Shad Roe dinner in the spring, Isaac Asimov presiding at the early dinners. As with the Sherlockian scions, regional chapters (called "racemes," using a term from flower-bearing) of the Wolfe Pack have been established.

Unlike many fan organizations, the Wolfe Pack remains healthy today. It arranged to have a plaque placed at 454 W. 35th Street (Wolfe's address according to its scholarship) by New York's Park Commissioner. Bimonthly book discussions of Wolfe stories are held at O'Casey's restaurant in Manhattan. Inevitably, tote bags, t-shirts, and sweatshirts are sold at its website.

The Thorndyke File (1976–?) and *John Thorndyke's Journal*

In spring 1976, Philip T. Asdell of Maryland launched *The Thorndyke File*, a journal devoted to R. Austin Freeman and his series detective, the medico-legal expert Dr. John Thorndyke. In addition to publishing scholarship, the journal, led by reader

Frank Archibald of Needham, Massachusetts, waged a successful campaign to have a stone placed at Freeman's unmarked grave in England. When other commitments forced Asdell to relinquish editorship of *The Thorndyke File*, John McAleer took over in 1980 and soon doubled the subscribers to 156, half of whom were medical doctors. Though *The Thorndyke File* is no longer published, a fan magazine, *John Thorndyke's Journal*, was published in England until recently by David Ian Chapman of Aldershot, Hampshire.

Simenon Organizations (1976–)

Though most of his mysteries, especially his Inspector Maigret series, are set in France, Georges Simenon was Belgian. Among several Simenon organizations in Belgium is **Le Centre D'études Georges Simenon** in Liège. It was established in 1976 "for the development and dissemination of Simenon's work." They sponsor a colloquium every two years and publish an annual review *Traces*. Scholarly information can also be found in Liège at a foundation, **Le Fonds Simenon de l'Université de Liège**, which provides access to over 7,000 works of Simenon. About 400 fans, readers and scholars belong to **Les Amis de Georges Simenon**, in Beigem, Belgium, which was founded in 1986. They publish *Les Cahiers Simenon* annually.

The Dorothy L. Sayers Society (1976–)

The popularity of Lord Peter Wimsey on British and American television, beginning in the 1970s, led to renewed interest in Dorothy L. Sayers. Biographies and collections of her letters have been published. The Dorothy L. Sayers Society was established in 1976. Located in West Sussex, England, it sponsors regular meetings, an annual conference, and a bimonthly newsletter. There are archives open to members. The Dorothy L. Sayers Centre in Essex, England, has a collection of works by and about Sayers.

Mohonk Mystery Weekend (1977–)

Because it started in 1977, the annual Mohonk Mystery Weekend at the Mountain House at Lake Mohonk, in New York State's Catskill Mountains, was probably the first non-Bouchercon general mystery convention. It was originally organized by Dilys Winn and Carol Brener of the Murder Ink bookstore in Manhattan. When first held as a "Dead of Winter" weekend, January 27–30, 1977, there were panels about the mystery, famous authors such as Phyllis Whitney and Isaac Asimov, and people knowledgeable *about* mystery fiction, including Otto Penzler and Chris Steinbrunner. The setting was an atmospheric 108-year-old hotel, and the event quickly proved popular, selling out each year within two hours of the hotel accepting reservations.

The first Mohonk was not entirely learned discussions of mysteries. There was a ghoulish cooking lesson by Winn, a talk by a safecracker, a ski tour, and a demonstration with raptors called, inevitably, "Maltese Falconry." However, increasingly, murder games predominate at these weekends. Mohonk continues to draw noted authors, but they often are there to participate in contests in which "murder" is committed in full view of attendees, who then try to solve it, often in teams. These murder events have proven popular at other hotels, on cruise ships, as corporate events, and even at an occasional Bouchercon.

Phyllis Whitney set her novel *The Stone Bull* (1977) at Mohonk, though she called the resort "Laurel Mountain House." Max Allan Collins was invited to be the "killer" at one of these weekends, and a few years later returned the favor with *Nice Weekend for a Murder* (1986) set there, with his detective Mallory playing a "suspect."

The August Derleth Society (1977–)

In 1977, a Connecticut school administrator, Richard Fawcett came upon *Walden West* by August Derleth, a book that so impressed him he called it "the heart beat of middle America preserved in amber." This was a non-mystery by the author of the Solar Pons pastiches and the Judge Peck mysteries. Fawcett was determined to find other fans of this prolific author and founded the August Derleth Society later that year, becoming editor-publisher of *The August Derleth Newsletter*, which includes material regarding Derleth's mysteries but also about his other fiction. The society, with several hundred members, has annual meetings in Sauk City, Wisconsin, the midwestern city where Derleth lived and about which he wrote, calling it "Sac Prairie."

Notes for the Curious: A John Dickson Carr Memorial Journal (1978)

This chapbook was published and edited by Larry L. French in 1978 to commemorate Carr's 1977 death. In addition to bibliographic material and a chronology of Carr's life, there were comments about him from most of the important names in fandom, including Hubin, Penzler, Breen, Nevins, Shibuk, and Briney. French was at work on a book about Carr, tentatively titled *The Grand Master of Mystery,* when he died.

Tony Medawar also produced a magazine devoted to Carr, titled *Notes for the Curious.* In its only issue, dated Autumn 1995, Medawar said it was "published by the Noughts-and-Crosses Club." That is the name of a fictional club that Carr had used in at least one novel and two short stories. Medawar also said that purchase of that issue "entitles the reader to Club membership which, at the moment, has as yet no significance whatsoever other than providing a convenient peg on which enthusiasts are warmly invited to hang their hats and coats." Neither the club nor the magazine went further, and both were dissolved.

The Holmesian Federation (1978–1980)

Surely the strangest Sherlockian publication of the 1970s was *The Holmesian Federation,* whose brief life began in November 1978. This "admittedly weird hybrid," as editor-publisher Signe Landon of Oregon called it, attempted to combine "two of my favorite universes": Sherlock Holmes and the TV series *Star Trek.* It was partly nonfiction with such articles as "A Study in Harlots" by Frankie Jemison, purporting to be "a shocking account of the real circumstances surrounding the meeting of Holmes and Dr. Watson" and "Holmes Was a Vulcan," a study by Priscilla Pollner. The fiction either transferred *Star Trek* characters into Victorian times or placed Holmes and Watson in the future. A second issue did not appear until October 1980, and I have no record of subsequent issues.

The Not So Private Eye (1978–198?)

Andy Jaysnovitch of New Jersey, a fan of private eye fiction and early television series, and a collector of almost everything, started *The Not So Private Eye* in 1978. His goal was to promote the private detective story, which seemed to have fallen on hard times. (This was before the popularity of books by Marcia Muller, Sue Grafton, and Sara Paretsky and the founding of the Private Eye Writers of America.) His illustrated magazine had continuing features such as "Series Spotlight," by Jim McCahery, who wrote about great private detectives of the past. Paul Bishop contributed articles on current private eyes. There were also interviews. In 1980 Jaysnovitch announced the demise of his magazine, but it was resumed in 1982 and continued to appear irregularly, though it did not survive past the 1980s.

Paperback Quarterly (1978–1982)

In 1978 Charlotte Laughlin and Billy Lee of Brownwood, Texas, launched *Paperback Quarterly*, calling it the "Journal of Mass-Market Paperback History." The first magazine devoted to collectible paperbacks, it ceased publication suddenly after Vol. V No. 2 (Summer 1982). At least half of the articles in it were mystery-related, including "Dashiell Hammett in the Dell Mapbacks" by William Lyles, "Skeleton Covers" by Bill Crider, "The Paperback Dr. John Thorndyke" by Daniel G. Roberts, and "Avon Classic Crime Collection" by Don Hensley.

813: Les Amis de la Littérature Policière (1979–)

Over 800 French writers and fans belong to 813: Les Amis de la Littérature Policière, founded in Paris in 1979. Their quarterly journal is also called *813*, the title of a 1910 Arsène Lupin novel by Maurice Leblanc.

The John Buchan Society (1979–)

Founded by Eileen Stewart on March 3, 1979, at Edinburgh University, this is a group of devotees of the author of *The 39 Steps* and other thrillers. Buchan was born Baron Tweedsmuir and became Governor-General of Canada. The membership has grown to almost 500.

Mystery (1979–1982)

Mystery, a slick-paper magazine published in Los Angeles, made its appearance with the November-December 1979 issue. Few of the articles about the mystery were well done, and up to a third of each issue was fiction. The first issue had the beginning of a continuing story, "Ace Carpenter, Detective," by Hamilton T. Caine, a pseudonym of *Mystery*'s editor-publisher Stephen L. Smoke.

Though supposedly professionally produced, *Mystery*'s schedule was as erratic as many amateur journals. In 1982 it was converted, without explanation, into a digest-sized magazine and then ceased publication in July. Unused subscriptions were transferred, without permission, to a west coast book review. The final issue included an ad for a book by Smoke, raising questions as to whether the magazine had only been a means of promoting his writing career.

13 Bouchercon: 1980s

1980: Washington DC

Bouchercon XI, October 10–12, proclaimed that it was in "Washington, DC, Where Crime Is Your Government's Business." Some thought there would be echoes of Watergate, but the panels on true crime emphasized law *enforcement*. One was about a successful "sting" operation, and another, "Support Your Local FBI," featured two FBI agents, but also author Al Nussbaum, once on the FBI "Wanted" list.

There was a Cold War panel on spying, with an FBI agent who worked in intelligence operations and a retired CIA agent. One of Bouchercon's co-chairmen, Jon L. Lellenberg, who moderated the panel, described himself as "a strategic analyst at a Washington, DC, national security research organization." The other co-chairman, Peter E. Blau, a geologist and journalist, is, like Lellenberg, a member of the Baker Street Irregulars.

At the Bouchercon site, the National Press Club, about 280 people attended, more than three times the 1970 figure. John Nieminski said that its original organizers must be pleased because "Their seedling root took firm hold and the Bouchercon has flourished, blooming annually for over a decade now, and sprouting up in locales as far removed from its West Coast birthplace as Boston, Chicago and New York."

On Friday night, in addition to the get-acquainted party, there was a panel on screen adaptations, with horror stories by Brian Garfield, James Grady, and Michael Hardwick on what was done to their work.

Phyllis White explained on Saturday morning why her late husband, born William Anthony Parker White, adopted his Boucher pseudonym. Realizing how many authors were named William White, he decided a fledgling writer needed a less common name, so he chose Boucher, the name of a relative on the maternal side of his family.

Because of my interest in regional mysteries, I was chosen to lead a panel on mysteries set in Washington. Since there were six writers on the stage, my job was more traffic manager than moderator. I still regret that I did not reduce the panel by one when Warren Adler objected to being introduced as a "mystery writer," claiming he was a "novelist." I should have ushered him off the stage. In introducing another panelist, Patricia McGerr, I called her *Pick Your Victim* one of the best and most unusual mysteries ever written. Later, a member of the audience showed me a used copy of the book, which she had purchased in the bookroom for $5. She hoped she would find it worth the price.

We had disagreement Saturday during a panel called "The Care and Feeding of Mystery Fans." Otto Penzler, on his way to being a successful publisher and bookseller (his Manhattan store had recently opened) opined that the mystery was in good shape, pointing to the emergence of mysteries on bestseller lists. Editor Michael Seidman took an opposite viewpoint, complaining of the corporate mentality in publishing. Seidman's telling the audience they should support writers by buying books brought a response from the third panel member, Art Scott, that there were enough good mysteries already published that fans did not have to purchase for that reason alone.

Saturday evening there was a live performance of William Gillette's one-act play *The Painful Predicament of Sherlock Holmes*, which originally played in New York in 1905 with Ethel Barrymore. Gillette had played Sherlock Holmes, as he did for many years. Sunday morning was partly devoted to Holmes, with a panel led by Blau commemorating the 50th anniversary of Doyle's death. Panelists worried that pastiches written to cash in on the success of *The Seven-Percent-Solution* might damage the reputation of the great detective.

On Sunday morning, William Ryan presented, albeit in a monotone, the interesting theory that Edgar Allan Poe had been murdered. Then, Guest of Honor Gregory Mcdonald, author of the Fletch series, spoke. He had harsh words for critics but was also amusing, telling how he was almost arrested for eating ice cream on Washington's food-free subway. Twenty-one years later, at another Washington-area Bouchercon, those subways were still clean—and food-free.

1981: Milwaukee

Mary Ann Grochowski, a child psychologist, ran this Milwaukee Bouchercon with the help of librarians Beverly De Weese and Gary Warren Niebuhr. It was held October 9–11 at the Marc Plaza and drew attendance of 212 people. Registration for the weekend was only $15 per person, a bargain compared to later Bouchercons.

Seventy-seven-year-old Helen McCloy was Guest of Honor, the first female selected. Frail physically, but mentally acute, she had many anecdotes to tell, including some regarding her stormy marriage to the late Davis Dresser who, as Brett Halliday,

Gary Warren Niebuhr and Mary Ann Grochowski.

created the Mike Shayne series. For the first time Bouchercon had a Fan Guest of Honor, and the choice was obvious: Allen J. Hubin, whose founding of *The Armchair Detective* led to mystery fandom as we now know it.

Grochowski wisely realized that Bouchercon's chances for success would be improved if it also had a "name" bigger than McCloy or Hubin. With the help of the Miller Brewing Company, she secured one of the best-selling writers of all time, Mickey Spillane. Spillane had acquired further celebrity by being featured in humorous television beer commercials. He proved friendly and not conceited, and his interview by Max Allan Collins was a highlight of this Bouchercon, which, incidentally, was called "Beer City Capers."

Another wise move was inviting William Campbell Gault, a former Milwaukee writer who had lived in Southern California since the end of World War II. Gault had given up mysteries to write juvenile sports stories in 1963 because he could make more money from them. He thought no one would remember his mysteries and was reluctant to come, finally agreeing to "patch up the holes in my topcoat" so that he could journey from his warm home to Wisconsin in the fall. Gault was considering returning to mysteries, and the reception he received encouraged him to do so. To his surprise, fans not only remembered and missed him, but also could discuss books he had written over twenty years before. Autographing books was becoming an important part of Bouchercon, and Gault and other authors were asking fans that presented old books to be signed, "Where did you find this one?"

Another Bouchercon highlight was the first of many slide shows by Art Scott, a leader in the branch of mystery fandom specializing in paperback cover art. On Saturday night I joined a congenial group at a restaurant called "The Safe House." Its decorations: espionage paraphernalia. When I left on Sunday, I found that Milwaukee had a used bookstore at the airport. I bought an old mystery to read on the plane.

1982: San Francisco

"Bouchercon-by-the-Bay" at the Jack Tar Hotel in San Francisco, October 8–10, used that city for much of its programming, as well as activities outside the convention site. There were two mystery-related walks: one following Anthony Boucher's footsteps in Berkeley, the other locations about which Dashiell Hammett wrote. Boucher, who never drove a car, walked all over Berkeley—and San Francisco when he crossed the Bay. Ever the reader, Boucher read while he walked the Berkeley streets, leading one to marvel that he survived. I took the Hammett walk myself on a hot day (October is San Francisco's "summer") and ended up meeting other fans for beer at the S. Holmes, Esq. Pub, where there is an excellent recreation of 221B Baker Street, including the sounds one might have heard in London during Holmes's time.

Don Herron, who runs the Hammett tour, chaired this Bouchercon, aided by local bookseller Bruce Taylor and the Maltese Falcon Societies of San Francisco and San Jose. Attendance was about 600. The committee reached 3,000 miles for its Guest of Honor, bringing in Robert B. Parker of Boston.

Friday night included, appropriately, an Anthony Boucher panel, with his sons Lawrence and James White among the speakers. Saturday, for the first time, there was two-track programming, which included Hammett and Holmes panels, another Art Scott slide show called "The Babe on the Paperback Cover," and a panel on California mystery writers. Private Eye Writers of America (PWA), founded by Robert Randisi, presented its first Shamus Awards.

Other topics for weekend panels included collecting, pulp magazines, and "The Current State of the Mystery." At a panel on reference books, Walter Albert, author of the definitive book on secondary sources *about* the mystery, declared himself "a passionate bibliographer."

This Bouchercon had an especially good selection of mystery films. They included the two film versions of *The Maltese Falcon* that preceded the 1941 Bogart film, and *Charlie Chan at Treasure Island*, with its background of the San Francisco area.

Despite the appeal of panels and movies, much that was enjoyable occurred outside the meeting rooms. Friday night dinner for many was at "The Shadows," a restaurant near landmark Coit Tower, where they served an unlikely, but delicious, green clam chowder. There were the usual parties held by the *DAPA-EM* group, at one of which I called *The Maltese Falcon* "a good, not great, book." Perhaps when I finally read it, I was overly familiar with the plot due to having seen several movie versions. It's a line *DAPA-EM*ers have never allowed me to forget. After Bouchercon was over, Art Scott invited a group to his home in Livermore, where people drooled over his collection of vintage paperbacks.

1983: New York City

Bouchercon returned to New York, courtesy of co-chairmen Otto Penzler and Chris Steinbrunner, to the Barbizon-Plaza Hotel on Central Park South, October 21–23, and was successful, with about 450 in attendance, despite having to abandon Columbus Day weekend because hotels were not available. Advance publicity was good, though an article by Eric Pace in the *New York Times* was the usual attempt at humor that newspapers favored; he pretended he was a private eye investigating Bouchercon.

John D. MacDonald was the Guest of Honor. At the Sunday banquet luncheon, MacDonald revealed that his famous series character was originally named "Dallas McGee," but he changed the first name to "Travis" after John F. Kennedy's 1963 assassination.

Various media were used, beginning with a Friday night radio mystery "Kiss My Face with Bullets," performed by a group associated with Bogie's, a Manhattan restaurant that attracted mystery fans and put on special events for them such as cruises and tours. There was a panel on the "Golden Age of Television," with excerpts from several crime shows. A Saturday night tribute was paid to recently-deceased Jonathan Latimer with two films featuring Preston Foster as his series detective, Bill Crane. Walter Gibson performed one of his popular magic shows. Also "performing" were two NYPD dogs. Police dogs proved a popular attraction at later Bouchercons.

Donald E. Westlake read a paper in which he suggested that the private eye novel was dead, and that writers of hardboiled novels were now merely following past greats and needed to set out in new directions. His talk was followed by panels about hardboiled mysteries at which there was agreement and disagreement with what he said. One of those agreeing was James Ellroy, who showed up wearing the baggy knickers favored by golfers in the 1920s. Another panelist, William Campbell Gault, agreed with Westlake about the overuse of metaphor by the late Ross Macdonald. Gault used a metaphor of his own when he said mysteries were minor league writing compared to the major leagues of Ernest Hemingway and F. Scott Fitzgerald. However, he seemed pleased to be in the minors in his resurrected career, because he told me happily that he had sold two new mystery novels to Walker. Later, there would be much discussion of Westlake's opinion in fan magazines.

Saturday night there was the usual noisy *DAPA-EM* party. During this one a German runner came to the door and begged for quiet because, "I have to run twenty-six miles tomorrow." He was entered in Sunday's New York City Marathon. After the convention, many attendees boarded subway trains for Brooklyn and a party at the home of Jeff and Jackie Meyerson.

1984: Chicago

It's hard to be objective about Chicago's third Bouchercon, called "Second City Skulduggery," since I was Fan Guest of Honor, only the second person so honored. I have fond memories, including a spontaneous round of applause from a *DAPA-EM* contingent in the lobby.

430 people attended October 26–28 at the Americana Congress Hotel. Three friends, Mary Craig, Ely Liebow, and John Nieminski, produced an especially well-run Bouchercon. Bill Pronzini was Guest of Honor, and he made himself readily available to fans. At Sunday's luncheon-banquet he read more examples of "alternate classics," bad mystery writing like that in his hilarious book *Gun in Cheek.*

For the first time Phyllis White couldn't attend Bouchercon; she was hospitalized with a case of shingles. Instead of her opening remarks on Friday night, Bob Briney read some of Boucher's reviews and other writing as tribute to him. The other Friday highlight in a convention with single-track programming was "Make a Mystery: An Improvisation Workshop" run by two Chicago-area actors.

In order to ensure good attendance at the first Saturday session (8:30 AM), "The State of the Mystery—1984," free paperbacks were given to early arrivals. The panel included an agent and an editor. It was clear the publishing world was beginning to notice Bouchercon. Other noteworthy Saturday sessions included Bill Crider's interview with Pronzini and what would become an annual event, a panel on short stories that included the sub-genre's most prolific writer, Edward D. Hoch.

As Fan Guest of Honor, I was interviewed by Nieminski. He elicited the story of the coincidences that happened to me in 1980. I had just published an article about fictional mysteries with operatic backgrounds, "Murder at the Opera," in the July issue of *Opera News* when a week later a violinist was murdered in the Metropolitan Opera House. *The New York Times* mentioned my article and the coincidence of the Met's first murder shortly after my article about crime and opera appeared. But the coincidences were not over. Five weeks later, the police arrested a suspect, and he was someone who lived on the same floor of the Bronx apartment building in which I had lived until eighteen months before the murder. I had often said good morning to him while waiting for the elevator. He was found guilty of felony murder. And I am the fan who decries coincidences in my mystery reading!

There was another coincidence to go with this Bouchercon, the publication of *Kill Your Darlings*, a mystery novel by Max Allan Collins, set at a Chicago Bouchercon. Collins said he started it before he knew that Bouchercon would be held in Chicago in 1984.

Sunday's schedule included a panel on collecting moderated by Otto Penzler. It included Allen J. Hubin, who amassed a collection of 25,000 mysteries before he had to sell them to fund his children's college educations. There was suspense at the closing session as attendees chose between two California locations, Berkeley and Los

Angeles, as the site of the 1985 Bouchercon. Berkeley won. The convention approved Bouchercon's first bylaws, as drafted by Len and June Moffat. The Moffatts had received many inquiries regarding Bouchercon organization and finances, questions which anticipated some of the later problems that would haunt those organizing conventions.

1985: San Francisco

The 16th Bouchercon was supposed to be held in Berkeley, but the convention committee had problems with the Claremont Hotel, and the convention was moved to San Francisco's Sir Francis Drake Hotel, October 25–27. Advance registration was still only $25, and a single room at the Drake could be had for $70 per night. A new record was set for Bouchercon attendance: 875 people. Bookseller Bryan Barrett was chairman, with help from Bruce Taylor and a large committee. Advertising referred to Bouchercon for the first time as "The World's Mystery Convention."

Bouchercon honored the California Crime Novel as "Guest of Honor," though it singled out Joe Gores, Joseph Hansen, and Collin Wilcox as exemplars of that sub-genre.

Cornell Woolrich fans Marv Lachman (l.) and Don Yates.

Fan Guests of Honor were June and Len Moffatt, who had been so important in founding Bouchercon.

There was a return to dual-track programming, with a third track devoted to almost continuous showing of crime films. Two panels were devoted to the California Crime Novel. Other panels topics included humor, cops, pulps, and Sherlock Holmes. Don Yates and I discussed Cornell Woolrich. A first was the hotly contested trivia contest, with prizes awarded to the winning team: Steve Stilwell, Bob Samoian, Jon L. Breen, and me.

The Saturday night banquet was held in an extremely crowded room with only one exit, and the peace of mind of those attending was not helped by a fire alarm going off and wailing for ten minutes. Fortunately, it was a false alarm. Meal service was poor, leading a frustrated author, J. J. Lamb, to let out an ear-shattering whistle when he had not received his entrée. There was another funny talk by Toastmaster Tony Hillerman about inept criminals and police officers in the Southwest.

1986: Baltimore

Attendance dropped to about 450 at the 17th Bouchercon at Baltimore's Sheraton

Inner Harbor, despite a return to Columbus Day weekend, October 10–12. Lack of adequate publicity kept the attendance relatively low, but for many 450 was the right number for a convention. In *TAD*, Edward D. Hoch reflected, "perhaps that was about the right size for a Bouchercon after all. A decade from now, when they do attract thousands of delegates, I have a feeling we'll look back on these smaller gatherings with fond recollection." Hoch proved prescient.

Gail M. Larson of The Butler Did It bookstore in Columbia, Maryland, was chairwoman, and unlike San Francisco, which had twenty-two people on its committee, she had one person, Bill Deeck, who did a superb job of programming. Larson didn't seem to feel any pressure. In the program book she described herself as "the short blond who can probably be found with a cigarette in one hand and a drink in the other asking, 'Are we having fun now?' "

Donald E. Westlake was Guest of Honor, and Chris Steinbrunner was Fan Guest of Honor. A film and television producer, and occasional professional writer, Chris said he preferred to think of himself as a "mystery activist," rather than a fan. He did not appear to enjoy himself, perhaps because he was already suffering from the depression and ill health that plagued him until his death in 1993. He certainly deserved recognition for many reasons, including bringing the films that were so important to early Bouchercons

Another notable attendee was Richard S. Prather, the creator of private eye Shell Scott. Prather had not published in about ten years while he fought a lawsuit against his publisher. Successfully concluding it, he had just published a new hardcover mystery. He was doubly pleased in Baltimore because PWA gave him The Eye, their lifetime achievement award, and he was remembered by many fans, who brought his books, especially the Gold Medal paperback originals, to be autographed. PWA, in conjunction with St. Martin's Press, imaginatively scheduled their annual Shamus luncheon to take place on a harbor cruise.

Though there was only one track of programming Friday night and Sunday morning, there were three tracks on Saturday. All panel titles were cleverly taken by Deeck from books or stories by Westlake. Thus, the opening panel, during which Patricia Moyes, Francis M. Nevins, Robert E. Briney, and I discussed Boucher's career, was called "The Busy Body." When Douglas Greene discussed John Dickson Carr, Deeck called it "Lock Your Room," after a Westlake short story. Publishers donated free books, but they were placed in the rooms of attendees, causing concern by some about who had entered their rooms.

Larson initiated a mystery award, the Anthony, named after Boucher. About 200 people voted for the first Anthonys, which were presented at the Sunday luncheon. Some fans don't approve of the Anthonys, considering them popularity contests, unlike the Edgars, in which a committee is charged with reading *all* the books or stories in a category before voting.

There was a coda to the Baltimore Bouchercon that left a bad taste in the mouths of those who read about it and those who chaired prior and future Bouchercons. There were precedents and a bylaw requirement that profits of one Bouchercon be turned over to future Bouchercons. *MDM* published an open letter to Larson from Barrett, Taylor, and Donna Rankin of the 1985 Bouchercon committee and Steve Stilwell and Becky Reineke who were co-chairing in 1987. They said they were troubled that, despite Baltimore having been profitable, "we are at a loss to explain how you managed to pass on to Bouchercon XVIII less money than was passed on to you from Bouchercon XVI." Having sought an accounting of funds for almost a year, they wrote, "Your failure to respond to what we felt is a reasonable request for an accounting has forced us to make this a public matter." Stilwell and Taylor told me they never received a response.

1987: Minneapolis

To some, the 18th Bouchercon, held at Minneapolis's Ritz Hotel, October 9–11, will always be remembered as "the convention with the magician." The convention was well run by Steve Stilwell, in charge of programming, and Becky Reineke, handling hotel and registration arrangements. Well, there *was* another problem, and that had to do with the Guest of Honor.

Lawrence Block had the writing credentials; he was author of the popular Matt Scudder and Bernie Rhodenbarr series. Still, the Guest of Honor must interact with fans. Apparently Stilwell had reservations about him for in *MDM*, announcing Block's selection, he wrote, "I think he is a good choice. Bright, witty, articulate, well-known, and he should be accessible and easy to work with. We shall see."

Before anyone could evaluate Block's "performance" in Minneapolis, the choice of another male Guest of Honor brought the committee grief. There was a letter from Carol Brener of New York's Murder Ink in which she jokingly (I assume) threatened to bash Stilwell's head in with a copy of Hubin's heavy bibliography. Brener said that if it weren't for the insult to Block, "I would urge fans to boycott Bouchercons until women are given at-least-token equal representation."

Block seemed uncooperative during his Bouchercon interview, giving one-word answers to many of Sandra Scoppettone's questions. The following year when Block published a very "New Age" novel, *Random Walk,* many wondered whether his behavior at Bouchercon wasn't due to a new philosophy. He wasn't much more outgoing at the banquet, claiming he didn't know he was supposed to give a speech and giving one that was brief. It should be noted that at conventions during the 1990s Block was far more open.

Many attendees wished the Fan Guest of Honor could have been there because John Nieminski, who died the previous December, was honored posthumously. No one enjoyed Bouchercons more than Nieminski, and his friends never felt the convention was under way until they saw him. Because many considered him the best writer in mystery fandom, a chapbook of his writings, *John Nieminski: Somewhere a Roscoe*, was distributed to all registrants.

Friday night opened with panels regarding Minnesota and Midwestern mystery writers. On Saturday when there were two tracks, plus movies, there were panels on the British and Canadian crimes scenes, one on hard-boiled female writers, and four Sherlockian panels in honor of the 100th anniversary of *A Study in Scarlet*. The first auction to benefit a charity was held, raising $1,500 for the Minnesota Literacy Council. Otto Penzler and Bruce Taylor were auctioneers, and an "item" auctioned off by authors, due to become standard at Bouchercon auctions, was the opportunity to have one's name used as a character in a mystery.

As toastmasters, Mary Craig and Max Allan Collins did everything to keep the Saturday banquet moving. The amateur magician brought things to a grinding halt. Not only was he boring, but he was inept and could not even do simple card tricks. Yet he was unwilling to leave the stage. Richard Moore said that the year he served in Vietnam was shorter and more fun than the magician's act. Many people walked out. Stilwell has had to put up with many years of kidding because of his role in scheduling the magician. Stillwell later wrote, "Two years of my life went into planning this convention and what will people remember about it? The magician (sic) at the banquet."

Another occasion marked during this Bouchercon was the 20th anniversary of *TAD*. A Sunday morning panel, moderated by its founder, Al Hubin, had panelists who were early contributors. On sale at the convention was *TAD Schrift: Twenty Years of Mystery Fandom in The Armchair Detective*, edited by Randy Cox.

It was clear, despite Baltimore's drop in attendance, that Bouchercons were going to get bigger; 650 attended Minneapolis. Bouchercon was becoming more international, as well as more commercial. There were nineteen booksellers, two from England. Longtime Bouchercon attendees, while enjoying themselves, felt its flavor was changing. John Apostolou summed up the feeling of many when he wrote in *MDM*, "Bouchercon was more fun when it was a smaller event."

Other fans felt that Bouchercon was becoming more for writers and editors than fans. Stilwell said that most "fans" coming to the convention want to hear writers, not other "fans." It was clear from attendance at presentations by "name" authors and increasingly long autographing lines that many attended because of these authors. On the other hand, panels regarding the past or fannish activities, such as the *TAD* panel, drew fewer people.

A Sunday morning panel, "The Writer as Critic," moderated by William L. De Andrea, gave Gary Warren Niebuhr the impression that "some authors claimed they are the best reviewers because their understanding of the craft would make them more sensitive to their fellow authors." He wondered whether, as reviewers, they have the interest of book buyers at heart. Ann Williams said that if the issue of writers reviewing other writers isn't raised, "nobody will *ever* believe a review or a jacket blurb by another writer."

Some might miss earlier Bouchercons, but it was still an event to which fans looked forward. Ellen Nehr summed it up in *MDM* when she wrote, "I go to these affairs for conviviality. I've made friends at these conventions that I wouldn't trade for blood relatives, have met authors whose works have entertained me for years and could say to their faces, 'Thank you for the hours of pleasure you have given me.' " After Minneapolis, Williams expressed the view of first-time attendees. "I'm still reeling from my first Bouchercon, and I expect that it will take me at least a week to get back to 'normal,' assuming that I *ever* do."

1988: San Diego

"Murder Sunny Side Up" was the title of Bouchercon 19 (October 7–9) at San Diego's U. S. Grant Hotel, and the weather cooperated. Initially, the committee, chaired by Phyllis Brown, of Grounds for Murder Mystery Bookstore, and Ray Hardy, announced membership would be limited to 800, but they relented and eventually almost 900 attended, a Bouchercon record.

Charlotte MacLeod was guest of Honor, and Robert Barnard of England Toastmaster. Considering the mysteries they write, it was only logical that each moderated a panel called "The Mystery as Social Satire and Comedy of Manners." Bruce Taylor was Fan Guest of Honor.

There were three, at times four, tracks, but they were not enough to accommodate the number of professional writers (200+) who attended and wanted exposure. The presence of so many professionals again led to a perception by some that author dominance at Bouchercons was increasing. They pointed to the failure to acknowledge fans at the opening ceremony or to introduce Boucher's widow, Phyllis White, either then or at the banquet dinner. Along with name badges, attendees were given ribbons to attach based on their status as Author, Bookseller, Reviewer, Editor, or Panelist. Otto Penzler had so many ribbons that, according to Richard Moore, he "looked like a commodore in the Prussian Navy." There were no ribbons for fans, leading Moore to wonder, "Why create this class distinction at an event historically free of them?"

The most controversial panel had the longest title: "Fans, Readers, Aficionados: What Is the Difference? Is There A Difference? Who is Making 'Fan' a Dirty Word and Why?" Panelist Michael Seidman said that those who write and review for

Two Maryland fans, Bill Deeck and Kerry Littler, better known for her alter-ego, "Sherlock Hound."

fan magazines did not affect the sale of mysteries. Unanswered was my question from the audience as to whether fans had not done much good for professionals by founding Bouchercon and reviewing thousands of books since 1967, most favorably.

Seidman and moderator Robert Randisi told tales of fans bothering writers, including a story of one fan who allegedly trailed an author into the rest room to get an autograph. There was also no response to Art Scott's point from the audience that it was schizophrenic for writers to come to conventions to court fans while at the same time wanting to be left alone.

There were four private eye panels, including one asking, "The Traditional Private Eye: Is He Dead or Alive and Well?" There was also a panel, led by Sara Paretsky, called "The Mystery Writer as the Conscience of Society."

One of the memorable people at the San Diego Bouchercon (and others) was Kerry Littler, a tiny woman from Annapolis, Maryland, who dressed in a deerstalker and carried "Sherlock Hound," a stuffed dog, also in a deerstalker. For the most part she only talked to people through the dog. She had the disconcerting habit of barging into private parties. In San Diego, though not a subscriber to *MDM*, she crashed the Saturday party that its editor, Bob Napier, gave, and he asked her to leave. In the early 1990s people noticed she had stopped appearing at Bouchercon. Don Sandstrom, whose daughter lives in Annapolis, did detective work to track her, finding she had died of cancer in 1991. That news made some feel guilty that they had not tried to be kinder to her since she obviously had trouble with interpersonal relations.

There were late parties on Saturday night, but early Sunday morning people at the U. S. Grant were awakened at dawn by helicopters flying over the roof. Vice President George Bush was in San Diego to campaign for President, and helicopters were providing security. He moved into the hotel, and Mary Higgins Clark had to give up her suite to him.

The 1990 Bouchercon bid got much attention because London was bidding against Omaha which, as a Midwestern city, was next in rotation. London won, leaving some Americans annoyed that there would not be a US Bouchercon. There was a feeling that the Midwest was being denied its year since a Los Angeles bid for 1991 had already been approved. Sandstrom wondered, "Why did the Midwest have to lose its turn at bat?" However, many supported an international Bouchercon; it was now regularly calling itself the World Mystery Convention. Bruce Taylor and Steve Stilwell, who had put on US conventions, were among the strongest supporters of London, promising to help. Stilwell asked in *MDM*, "Why shouldn't British fandom have a shot at enjoying what we've enjoyed all these years?"

1989: Philadelphia

The 20th Bouchercon reached a milestone when over 1,000 people attended, October 6–8, at Philadelphia's Society Hill Sheraton. Deen and Jay Kogan, a Philadelphia couple active in local theatre, chaired the convention. "Give Me Liberty or Give Me... Death" was the convention slogan, and it was used on t-shirts and sweatshirts for sale. There were also bumper stickers, one of which my wife bought and placed on her car because it said, "Take Pity on Me; My Spouse Collects Books." In 1990 the Kogans applied for and obtained a trademark for Bouchercon.

Simon Brett, the British mystery writer was Guest of Honor. Not only did he give an amusing speech, much of which was in the form of a poem, but he wrote a witty article for the program, as by his series character, explaining why Charles Paris couldn't attend. Beginning a trend toward multiple honorees, Philadelphia also honored Dorothy Salisbury Davis with a Lifetime Achievement Award, editor Joan Kahn for "Distinguished Contribution to the Field," and William Link, co-creator of *Mannix*, *Columbo*, and *Murder, She Wrote*, with a performance award.

There were two Fan Guests of Honor: Linda Toole, of Rochester, New York, an ardent fan of Rex Stout, and witty William F. Deeck of College Park, Maryland. When toastmaster Bruce Taylor introduced Deeck at the banquet, he joked about the latter's affinity for the unintentionally funny books of James Corbett. Deeck's reply, "But he doesn't mind selling me the books," drew many laughs.

In the past, Bouchercon started on Friday evening, allowing people to travel on that day. With authors so anxious to be on panels, a full third day was deemed necessary. Philadelphia started at 9:30 AM Friday. There were four tracks, with videotapes also shown. In response to requests, Friday's programming included three fan-oriented panels: a retrospective on twenty years of fandom that I moderated; one on fan magazines, led by Deeck; and collecting from the fan perspective, moderated by Toole. People spent much time (and money) in the booksellers' room. Many attendees wanted to purchase the books of authors at Bouchercon and have them autographed. Carl Melton, attending his first Bouchercon, set a $200 limit for book purchases but found the book room so tempting that he spent that amount in his first hour, leaving him unhappy on future trips when he saw more books he wanted.

At a panel called "After Equality What?" Sandra Scoppettone "outed" herself, revealing she had written three mysteries under the pseudonym "Jack Early" because she found it easier to get published using a man's name. She also revealed she would be using her own name hereafter and was writing a private eye novel with a lesbian protagonist.

Another notable panel was booked as an interview of writer Michael Avallone by Mike Nevins. Those who attended wondered what to expect because of Avallone's vituperative letters to *MDM*. It was a mellow, charming "Avo" in Philadelphia, but he hardly allowed Nevins to get a word in. Bruce Taylor described Nevins's efforts to conduct the interview as "like trying to hold fifty pounds of water in a thirty pound sack." It was amusing to see Nevins almost speechless as Avallone talked enthusiastically, but without stop, about movies and his books.

The Kogans scheduled innovative activities. Charlotte MacLeod was hostess for "Tea and Bloody Marys," at the Edgar Allan Poe House, where Poe lived when he wrote what is generally recognized as the first detective story. Two short stories by members of Sisters in Crime, a new organization to promote female writers, were dramatized at the Kogans's Society Hill Playhouse. "Boucher's Corner" was a room where times were scheduled for fans to meet and talk to the writers of the kinds of books they liked.

The banquet, for the first time, had assigned seating. Some were upset at not being able to sit with friends. However, others liked the practice because the randomness allowed them to meet people they might not have met otherwise. For example, we sat next to a new novelist, Anita Zelman, and her husband and have been friends since.

The controversy regarding the selection of London resumed in 1989 with rumors that there would be attempts in Philadelphia to overturn the vote. In *MDM*, Max Allan Collins called the selection of London "elitist." He said, "I sincerely hope London can be voted down or that an alternate con (perhaps sponsored by PWA) will offer the continental United States an option."

Fortunately, the advice of Taylor, Stilwell, et al, was heeded, and there was no attempt to derail the London Bouchercon. For those choosing not to go to London, there would be 1990 convention choices not conflicting with Bouchercon.

No report on Philadelphia is complete without mention of its large lobby. For the first time, fans, especially those who wrote to each other in *MDM*, gathered in one place and talked for hours. A relatively young fan, Gary Warren Niebuhr, reported that he "sat at the feet of" Charles Shibuk, Bill Deeck, and myself. He generously said, "So much information was flying through the air I felt like someone should be making an oral history of the conversation." One of the most active fans during late-hour lobby discussions was Orietta Hardy-Sayles, who could have been speaking for many in Philadelphia when she wrote, "I had a terrific time at Bouchercon. I didn't get any sleep."

Observant Linda Toole reported that a month after Bouchercon, on November 19, an episode of *Murder, She Wrote* was set at a San Francisco "Boucheron." Television not only misspelled the convention's name but also gave it a French pronunciation, whereas Anthony Boucher pronounced his pseudonym to rhyme with "voucher."

14

Mystery Readers International (1981–)

In 1981, Janet A. Rudolph of Berkeley, California, started this umbrella organization of fans, authors, booksellers, and others "dedicated to enriching the lives of mystery readers." It has grown into the largest mystery fan organization, with 1,500 members, located in all fifty US states and twenty-two foreign countries. Rudolph has edited and published her organization's journal since the Fall 1985 newsletter, *Mystery Readers of America*. It then had several title changes and for two years was *Mystery Readers of America Journal*. (It had been bimonthly but became quarterly with the start of its third year.) With Vol. 4 No. 2 (Summer 1988), it became *MRA Journal*, then with Vol. 5 assumed its present title, *Mystery Readers Journal*, as it was no longer restricted to America.

Each issue since February 1986 (about art mysteries) has focused on a specific theme. Some topics, for example, religion, medicine, gardening, sports, and legal mysteries, are so popular they have been the subject more than once. Often, the response is so great Rudolph has to devote two issues to a theme. Whatever the topic, she finds people willing to write reviews and articles about it. This includes many fiction writers who write when it matches their books. For an issue on religious mysteries, Rochelle Krich wrote "Coming Out of the Orthodox Jewish Closet." Regarding music, John Harvey wrote on jazz, and Reginald Hill wrote, "Me, Music and Mahler."

Whatever the subject, Philip Scowcroft of England manages to match it with British mysteries. Early in the life of *Mystery Readers Journal*, Bill Deeck wrote retrospective reviews of older books. He also compiled an index of *MRJ*'s first ten volumes. Since 1989, I have contributed a column, "In Short," discussing short stories about the issue's theme.

MRI Director Janet A. Rudolph.

The *Journal* is also one of the best sources of news, with listings of conferences and book discussion groups, bookstores, reference works, prizes awarded, and publishing information about its members. Since 1985, the readers of *MRJ* have voted on the Macavity Awards, presented at Bouchercon.

15 Mystery News (1982–)

By the 1980s, as mysteries grew increasingly popular, the fan revolution led to new journals not designed for articles and letters. The established magazines were providing the scholarship, as was an array of new reference books. With more mysteries published than ever, readers felt they most needed reviews. Once, Boucher's columns were the "gold standard" for recommendations. By 1980 there was no single person who carried his critical stature, though Allen J. Hubin and Jon L. Breen were well regarded. 1982 saw the birth of two prize-winning journals consisting mainly of reviews, and they have shown remarkable staying power.

The purpose of *Mystery News*, as stated by editor-publisher Patricia Shnell of Sparks, Nevada, in its first issue (January-February 1982) was to inform "about as many new mystery books, those recently published and those about to be published, as possible." She also included news and interviews. Despite changes of ownership, *Mystery News* remains consistent in filling these goals, though it now provides more information about mystery conventions and awards. It remains a tabloid newspaper, published bimonthly.

In 1988 Harriet Stay, a US Postmaster from Port Townsend, Washington, and her husband Larry took over *Mystery News* as editor and publisher respectively. Harriet conducted interviews and wrote reviews and editorials. An important feature was "Previews," which in some issues occupied almost half of the space. These were brief plot synopses of forthcoming books.

With the July-August 1997 issue Lynn Kaczmarek of Illinois and Chris Aldrich of Levittown, NY, operating as Black Raven Press, took over *Mystery News*, which had not been published for a year, honoring subscriptions from the previous owners. They changed little about it, but increased the number of pages, sometimes to forty. Kaczmarek writes an editorial called "Quoth the Raven," while Aldrich provides "Mystery Calendar" and other news in her "Mysterious Stuff." There are a few columns. Since1998 I have written about books and authors of the past. At first I called it "Classic Corner" but changed it to "Out of the Past." Starting in the March-April 1999 issue, Stephen Miller has interviewed authors of first novels under the heading "In the Beginning…".

There is the occasional article, but *Mystery News*'s stock in trade is its reviews and previews, with such excellent reviewers over the years as Frank Denton, Virginia R. Knight, Sally Fellows, Barry Gardner, Don Sandstrom, Barbara Peters, and Gary Warren Niebuhr. Interviews continue to be important, and have increased in number, with a regular cover interview featured. In 2001, *Mystery News* won an Anthony as best fan journal. As of the end of 2004, it had a circulation of 1,380 copies.

16 The Drood Review of Mystery (1982–)

The other review journal that began in 1982 was *The Drood Review of Mystery*, founded by Jim Huang of Boston. From 1977 through 1980, when he lived in New Jersey, Huang published *Cloak and Dagger*, which was primarily, according to him, "a mystery news 'zine." Besides news of forthcoming books and television shows, there were reviews, occasional short stories, and a column by Stuart Kaminsky on mystery films. Huang had fewer than 100 subscribers then.

In 1982 Huang began to publish *Drood*, almost as a cooperative with other mystery fans. It has always consisted mostly of reviews and one of the most complete listings of forthcoming mysteries available anywhere. Articles are few, though in 1987 I wrote a four-part series on the "Nameless Detective" books of Bill Pronzini.

Drood has often been accused of political correctness. Huang once called himself "the last bastion of liberalism," and sexism and racism were mentioned in his editorials. For example, he said in April 1985 that he finds sexism in a disproportionate number of reviews by men.

Social issues found their way into *Drood* reviews, for example Ed Blachman's "So Far We've Come, So Far We Have to Go: Women, Feminism and Mystery" in February 1989, his review of three books. Another example was Blachman's "Mysteries with a Conscience: Social Problems in Today's Crime Fiction" in October 1990. In that issue Brad Skillman in "Pedagogic Entertainment" and Kevin R. James in "Voodoo Social Policy" cautioned crime writers to be aware of the potential social message of their work.

Drood Review editor Jim Huang.

Letters in *MDM* and elsewhere criticized *Drood*'s viewpoint. Some found academic pretensions in some of the above as well as pieces such as "The Novelist as Ethologist" and a reprint of Peter Dickinson's Boston Mystery Festival speech, "Mysteries and the Social Fabric."

Drood eventually moved with Huang from Boston to Ann Arbor, Michigan, and then to Carmel, Indiana, where he sells books as The Mystery Company and publishes as Crum Creek Press. *Drood* has remained much as it once was, though increased in size to an average of twenty to twenty-four pages per issue. Social issues do not seem to appear as often in editorials or the reviews of Drood's strong regular staff, which includes Ted Fitzgerald, Jeanne M. Jacobson, and Susan Oleksiw. In 1990, *Drood* was honored as a fan magazine at the first Midwest Mystery & Suspense Convention. Its circulation was 1,440 at the end of 2004.

17 Mystery & Detective Monthly (1984–2003)

The "juice" seemed gone from the letter column of *The Armchair Detective*. Correspondents waited two or three issues to see their letters published, and there was little controversy. Fortunately, "Cap'n Bob" Napier, a former Army enlisted man who was given his "rank" as a nickname while on a gold-prospecting trip, filled the gap. He launched *Mystery & Detective Monthly (MDM)* in June 1984, with sixty-one subscribers, as a magazine for letters by fans. Napier said, "*MDM* was specifically designed so people who would never consider preparing an article for a fanzine could still find a forum for their ideas and opinions." He later punnily called it "the magazine of great letterature." In the second issue, I called *MDM* "Bouchercon Through the Mails."

Jeff Smith wrote the valuable "New Releases" column, describing recent books, for most of the first fifty issues. Then, Bob Samoian handled the column until issue #110 in the month of his death, February 1995. Napier took over in issue #112 and continued until Kelly Wolterman stepped in for issues #167 (August 2000) through #200.

MDM grew steadily. At first, Napier offered a free issue to anyone who contributed a letter of 100 words or more. By issue #13 he was receiving thirty letters, most more than 100 words, and it became an economic necessity that, with issue #15, he stop giving free copies in return for letters. However, he did permit subscribers to run free ads. Though *MDM* occasionally had columnists, they did not last long. Ed Gorman had a column, "The Criminal Element," for only three issues, beginning with #14 (September 1985). Frank Denton's column, "D.O.A." began in #18 (January-February 1986) and ran until #41 (April 1988). *MDM* remained, in addition to "New Releases," primarily for letters and Napier's editorials ("My Word").

From the beginning, the letters (there were eleven in the first issue) were lively, controversial, and fun to read and answer. A feature from the start was a humorous heading by Napier above each letter. (June Moffatt said he should be called "Caption Bob.") Napier attracted fans, but he also received letters from professional mystery writers.

MDM contained accounts of mystery conventions, opinions on books, reports on correspondents' writing careers and personal lives, and stories of book hunting. Some opinions were well informed. For example, LAPD detective Paul Bishop wrote about errors and lack of authenticity in Elizabeth Linington's police procedurals. Other opinions were outrageous, apparently meant to provoke debate. In issue #4 Robert Randisi said he "detested" English mystery writers. There were helpful letters, as when Art Scott wrote on how to catalog one's collection, using a computer database. Even obscure questions, such as the identity of the dedicatee of an Aaron Marc Stein mystery, were usually answered.

An area of controversy involved fans of hardboiled mysteries versus those who preferred an emphasis on detection. Joe R. Lansdale was popular with many *MDM* readers, but Bob Samoian said of one of Lansdale's stories, "This kind of vulgar writing belongs, if anywhere, in an adult bookstore, or a garbage can, but not in my library." Lansdale's editor, Wayne Dundee, defended him and his own judgment and then attacked Barry Pike and Meredith Phillips, who had agreed with Samoian, calling them "cozy readers" with a contempt for hardboiled and "blue collar" writers.

Herb Resnicow was also involved in the *MDM* debate sometimes characterized in simplistic terms as cozy vs. hardboiled. Resnicow, who wrote well-plotted detective puzzles, criticized what he termed "GEMSAV (Gratuitous Explicit Mindless Sex and Violence)." Another debate concerned the balance in crime fiction between plot and character. I thought plot the most important part of a mystery, but Michael Seidman advocated emphasizing character development, saying, "Plots are for graves."

MDM regulars thought of themselves as part of a family, especially after the gathering in the Holiday Inn lobby at the first Omaha convention. The next year, Cap'n Bob was honored at that convention for his work on *MDM*, and his readers provided him with a special copy of *MDM*, numbered 72½. Inspired by Orietta Hardy-Sayles, it was a written "roast" of Napier.

On the night before the 1991 Pasadena Bouchercon, people who wrote letters for *MDM*

The infamous MDM take-over of the Omaha Holiday Inn lobby at the Midwest Mystery & Suspense Convention in 1990. Facing the camera (l. to r.) Ann Smith, Jeff Smith, Jo Ann Vicarel, Marv Lachman; with backs to camera June Moffatt (l.) and Mike Nevins.

were invited to Bob Samoian's home and provided with food, drink, and a tour of his library of 23,000 mystery books. Also memorable was a hilarious informal dinner of *MDM* contributors at a Japanese restaurant at the 1992 Toronto convention. At the 1994 Seattle Bouchercon, Cap'n Bob arranged an *MDM* dinner on Bainbridge Island, following a scenic ferry ride.

Subscribers felt free to share life experiences, happy and sad. Josh Pachter wrote of his heartache during a custody fight over his infant daughter. Ann Williams told of her husband's terminal illness, but a few years later she shared the good news that her first novel was to be published. Arnold Marmor's widow sent a letter announcing his death, and telling how much reading *MDM* and writing for it meant to him. Paul Bishop described what it was like to be on duty on the streets of Los Angeles during the riots following the verdict in the trial of the policemen accused of beating Rodney King. When Bill Crider was wondering whether to retire, he shared his uncertainty with *MDM* readers. In one issue David McKean wrote why he was closing his bookstore, while Sue Feder reported she was buying one. Correspondents wrote of their illnesses so often George Kelley suggested that *MDM* stood for "Medical Diagnosis Monthly." Samoian said that *MDM* kept him going during his final illness.

As in all families, there were disagreements and misunderstandings in the *MDM* "family," making for lively reading. In 1985, Napier announced his editorial decision to ban mention of writer L. A. Morse from his pages. Morse had gone to Canada to avoid the draft during the Vietnam War. Napier opposed mentioning "the ones who deserted their country in a time of crisis, and who left other of their countrymen to take their place." Guy M. Townsend called Napier's position "reactionary" and cancelled his subscription to *MDM*. The issue was debated in *TMF*, but not in *MDM* because of Napier's ban on mentioning Morse. By 1989 Napier was willing to let Morse's name appear. *MDM* had won an award from *Mystery Scene* as best fanzine, and he felt, having "achieved a level of prominence," he must cater more to the views of his readers than to his own feelings.

Some of Michael Avallone's letters were almost four pages long. He claimed that he was cheated out of royalties by publishers and then blacklisted because he complained. Avallone sent long letters with his complaints to individual fans, but *MDM* gave him a wider audience. Napier preferred not censoring letters, but possibly libelous material from Avallone, as well as the length of his diatribes, sorely pressed his patience, and he occasionally was forced to use the editorial blue pencil until Avallone left on his own. Before he left, Avallone criticized Anthony Boucher and, in what seemed to be envy, currently successful writers Mary Higgins Clark, Lawrence Block, Sue Grafton, and Bill Pronzini. What was valuable in Avallone's letters were his personal reminiscences of mystery writers of the 1940s and 1950s, especially Cornell Woolrich.

Robert Randisi failed to appreciate Herb Resnicow's heavy-handed humor when he urged Randisi to return to MWA, "We need you. To hell with personal problems; a divorce you can always get. Or you can make an appointment to be home one night a month; if that doesn't satisfy Anna, she's isn't fit to be the wife of a mystery writer." Randisi took offense and, denying that personal problems caused him to quit MWA, said, "I will never again write a letter to *MDM*, or any other fanzine."

Randy Russell wrote a letter that implied that he and Joan Hess had a personal relationship at an Omaha mystery convention. Hess indignantly denied it and said she resented what "I perceived of as a snide attack on my reputation." Russell subsequently apologized in *MDM* for his attempt at humor. Later, Russell had "words" with Hal Blythe and Charlie Sweet, who write fiction as Hal Charles, but he soon disappeared from *MDM*'s pages and from the mystery scene.

When, in 1998, I questioned Mickey Spillane's influence on the mystery, Max Al-

Ian Collins responded by referring to my assertions as "absurd." Knowing that Collins feels strongly about Spillane, I chose not to take what he had written personally, responding that I wasn't referring to his impact on publishing but to the quality of his work, calling Spillane "a writer for the 16-year-old in the American reader." There was little comment about our controversial remarks, an ominous sign for *MDM* and fandom.

Some correspondents who were professional writers and editors reacted to what they considered negative reviews of their work by fans. They thought writers should only be reviewed by their peers. Most strident in this regard was William Campbell Gault, who was cantankerous in print, though well liked personally. In issue #18 he wrote, "For those vitriolic fans with cast iron opinions, who rave on endlessly in your columns, may I suggest they spend their energies more fruitfully by writing mysteries (or whatever) instead of opinions." Later, he wrote, "I don't need the support of amateurs to keep me going. Or fanzines." Gault was quick to criticize, but equally quick to apologize, as when he suggested that Paul Bishop needed a remedial reading course. He had a second feud with Paul Bishop when the latter criticized one of his stories. When a Canadian, Charles MacDonald, criticized his novels, Gault called him "that puke from British Columbia." His increasingly thin skin led Gault to stop writing for *MDM*, but urged by its readers, he returned. When he no longer could get published (his later novels *were* weak), he still wrote to *MDM*, saying, "I have to write; that is the nature of this critter." He wrote of his felt need "to educate your opinionated readers." Sometimes he had two letters in an issue of *MDM*, also using one of his pseudonyms, Roney Scott or Dial Forest.

Randisi and Collins objected to criticism of Gault in the pages of *MDM*. Randisi belittled fan reviewers, saying "when it comes to commenting on writing—good or bad—they should leave that to the professional reviewers and critics." He distinguished between readers and fans, calling the latter "that breed of 'reader' who, when they don't like a book, write to a fanzine or go to a convention for the purpose of telling that writer how bad his book was, and what he should have done." Far less stridently, Carolyn G. Hart suggested that authors should review. "The point is not to protect poor writing, but to afford an author a thoughtful judgment by a peer."

Fans gave as good as they got, recommending that no writer be considered above criticism. Ann Williams objected to Randisi's premise that fans can't tell good writing from bad. Michael Reilly said, "Appreciation of good writing, and recognition of bad, comes from close and intelligent reading rather than from joining the 'professional reviewers' union." I paraphrased Clemenceau regarding generals in war when I said that mystery reviewing was too important to be left to mystery writers alone. They could judge how difficult it is to *write* a mystery, but fans are best able to judge the final product. Randy Himmel pointed out that most reviews in fan journals were favorable and provided good publicity.

Bill Deeck used sarcasm, writing, "Still it's nice that Randisi accepts most of the fans despite their being unpleasant, opinionated, and wrongheaded." Jo Ann Vicarel feared "The danger here is that fan is becoming a dirty word and something that no right thinking lover of mystery fiction wants tacked onto her name." Several fans writing to *MDM* reported a noticeable anti-fan bias at San Diego's 1988 Bouchercon.

Some *MDM* subscribers were bothered by the controversies. Maryell Cleary, a minister, announced that she would not resubscribe, partly because of the "feuds." She was told she'd be missed and changed her mind. Through *MDM* she met Ellen Nehr, whose tastes in mysteries she shared, and Nehr loaned books to her.

Eventually 232 people contributed letters to *MDM*, but there was a small group of fans that wrote often. Bill Crider never missed an issue. Carolyn G. Hart described the plight of new readers to *MDM*: "It's like dropping into a cocktail party late and overhearing snatches about people you know." Using the same metaphor, Margaret Maron likened *MDM* to "a nicely raucous cocktail party where one may barge in on conversations." *MDM*'s regulars were welcoming, and newcomers quickly felt at home.

In September 1993, Napier raised the possibility that he might have to discontinue publication after that issue, #96. Many letters in #97 expressed dismay at the news, but Napier decided he could continue. He again considered ending *MDM* in 2000 because, with job and family commitments, it was too time-consuming. However, Kelly Wolterman's agreeing to handle "New Releases" shifted enough of the burden to allow *MDM* to continue. In February 2001 Napier announced an irrevocable decision to cease publication, though not until after issue number 200. By 2001 only about a dozen people wrote letters for each issue; in the late 1980s several issues had thirty-three letters. There were only ten letters in #190, but fourteen pages listing "New Releases."

Twenty-five people contributed to the final issue in October 2003, heaping praise on Napier. Art Scott pointed out that he was "the sole loony in mystery fandom" who had been putting out a publication (*DAPA-EM*'s mailing) longer than Napier's almost twenty years. Beth Fedyn wrote, "Bob and *MDM* have introduced me to a lot of wonderful people. I treasure the friends I've made through these pages." Blythe and Sweet, who wrote together, asked, "Where could you find a more knowledgeable, friendly group than we've encountered here over the years?" Bob Adey wondered where he would now get "this class of scuttlebutt" about the mystery. I wrote that, as part of my research for the book you are now reading, I reread *MDM* from the first issue and "many letters are just as interesting now as they were the first time."

In October 2003, at the Las Vegas Bouchercon, the final *MDM* gathering took place, a breakfast organized by Fedyn honoring Napier. He downplayed his own role, graciously repeating, in essence, what he had written in the last issue: "I've gotten back tenfold what I've put into *MDM*."

18

CADS (1985–)

In July 1985, five years after Ethel Lindsay discontinued the first general British fan magazine, Geoff Bradley, an Essex school teacher (now retired), launched *CADS (Crime and Detective Stories)*. In his first editorial, Bradley described himself as a longtime reader of fanzines such as *The Armchair Detective* and *The Mystery Trader*, but he promised not to use "that horrible word fanzine" again. He decided not to offer subscriptions or follow a strict schedule, removing the pressure of deadlines. However, occasionally even he has seen fit to "apologise" for long delays.

In addition to encouraging articles on any subject related to crime fiction (he offered complimentary copies to those writing them), Bradley was especially anxious to receive letters, which he called "the life-blood of any magazine," and his readers responded, often disagreeing with each other, as well as supplying corrections and additional information. Because *CADS* was lively, readers, including Al Hubin, quickly compared it to the early issues of *TAD*. American reader Myrtis Broset said in issue #7 (December 1987) that "I get information I cannot find in a publication here." Others noted *CADS*'s "personal touch," something *TAD* had lost. By his third issue, Bradley had more articles than could be included in one issue, and that has continued for the twenty years of *CADS*'s existence. His circulation was about 300 as he prepared issue #47 early in 2005.

Some writers appeared in virtually every issue. Philip Scowcroft of Yorkshire, since the second issue, has found mysteries about such unlikely subjects as Parliament, walking sticks, trams, and snow to discuss interestingly. His series on British regional mysteries cries for book publication. Peter Tyas had an article or letter in every issue of *CADS*, including #28 (May 1996), which, sadly, announced his death. Bill Deeck was one of *CADS*'s best and most varied contributors. He wrote, with tongue in cheek, "The Genius of James Corbett" and "Further Gems from the Literature." Deeck also wrote "Mysteries with Magicians: A Mildly Annotated Checklist." He was a frequent reviewer and assumed the task, in one of *CADS*'s columns, "Checking the References," of correcting the dozens of mistakes in *Sleuths, Sidekicks and Stooges* (1997) by Joseph Green and Jim Finch. Deeck indexed *CADS*'s first thirty issues.

Bob Adey is a frequent writer about his specialties: impossible crimes and locked room mysteries, and he also writes reviews of obscure short story collections. He is one of *CADS*'s literary detectives, reporting bibliographic discoveries, something done rarely, if at all, in other

British fans Bob Adey (l.), impossible crime specialist, and Geoff Bradley (r.), founder of *CADS*.

fan journals. Adey reported on his discovery of what was probably the second book about mystery fiction: *Masterpieces of Detective Fiction*, by C.A. Soorma. It was published in 1919 in Rangoon, Burma, by the American Baptist Press. Paul Moy was the first of these sleuths, discovering in issue #7 a lost John Dickson Carr novel written under the pseudonym Nicholas Wood.

Chief literary sleuth for *CADS*, writing under the title "Serendip's Detections," is Tony Medawar, who discovered a new Roger Sheringham story by Anthony Berkeley, a Nigel Strangeways radio play by Nicholas Blake, an Agatha Christie short story as well as information regarding a Christie play that was destroyed, a Carr short story, a John Rhode radio play and another pseudonym for Major Cecil Street, who wrote as Rhode and Miles Burton. In #37 (May 2000), another *CADS* detective, Thea Clayton, wrote engagingly of her research into the life (and death) of Herbert Adams, the leading author of golf mysteries. She traveled to interview Adams's nephew (age eighty-eight) just a few days before his death.

Other scholars who have contributed to *CADS* include Barry Pike, Ian Godden, and Malcolm Turnbull, as well as the two leading scholars of John Dickson Carr: Douglas Greene and James Keirans. Many leading British fiction writers, such as H. R. F. Keating, Martin Edwards, and David Williams, have written articles or letters.

Several features from *The Mystery Fancier* moved to *CADS* when it ceased publication in 1992. William A. S. Sarjeant continued his series "Crime Novelists As Writers of Children's Fiction" with articles on Patricia Moyes, Gladys Mitchell, J. S. Fletcher, and the Lockridges, among others. In March 1993 my obituary column, "Death of a Mystery Writer," began to appear in *CADS*, where it is still published. I include critics, reviewers, actors, directors, and others with a relationship to mystery fiction. I have help from many fans, especially *CADS* readers, people I dub "Lachman's Obituarians," coining the latter word because it flows more easily than the correct word "obituarists."

My column inadvertently started a political controversy in *CADS*. In writing of the deaths of people who worked in movies or television, I mention, if factual and important to their careers, whether they had been "blacklisted" in the McCarthy era. Rinehart Potts, with whom I had clashed in *The Poisoned Pen*, took exception to the use of "blacklist" and pointed out that many of these people denied employment had been members of the Communist Party. He compared them to spies who had worked for the Soviet Union, but in response to requests by Bradley and myself failed to "name names" of any in the arts who had been Soviet agents. Potts decided not to read *CADS* anymore; he had been getting it from Bradley in exchange for his *Linington Lineup*.

Since the ninth issue, Bob Cornwell has contributed good artwork on the front covers of *CADS*. He also conducts "The Questionnaire," an interview column. Cornwell's political views are often apparent in his reviews and letters, and they also seem behind one of the questions he asks all writers he interviews: "Are you in favour of the death penalty for murder?" All he interviewed are against it, with the exception of Dick Francis who suspected Cornwell's motives when he replied, "Is this the real question to be answered camouflaged amongst all the others? The answer is 'Yes,' but not as a mandatory sentence for all murder as it was prior to 1965. Particularly brutal crimes demand brutal punishment."

A non-political controversy was sparked by John Hogan's letter in #19 (October 1992) in which he objected to obscene language in Robert B. Parker's Spenser series. Most writers who responded disagreed with Hogan, who then replied in rather intemperate fashion questioning their moral values. Hogan died in September 1993; the announcement of his death appeared along with a reasonable response from Barry Gardner who said that many accepted Parker's language in their reading without routinely using such language themselves.

Though *CADS* devotes more space to Golden Age writers than other journals, it also discusses recent mysteries. Cornwell wrote in #26 (September 1995) that he wanted "more realism, blood, sex and violence" in the mystery. Before printing John Boyles's "The Drift to Realism," an article about James Crumley in #36 (November 1999), Bradley wrote that the language might offend some readers.

CADS is important in establishing ties between mystery fans on both sides of the Atlantic, with Americans significant contributors to it. Americans visiting England often meet with Bradley, Adey, and Pike, and other English fans. *CADS* has also helped to publicize British mystery conventions which began in 1990.

19 Mystery Scene (1985–)

Though containing material of interest to fans, *Mystery Scene* was started by writers Ed Gorman and Robert J. Randisi and devoted much space to promotion of writers. In the first issue, dated 1985 and mailed with *MDM*, Randisi stated its goal was "to entertain and inform mystery writers *and* readers as fully and completely as possible with publishing news, stories and, when necessary, rumors, as well as book reviews, articles, and interviews." Publishing news made up most of the first issue, which included an article by Ray Puechner, "Finding an Agent."

Mystery Scene, looking to increase its subscriber base, in the second issue (twenty-four pages) added "The Horror Scene" and reported on the World Fantasy Convention. Still, there were profiles of mystery writers and Ellen Nehr's column "Murder Ad Lib," containing news and reviews, mostly of "cozy" books, providing contrast in a magazine that seemed to tilt in favor of hardboiled material. Michael Seidman and William Campbell Gault began columns in the second issue.

By the third issue in 1986, *Mystery Scene* had almost 200 subscribers and was fifty-two pages. A new columnist was Warren B. Murphy, writing "Curmudgeon's Corner," giving them two curmudgeons because Gault fit that description too. The magazine continued expanding its definition of the mystery scene with Kevin Randle's article on "The World of Action Adventure." More mystery-related was Josh Pachter's new short story column "The Short Sheet." In Issue #16, Bill Pronzini showed that he was a fan as well as a writer with his article on forgotten short story writer Bryce Walton.

I was not alone in perceiving an early bias against fans in *Mystery Scene,* though it never extended to refusing our subscription payments. I criticized that and the inclusion of horror and fantasy in a magazine titled *Mystery Scene.* Michael Seidman responded, taking umbrage, especially at my calling him "Mike," which I had heard people do at Bouchercons. He also objected to my characterizing as "whining and doomsday forecasting" the remarks he made at Bouchercons about the state of the mystery, when he admonished fans to support writers by buying their books. In the January 1987 issue, he launched his strongest attacks on fans, saying the majority were negative and that "Ultimately, those who label themselves fans do not have the power to create. They are vampires, sucking the very essence of life from those and that which they adulate."

Not willing to let Seidman have the last word, I wrote a letter for the eighth issue about his artificial distinction between "aficionados"—whom he regarded favorably—and "fans," whom he denigrated. I said he was ignoring the time and money fans had put into writing for fan magazines and putting on Bouchercons, activities that benefit writers. I also mentioned a gratuitous dig by Gault at fan magazines in *Mystery Scene.*

It was difficult to keep up with the changes in format of *Mystery Scene.* What started as a four-page first issue had grown to a ninety-eight-page publication, with a slick cover, by the fourth issue. Then, the fifth issue morphed into a tabloid newspaper without issue number, date, or table of contents, but the sixth issue was a magazine again, now with a comic book section, as well as an original short story. In January 1987 it was a tabloid again, and had added eight pages about Westerns. Then, in March 1987 the eighth issue was called *Mystery Scene Newsletter*, and it was in the form of a magazine. Randisi described it as containing "48 pages of information about the mystery and horror publishing scene, essays, columns, interviews and reviews." He promised eight issues a year. The fiction was omitted, to be included in a new quarterly magazine to be called *Mystery Scene Reader*. Fiction occasionally returned, as with a 20,000-word story by Dean Koontz in 1999, followed by two issues in which *Mystery Scene*, in its promotional mode, included first chapters of many novels.

The "Newsletter" concept did not last long, nor did the *Mystery Scene Reader*. By the 13th issue, it was back to simply *Mystery Scene*, and it still did not give the month of the issue. The fans vs. writers "feud" was apparently over, but *Mystery Scene* was, in the words of Jon Breen, "a

Jon L. Breen, frequent contributor to *Mystery Scene* and *EQMM* reviewer..

lightning rod for controversy." Warren Murphy in his column criticized Harlan Ellison, drawing a heated response followed by an apology from Murphy for what he admitted was "a gratuitous cheapshot." Other early feuds included Seidman vs. MWA, and Joe Lansdale vs. Jo Ann Vicarel on the subject of Elizabeth George. Barbara Mertz, Linda Grant, and Laurie R. King wrote of their perceptions of male sexism.

In #15, *Mystery Scene* was soliciting votes from their readers for "The American Mystery Awards," which were awarded for about five years. One category was for "Best Fan Publication," and *Mystery Scene* got the most votes for 1987. They decided not to accept the award, but it was apparently due to modesty, not because Randisi said they weren't a fan magazine. (At the 1986 Bouchercon, Randisi emphasized that *Mystery Scene* is not a fan magazine.) Editing was casual, and they admitted they could improve their proofreading; they reported the death of Elizabeth "Lenningston" (Linington).

Anthologist Martin H. Greenberg replaced Randisi as publisher, with Ed Gorman soon sharing editorial duties with his son Joe. Ed referred in issue #31 (October 1991) to "the new, improved *Mystery Scene*," which would be published seven times yearly. (In his 2002 article on the history of the magazine, Breen found there had been an average of 4.4 issues per year.) Gorman said he was incorporating suggestions from Scott Winnette, who had experience with the science-fiction magazine *Locus*, and who felt that (in Gorman's words) *"Mystery Scene* wasn't so much a magazine as a grab bag of pieces that happened to interest Ed Gorman." The amount of non-mystery material was reduced. Still, contributors came and went from the pages of *Mystery Scene.* As Breen said, *"Mystery Scene* would pick up and lay down reviewers and columnists in numbers too dizzying to keep track of." My short story column was a casualty in 1993.

Whatever the problems of *Mystery Scene,* perhaps in tribute to Gorman's flexibility, it published for seventeen years. With health problems in 2002, Gorman decided to cut back on his work and sold the magazine to Kate Stine, former editor of *The Armchair Detective,* and her husband, computer-expert Brian Skupin. Their first issue (#76) was dedicated to Gorman and included tributes by many writers, most of whom had never met him (something of a recluse, Gorman seldom leaves Cedar Rapids, Iowa). However, Dean Koontz had been there, and he wrote humorously about his visit.

The cover of #76 proclaimed "See Our New Look!" and it was an attractive, well-illustrated ninety-four pages. It included Jon Breen's column "What About Murder?" and Tom Nolan and Dick Lochte's column reviewing mysteries on tape. Both had been in *TAD.* It also featured material about a neglected area of the mystery, the stage. Gorman remained with a column called "Gormania," which was part of a large section, "The Writing Life," that showed *Mystery Scene* was still more focused on publishing than other fan journals. So did articles by James Grippando and Adam Meyer on their writing lives.

However, other articles provided more historical perspective, including in #77 Breen's history of *Mystery Scene* and Mike Nevins's article on Harry Stephen Keeler: "Nut King of the Universe." In #81 Elizabeth Foxwell wrote of Metta Fuller Victor, who, as Seeley Register, wrote what is generally considered the first American detective novel.

Mystery Scene has the largest circulation of any magazine about the mystery, with a circulation of approximately 7,000 copies. In addition, it is carried in 185 libraries.

Other Fan Magazines &
Organizations: 1980s

Clues (1980–)

Though fans wrote for it and subscribed to it, *Clues* was an academic publication, edited by Pat Browne and published by Bowling Green State University of
Ohio. *Clues* began with the Spring/Summer 1980 issue and maintained a semiannual
schedule until it halted publication in 2002. In his bibliography of secondary sources,
Professor Walter Albert said, "*Clues* is criticized by fans for being too academic and
by academics for not belonging to that unstable list of 'prestige' journals beloved of
university tenure and review committees." Many of the articles may have been written under "publish or perish" strictures. However, the contents included articles not
out of place in strictly fan journals, for example Martha Alderson's "Death at the
Stage Door" about theater mysteries by Anne Morice and Simon Brett.

After a brief hiatus *Clues* returned in 2004, now published by Heldref Publications of Washington, DC, with Elizabeth Foxwell as Managing Editor. The new version will apparently be devoted to individual authors, such as Margery Allingham,
subject of its Fall 2004 issue. Dashiell Hammett and Sara Paretsky are scheduled for
future issues.

The Wilkie Collins Society (1980–)

In 1980 this group—still active—was founded in London to promote interest in
the life and work of this author of 19th century crime novels, including *The Moon-
stone* and *The Woman in White*. A 2004 musical version of the latter, by Andrew
Lloyd Webber, can only increase interest in Collins.

Cloak and Pistol and *Pulpette* (1981–198?)

1981 saw the start of two more magazines devoted to appreciation of the pulps,
both produced by Joseph Lewandowski of San Juan Capistrano, California. *Cloak
and Pistol* was professionally produced and well-illustrated, with cover art by Frank
Hamilton. The first, and apparently only, issue included articles about The Shadow,
Secret Agent X, and The Phantom. *Pulpette* had reproductions from old magazines
as well as detective fiction written in the style of the pulps. It continued for several
years.

The Bony Bulletin (1980–1988)

Having left *The Thorndyke File*, in the early 1980s Philip Asdell started another fan
journal, "published at irregular intervals for Bony and Upfield enthusiasts." Asdell's
audience, of course, knew that he referred to Australian writer Arthur W. Upfield
and his series detective the part-aborigine Napoleon "Bony" Bonaparte. He dedicated his 25th issue (July 1988), the last one of which I have record, to Bony fan Betty

Donaldson, who had encouraged him.

The Maltese Falcon Societies (1981–)

The **Maltese Falcon Society** was organized by Don Herron and others in San Francisco. It had its first meeting on May 20, 1981. At its peak, it had between 100 and 150 members. Originally it met monthly, but after about a year, as the initial enthusiasm

tapered off, its meeting schedule was irregular. Speakers included Charles Willeford, Bill Pronzini, as well as Dashiell Hammett biographers William F. Nolan and Diane Johnson. Its last meeting, May 27, 1986, coincided with Hammett's 92nd birthday. His daughter, Josephine Marshall, spoke. Jiro Kimura, arguably Japan's leading fan, founded the **Maltese Falcon Society of Japan** in 1982, and it still is active, though he is no longer in charge. It issues *The Maltese Falcon Flyer* almost monthly.

The Crime File (1982–1991)

The Crime File was born in June 1982 as the monthly newsletter of The Mystery Club, a group sponsored by the Grounds for Murder Mystery Bookstore in San Diego. Annual dues of $6 included the newsletter and attendance at twice-monthly meetings. Laurie Mansfield Gore, the club's secretary-treasurer, published

Don Herron, Dashiell Hammett fan.

it, at first for members only. By August 1987, *The Crime File* was described as "an independent newsletter." Most of the material was written by Gore at first, though in October 1987, Tom Nolan wrote of the old radio show *Yours Truly, Johnny Dollar*. Gore did interviews, wrote reviews, and accounts of Bouchercons she attended.

I started writing my column "The Short Stop" in January/February 1989 (*The Crime File* had gone bimonthly) and continued it until the magazine ceased publication. With the undated first number of Vol. 10 (apparently in 1991), it had become a quarterly. Beginning in that issue, George Easter conducted the "Future Investigations" column, listing and reviewing new books. *The Crime File*'s publishing life was marked by frequent delays. At one point, Gore asked readers to excuse her "apparent disappearance." Most issues were sixteen pages, though some were shorter. Unspecified problems, the bane of existence of fan magazine publishers, beset Gore. An undated "Special Double Issue," copyright 1991, ended *The Crime File*'s run.

The Thieftaker Journals

Paul Bishop, the Los Angeles police detective with more energy than any person should have, was a marathon runner and mystery fan. He published *The Thieftaker Journals* as his *DAPA-EM* magazine and then, after leaving that group, partly because he felt it was insufficiently appreciated, he published it independently in the early

1980s, using distinctive green covers. Bishop was a great fan of horse racing mysteries, and his May 1983 issue was dedicated to that subject, with articles by him and by Jon L. Breen, equally devoted to that small sub-genre. Bishop went on to become reviewer for *Mike Shayne's Mystery Magazine* and later a successful writer of fiction, but he kept his hand in fandom, especially with letters to *MDM*.

Echoes (1982–2004)

The time, effort, and expense of publishing cause many fan magazines to come to an end quickly. An exception was *Echoes*, the fanzine started by Tom and Ginger Johnson of Texas in June 1982; it lasted 176 issues, until December 2004. That it lasted was due to the efforts of the Johnsons, not because they grew wealthy. In an editorial, they said, "The magazine must break even if it is to survive." At one time they drove 424 miles to get it printed at a price they could afford. Still, they lost $500 their first year.

This was a nostalgia magazine, and though it was mostly about the pulps, there was also material for fans of old films, old-time-radio, and collectors of juvenile series. About half of each issue involved crime fiction, often about Doc Savage, Operator #5, and The Spider. There were also articles on such unusual crime-related pulp magazines as *Gun Molls* and *Underworld Romances*. I wrote an article on *Dime Detective* which, because it was regarded as the second best pulp magazine after *Black Mask*, I called "The Avis of Detective Pulps." *Echoes* attracted the people who wrote for other pulp fan magazines, including Robert Sampson, Will Murray, Nick Carr (a cousin of John Dickson Carr), Link Hullar, and Rex Ward.

At its peak, *Echoes* had almost 300 readers, including two in France and one in Australia. Controversy, largely absent from the pages of *Echoes*, surfaced with issue #96 (December 1997) after readers complained about sexy covers drawn by Ron Wilber. Many liked Wilber's work, though one inappropriately compared objections to Wilber's covers to the Nazi holocaust. Tom Johnson defended his publishing the covers and then at about this time had to defend himself from bad reviews in the Pulp Era Amateur Press Association mailing. In issue #97 he expressed his dismay at the "infighting" and announced he would stop *Echoes* after #100, turning it into a smaller advertising/news magazine. He stopped publishing letters for issues #98–100. In issue #100 (August 1998), he said that it was not only the "infighting" that caused him to cease publication; there were also health reasons. Despite this, Johnson continued *Echoes* as an 8-page monthly newsletter for pulp fans for over six more years.

The Elizabeth Linington Society and *Linington Lineup* (1984–2004)

In 1984 Rinehart S. Potts, of Glassboro State College in New Jersey, began this group and the quarterly newsletter devoted to study and discussion of Elizabeth Linington, the author of police procedurals who was equally famous under her Lesley Egan and Dell Shannon pseudonyms. Potts seemed to share the right-wing political views that Linington held, and this led him into disputes that I wrote about in connection with *The Poisoned Pen* and *CADS*. The society remained active long after Linington's death in 1988, thanks to the efforts of Potts. However, Vol. 21, No. 6, November/December 2004, was his last issue, due to his advancing years and declining health. He said he would reimburse for unfulfilled subscriptions.

I Love a Mystery (1984–)

Sally Powers was casting director for the successful television program *Hill Street Blues* and a mystery fan also. In February 1984, she started a fan magazine with the catchy title *I Love a Mystery*, a title once the name of a popular radio show. At first, she wrote mainly about the Southern California scene, but she began to go farther afield when she attended the first Boston Mystery Festival, interviewing Robert B. Parker there and taping and printing a talk by Guest of Honor Jane Langton. She later visited, wrote about, and photographed the 1984 and 1985 Bouchercons, the Edgar presentations, and two more Boston Mystery Festivals.

Using the title of my *DAPA-EM* magazine, "Just in Crime," I started a review column for *I Love a Mystery* in May 1985. My column included "Doom with a View," my reviews of television and film mysteries, and the mystery obituaries that I still write. Powers stopped publishing *I Love a Mystery* as a magazine after May 1986, though she brought it back as a review newsletter for at least nine issues in the early 1990s. It later became an online-only newsletter and remains so in 2005.

Stephen Wright's Mystery Notebook and *Whitechapel Journal* (1984–2000)

This was one of the more personal journals. Its premiere in winter 1984 coincided with W. Somerset Maugham's birth date in January, and the issue was devoted to Maugham and James M. Cain, two of Wright's favorite writers. Most of the next issue (ten of twelve pages) was devoted to Dashiell Hammett, another favorite of the eponymous editor-publisher. More than half of Vol. 2, No. 3's eight pages were devoted to Wright's article "The Gay Detective Story." In Vol. 3, Wright began publishing his own novel *The Adventures of Sandy West*. This novel about a private eye, which Wright eventually self-published, was billed as featuring the first bisexual detective.

After a hiatus, Wright returned, now calling his magazine *Mystery Notebook*, saying he removed his name due to "modesty." He continued to run material about Maugham and also had an article about Oscar Wilde. Increasingly, non-mystery related material, often about gays, appeared and by his 24th issue, the magazine was titled merely *The Notebook*.

Another interest of Wright's was Jack the Ripper, and he devoted the 16th issue to his crimes. By the fall of 1996, *The Notebook* was gone, and Wright published the first issue of his new magazine *Whitechapel Journal*, a newsletter devoted to Jack the Ripper. It included some historical material and true crime in general, along with Ripperology. It ended in mid-2000 and mail to Wright was returned.

Hardboiled and *Detective Story Magazine* (1985–)

Hardboiled was started in the summer of 1985 as a fiction magazine by Wayne Dundee of Belvidere, Illinois. However, there were occasional articles *about* mystery fiction, for example on Jim Thompson and Robert J. Randisi in the first issue. Hardboiled fiction is also the great love of Gary Lovisi of Brooklyn. He started a magazine of hardboiled fiction in May 1988, using the name *Detective Story Magazine*. After the twelfth and final issue of Dundee's *Hardboiled* in 1990, it was combined with

Lovisi's magazine as *Hardboiled Detective* for three issues. Since March 1992, Lovisi has published it with the less restrictive title *Hardboiled*. For the first twenty issues of Lovisi's magazines, I wrote a column, "That's the Story," about short stories. I was given freedom to say anything I wanted, including my view that the generally accepted definition of "hardboiled" is far too narrow since, by my lights, Miss Marple, with her cynical and realistic view of human nature, is hardboiled. Many issues have contained some non-fiction about the mystery, for example, Art Hackathorn's brief article on Frank Gruber in issue #9 introducing a Gruber story never previously published.

Paperback Parade (1986–)

Lovisi, as part of his publishing empire called Gryphon Books, started *Paperback Parade* in 1986. It followed the pattern of *Paperback Quarterly*, and while there were issues devoted to science fiction, gay and lesbian, Western, and juvenile delinquent paperbacks, much of the content was mystery-related. The first issue had "The Mystery and Detective Paperback" by Jon White. Later issues included "Cornell Woolrich in Paperback," "Collecting Jim Thompson," a "Richard Prather and Shell Scott Special Issue," and a "Mickey Spillane Special Issue." *Paperback Parade* is still alive in 2005.

The Criminal Record (1986–1996)

This was the one-woman operation of Ann M. Williams of Denver. She called her pocket-sized, bimonthly magazine "A Newsletter *for* and *by* Fans of Mystery/Detective Fiction." It consisted mainly of reviews written by Bill Deeck, Mary Helen Becker, Sue Feder, Don Sandstrom, and Barry Gardner among others. As a reviewer for *TCR*, I had a rare instance of agreement with Rinehart Potts. I criticized what I thought was a poor mystery, one written with a grant from the National Endowment for the Arts, and said it gave me second thoughts about how the public's money is spent. Potts, remembering our disagreement in *The Poisoned Pen*, said he was astonished because I agreed with his position regarding government, literature, and the arts.

Williams wrote editorials, punny headings for the reviews, and Bouchercon reports. Though she occasionally had computer and printing problems, it was usually on time and a bargain at $1 (later $1.25) an issue.

There were times when Williams deviated from the basic review format. During the third year of *TCR*, her husband Bob was stricken with cancer, and she continued the magazine but occasionally told of his struggle with the disease and chemotherapy. He died shortly before the 1989 Bouchercon, but Ann went to Philadelphia, keeping her commitment to be on a panel about fan magazines. Though ill, Williams finished ten complete years of publishing with issue #60 in November 1996, before dying that month of a severe liver ailment.

Agatha Christie Fandom (1986–)

In 1986 Amy Lubelski of New York edited and published *Woman of Mystery*, a short-lived magazine described as a "compendium of ideas devoted to Agatha Christie." The *Christie Chronicle*, which began in 1993, lasted longer. It was the journal of the Agatha Christie Society, whose chairman was Mathew Prichard, Christie's grandson; the president was Christie's mother, Rosalind Hicks. Kate Stine edited the newsletter and acted as the society's US director. It included an article, "Teaching Agatha Christie," by Gordon Clark Ramsey, who in 1967 wrote the first of more than a dozen books about Christie. Other articles told of Christie celebrations, including the society's annual trip to see *The Mousetrap* in London and the yearly gathering of the society in Torquay, Christie's hometown. By 2003, the Society (and its magazine) had been disbanded, and replaced by an English website, AgathaChristie.com, called "The Official Online Home of Agatha Christie."

The Short Sheet (1987–1988)

Josh Pachter's column, "The Short Sheet," in *Mystery Scene* outgrew the space it was allowed, so in April 1987, Pachter, a fan as well as a writer and editor of the short story, started *The Short Sheet*. Though Edward D. Hoch had written a column about the short story for *TAD*, Pachter's publication was the first fan magazine devoted to the mystery short story.

News of the short story and summaries of anthologies and magazines was an important part of Pachter's magazine. He interviewed authors known for their short fiction, for example Brendan DuBois. An interesting feature was "Critic's Choice," which contained reviews of favorite past anthologies. Morris Hershman reviewed Ellery Queen's anthology *101 Years Entertainment* (1941), and I reviewed *The Pocket Mystery Reader* (1942), edited by Lee Wright.

In December 1987, Pachter wrote an "obituary" for *Espionage*, a digest-sized fiction magazine started in 1984 that, after a promising start, failed to attract enough subscribers to continue. Ironically, the next issue, January-February 1988, was the last for *The Short Sheet*.

The Margery Allingham Society and *The Bottle Street Gazette* (1988–)

This was a society that started in England but had an American branch. It began in 1988 "to celebrate the life and work of a great 'Queen of Crime.'" Barry Pike, author of *Campion's Career: A Study of the Novels of Margery Allingham* (1987), and Pat Watt were co-editors of the society's newsletter, *The Bottle Street Gazette*, which Pike now edits alone. Its title comes from the location of Campion's London flat. It has included biographical material about Allingham, candid photographs of her, and copies of her correspondence. In America, Maryell Cleary was editor of the US newsletter. The final issue of the US edition was Fall 1995, but the society remains active in England, with an annual dinner, trips, and publication of the semiannual newsletter. In 2004, the society celebrated the centenary of Allingham's birth with a traveling exhibition of visual and literary material from the Allingham archives; publication of a volume of articles and essays about her by other crime writers, friends, and fans; and the unveiling of a commemorative plaque at her former London home.

Pulp Vault (1988–1996)

Pulp Vault, one of the best pulp fan magazines, was started in February 1988 by Doug Ellis of Chicago. In addition to reprinting pulp stories, each issue had articles by knowledgeable fans and by pulp writers themselves. For example, there was a series by Hugh B. Cave "Magazines I Remember," and Theodore Roscoe's memoir "By Writing I Could Eat."

A poignant feature of issue #11 in 1993 was Michael Avallone's obituary for Robert Sampson (1928–1992), perhaps the leading fan writing about pulps. Sampson had written for virtually every magazine, usually about crime stories, and also wrote

Sue Feder, outstanding fan of historical mysteries, in 1999.

seven books about pulps for Popular Press, including six in the "Yesterday's Faces" series. Like some fans, Sampson had turned to fiction; he won MWA's Edgar for Best Short Story of 1986.

Pulp Vault promised it would be published "irregularly," and it lived up to its word; no issues have appeared since 1996.

Historical Mystery Fandom (1988–2002)

Sue Feder of Maryland, a one-woman advocate for the historical mystery, founded the **Ellis Peters Appreciation Society** in December 1988 because of her love of the work of Edith Pargeter, better known as Ellis Peters, the pseudonym she used for mysteries, including her series about Brother Cadfael. Shortly after the death of Pargeter in 1995, Feder suspended publication of *Most Loving Mere Folly: The Journal of the Ellis Peters Appreciation Society* after thirty-one issues. The title was taken from a Shakespearean quote that was also the title of a Pargeter novel.

In the spring of 1998, Feder founded a more general organization: **The Historical Mystery Appreciation Society**. Its magazine, offering news and reviews of historical mysteries, is *Murder: Past Tense*. The society has presented the Herodotus Awards, honoring the best in historical mysteries, at Bouchercon. The magazine and the awards were suspended in 2002 when Feder's illness forced her to take "a long sabbatical."

21 Malice Domestic (1989–)

By the mid-1980s, the success of Bouchercon led fans to consider starting conventions closer to their homes. The idea of smaller, more intimate conventions was also attractive. Some wanted a convention devoted to what they called the "traditional" mystery. Mary Morman, who felt Bouchercon emphasized hardboiled mysteries, was the catalyst that brought the idea to life. However, she gives credit to Barbara Mertz (better known under her pseudonyms Elizabeth Peters and Barbara Michaels) as the focal point around whom Malice Domestic was built. Morman published a newsletter called *The Friends of Barbara Mertz* and held a small (twenty-person) meeting called "Mertzcon" in 1986. It was there that the idea for Malice Domestic took root, with planning meetings beginning in the fall of 1987. Morman says Malice would never have succeeded without Mertz's hard work, especially in attracting famous writers.

The first Malice Domestic, chaired by Morman, was advertised as taking place in Washington, DC, though it was held April 21–23, 1989, at the Sheraton Northwest in Silver Springs, Maryland, close to downtown Washington. Phyllis Whitney was announced as Guest of Honor, but she could not appear due to illness, and Mertz took her place. Ellen Nehr was the Fan Guest of Honor. Tough-talking, she was nonetheless a great fan of cozier fiction, especially novels involving detectives she called "little old ladies" and "little old men." Robert Barnard of England was Toastmaster. At its first convention, Malice Domestic initiated the practice of honoring a dead writer from the past; Agatha Christie was "Ghost of Honor."

Three hundred and fifty people attended; Morman said seventeen were males. Most people enjoyed themselves, though there were complaints. Regarding hotel food service, Bill Deeck said, "the dining room was actually a waiting room, and when the food did arrive you wished you were still waiting." The hotel was just as bad elsewhere with, according to Morman, rooms without hot water, a meeting space that needed cleaning, and maids who left notes in the rooms asking guests to leave the room "as clean as possible."

At the banquet, Barnard lauded the "Ghost," joking that anyone who disliked Agatha Christie could not be his friend. Perhaps reacting to those who dubbed Malice Domestic "Biddycon," Barnard poked fun at PWA and its lengthy award ceremony in San Diego, wondering why critics refer to "the laconic American private eye."

Beginning in 1989, Malice Domestic awarded the "Agatha" Award for best "traditional" work in various categories. Nominees were selected by those who had registered and then voted on by those attending. Carolyn G. Hart won the Agatha for Best Novel, in the form of a teapot with a skull and crossbones on it. Editor Ruth Cavin announced that for 1990 St. Martin's Press would award a $10,000 advance against royalties for the Best First Traditional Mystery Novel in a contest jointly sponsored with Malice Domestic. (St. Martin's, in cooperation with PWA, also offers an award for Best First Private Eye Novel.)

Malice Domestic moved to the Hyatt Regency in Bethesda, Maryland, for 1990, and it proved to be a popular location, with its large atrium-lobby and glass elevator. About 400 people attended. Malice was made more affordable, with Ellen Nehr functioning as "Roommate Coordinator," so those who wished could share the cost of a room. Patricia Moyes was Guest of Honor. Phyllis Brown was Fan Guest of Honor. The "Ghost of Honor" was Dorothy L. Sayers. Phyllis Whitney, at age eighty-six, was now well enough to attend and received a Lifetime Achievement Award.

In 1991 Sue Feder, founder of the Ellis Peters Appreciation Society, appeared at Malice in a monk's cowl similar to that worn by Peters's Brother Cadfael. A most unusual panel was "Warning: Endings Revealed!" in which Margaret Maron, Barbara D'Amato, and Bill Deeck deliberately disclosed the endings of mysteries in order to discuss the craft of writers in resolving plots.

So recognizable had the name "Malice Domestic" become (it is now trademarked) that in 1992 the first of a series of original short story anthologies using that title was published. No editor was shown; it was "presented by" Elizabeth Peters. In her introduction, Peters called Malice Domestic an "Idea Whose Time Had Come" and attempted to define "traditional" mysteries. She felt the kinds of murders in books she called "cozy" involved the personal and private aspects of crime, as opposed to the public and impersonal found in books about serial killers, terrorists, assassins, and hit men.

More men were attending Malice. In 1992 Aaron Elkins was Guest of Honor, and Deeck was Fan Guest of Honor, delivering a hilarious speech about his favorite "bad" writer, James Corbett, who penned such lines as, "He was galvanized into immobility." Mary Higgins Clark was Toastmaster, and Margery Allingham was "Ghost" of Honor. There was an imaginative panel in which Ellen Nehr and her good friend Joan Hess pretended to argue, with Joan "murdering" her. They acted so well that some in the audience grew uncomfortable, not realizing at first it was scripted.

Reporting in *TAD*, Janet Rudolph mentioned "the special touches at Malice which make it stand out head and shoulders above the rest—including giving panelists Godiva chocolates and flowers for their rooms and serving champagne at the opening night reception." In 1992 Malice incorporated, establishing bylaws and a board of directors. By the early 21st century, it even had its own archivist, Ruth Sickafus.

By mid-January 1993, three months before starting, Malice was sold out. 535 people attended. It coincided with the Gay Rights March in Washington, and Marlys Millhiser said wearing her Sisters in Crime sweatshirt on the plane didn't stand out. Other passengers thought she was just making another political statement. Anne Perry was Guest of Honor. Mary Morman was Fan Guest of Honor. The unusual selection for "Ghost of Honor" was Shakespeare, whose plays are replete with murder.

Attendance at the sixth Malice Domestic closed shortly after January 1, 1994, with over 500 registrants, including 140 first-time attendees. In a letter to *MDM*, Deeck, one of the organizers, defined its purpose as "to celebrate what was felt to be a neglected aspect of the mystery.... Malice Domestic is a fan—some would prefer to say, a readers' convention, not an authors' convention. Certainly flogging books is not frowned on, but our primary purpose is not to increase book sales." Malice Domestic had now fixed its dates as the weekend after the Thursday night Edgar ceremony in New York, allowing those attending to come to Malice for the weekend.

Many attendees wore large hats, a throwback to fashions during the Golden Age between the World Wars that this convention celebrated. British writer Sarah J. Mason recalled that someone gave her a hat in the elevator, and she was so surprised that she had gotten off at her floor before she could identify the donor, whom she called "Anonyma." Steve Stilwell, a frequenter of the bars at Bouchercons, attended in 1994 and was amazed to find "no one in the bar at a mystery convention." Dorothy Salisbury Davis was Guest of Honor. Jim Huang was Fan Guest of Honor. Edgar Allan Poe was "Ghost of Honor." A Lifetime Achievement Award went to Mignon G. Eberhart.

There was great disappointment that ill health prevented Guest of Honor Edith Pargeter, who wrote as Ellis Peters, from attending in 1995, though there was a taped audio interview with her. In the centennial of her birth, Ngaio Marsh was "Ghost of Honor," and B. J. Rahn, America's leading expert on Marsh, portrayed her during an interview by Simon Brett. Rahn also scripted a Friday night event in which Toastmaster Edward Marston played the part of Roderick Alleyn, Marsh's sleuth. Dean James was Fan Guest of Honor and also won, with Jean Swanson, an Agatha for Best Non-Fiction for *By a Woman's Hand: A Guide to Mystery Fiction by Women*. The Agathas were announced by Sue Feder, wearing her Brother Cadfael monk's habit.

There was occasional disagreement about the definition of the type of book celebrated at Malice, and at one 1995 panel Stephen White and Frances Fyfield said that though their books were darker than many "cozies," they qualified. Panels also introduced fans to Sisters in Crime's official e-mail server and to DorothyL, the popular chat service for fans.

Proving that males were more than welcome, Jeff Abbott (he also won an Agatha for Best First Novel) was presented with the "Cozy-Boy Fan Club Award," with female attendees interrupting his panel to give him the award and then displaying t-shirts with the name of their club, whose purpose apparently was to honor male pulchritude. In 1994, Abbott had been the recipient of the first grant from Malice Domestic for unpublished authors.

The popularity of Malice was growing, and more than 700 people attended in 1996. Peter Lovesey was Guest of Honor. The Fan Guest of Honor was Shirley Beaird. Margaret Maron, often an Agatha winner or nominee, was Toastmistress, and Josephine Tey was the "Ghost of Honor." The program book contained a tribute to Malice's first Fan Guest of Honor, Ellen Nehr, who had died the previous December.

Attendance was over 725 in 1997. At the opening ceremony Malice founder Mary Morman was "murdered," and one panel was devoted to solving the killing. Carolyn G. Hart was Guest of Honor, and Jack and Judy Cater Fan Guests of Honor. Mary Latsis and Martha Henissart, the women writing as "Emma Lathen," received a Lifetime Achievement Award. In accepting it, Henissart said about attending their first convention, "If we had known it was going to be this much fun, we might have come to one of these affairs sooner." Frances and Richard Lockridge were 1997's "Ghosts of Honor." The Agatha Awards were presented by Carole Nelson Douglas and Parnell Hall, acting as the Lockridges' series characters Pam and Jerry North.

The tenth Malice Domestic in 1998 also had poignant moments. Longtime attendee Don Sandstrom had died the previous October. Kate Ross's *The Devil in Music* won the Agatha as best novel, but she, too, had died. Her father accepted the award for her in a moving speech. Robert Barnard was Guest of Honor, and Katherine Hall Page was Toastmistress. Maureen Collins was Fan Guest of Honor. Ellery Queen was "Ghost of Honor." Charlotte MacLeod received a Lifetime Achievement Award. With attendance now over 800, Malice had outgrown Bethesda and moved to the Renaissance Hotel in Washington. That remained the site through 2000, though it was not popular with many who felt it was in an unsafe, remote area.

Don Sandstrom, longtime Malice Domestic participant.

In 1998, those who had attended all ten Malice Domestics were given a special gold numeral "10" and a chain. Malice had its first stalker when someone followed Leslie Slaasted, a fan and member of the convention staff, and called her room at 1:30 AM. When the stalker did not follow hotel security's instructions to stay away, a hardboiled threat to knock his teeth down his throat by Richard Moore, one of those with a perfect Malice attendance record, succeeded.

In 1999, Mary Higgins Clark was Guest of Honor. M. D. Lake (pseudonym of James Allen Simpson) was Toastmaster. John Dickson Carr was "Ghost of Honor." The Fan Guest of Honor, Carol Harper, came all the way from Saudi Arabia, where she was living, to be honored. Patricia Moyes received a Lifetime Achievement Award.

Simon Brett, a frequent Malice Attendee, was Guest of Honor in 2000. Eileen Dreyer was Toastmistress. Sir Arthur Conan Doyle was the honored "Ghost," and Sheila Martin the Fan Guest of Honor. Dick Francis received a Lifetime Achievement Award, which was accepted for him by his son.

Malice Domestic moved to the Crystal Gateway Marriott in Arlington, Virginia, in 2001, with Margaret Maron Guest of Honor and Rita Mae Brown Toastmistress. Rex Stout was Ghost of Honor, and Patti Ruoco the Fan Guest of Honor. A Lifetime Achievement Award was given to Mildred Wirt Benson, who wrote the early Nancy Drew series, the first mysteries read by many people who attend Malice.

In 2002 Edward Marston was Guest of Honor, and Tony Hillerman received a

Lifetime Achievement Award. Annette and Marty Meyers were joint Toastmasters. G. K. Chesterton was honored as "Ghost." Gerry Letteney was Fan Guest of Honor.

The 2003 Malice Domestic was treated as a special event, with a separate section in the program, "Memories of Malice: 15 Years Celebrating the Traditional Mystery," largely the work of Tom O'Day, Chairman of Malice. Agatha Christie was "Ghost of Honor" a second time. Malice gave out its first Hercule Poirot Award, designed for those who made significant contributions to the mystery through other than writing. David Suchet, who acted Poirot so well on *Mystery!*, was the recipient. Barbara Mertz was a popular choice for the Lifetime Achievement Award. Donna Beatley was Fan Guest of Honor. During the Agathas, Guest of Honor Barbara D'Amato and Toastmaster Parnell Hall engaged in a funny pie-throwing sketch.

Malice Domestic stayed in Arlington in 2004, but moved to the Sheraton National with Dorothy Cannell the Guest of Honor, Marian Babson the winner of a Lifetime Achievement Award, Jan Burke Toastmistress, Linda Pletzke Fan Guest of Honor, and Erle Stanley Gardner the "Ghost of Honor." Carole Anne Nelson, recently deceased, was a "Special Fan Ghost of Honor." The second Poirot Award went to Ruth Cavin and Thomas Dunne of St. Martin's Press. Also at the Sheraton was a convention of followers of Louis Farrakhan, and several commented on the contrast between the typical Malice Domestic attendee, whom Richard Moore described, not meaning to be unkind, as "a white, middle-aged woman, often wearing a large, ornate, floppy hat" and the "young African-American men wearing bowties."

Sometimes derided for the allegedly "cozy" murders found in the books in which it rejoices, Malice Domestic has proven for seventeen years that these books provide superior escape reading to many.

22

Midwest Mystery & Suspense Convention (1990–1992)

Despite having lost its Bouchercon bid for 1990, Omaha had ambitions for 1993, and its committee, led by Chuck Levitt of the Little Professor Book Store, decided to prove Omaha's credentials by holding a convention. Don Cole, an important member of his committee, admitted that the first Omaha convention "did start out as a protest con, though we were not ready to admit it, but it quickly became an entirely new concept for the genre—fan conventions of a smaller and more intimate nature." Though Malice Domestic preceded Omaha by a year, it was limited to one sub-genre.

Omaha succeeded in its goal—not in the protest since it occurred three months before Bouchercon, and some people attended both—but in providing a memorable, relaxed convention. Cole described it as "not a regional, as such, but a new national convention for the mystery fan." Indeed, in addition to a large Midwest contingent, fans and writers came from both coasts, as well as the Southwest and Rockies. It was held May 25–27, 1990 at the Holiday Inn Central, in whose labyrinthine corridors attendees frequently became lost. Jeremiah Healy reported he called Room Service and, after placing his order, was asked for directions to his room.

410 people attended in 1990, but *MDM* correspondents were most noticeable. They took over the lobby, moving the furniture into a circle and talking and laughing late into the night. Ann Williams reported, "I never found myself wanting for a rowdy group in which to make a total fool of myself. But then what are conventions for?" Ori Hardy-Sayles couldn't remember ever laughing as hard. The imaginary fan George Kramer, invented at the 1989 Bouchercon, was discussed and became more "real" as Bob Samoian took out a subscription to *MDM* in his name and wrote letters for him. In one letter "Kramer" claimed that his first mystery was going to be published by "Orange Grove Press," an imaginary California publisher. Relying on information in *MDM*, Allen J. Hubin was going to include Kramer in his bibliography, but I spotted the entry in time to assure him it was a fake.

Omaha was a relatively inexpensive convention, with early registration $35. The Saturday night buffet banquet was only $18. Clive Cussler was Guest of Honor, and Jim Huang's *Drood Review of Mystery* was honored as a fan publication. At the banquet, authors were seated at various tables, allowing them to mingle with fans. Barbara Paul, who sat at my table, seemed unfamiliar with the hilarity and inside jokes of mystery fans, though she had attended science fiction conventions. The drawback of the banquet was a long-winded welcome by the representative of Omaha's mayor, one more appropriate if attendees were voters in that November's election.

Panels were good in Omaha, including Nehr leading a discussion of "Little Old Ladies of Crime." When Joan Hess missed the beginning of that early Sunday panel, she got caught up in Omaha's atmosphere and picketed the room, saying she had been thrown off the panel. Gary Warren Niebuhr moderated a hometown private eye

Fans at Omaha: (l. to r.) Orietta Hardy-Sayles, Leila Dobscha, Bob Samoian, Linda Toole, Marv Lachman, and Gary Warren Niebuhr.

panel, and there was a panel called "Murder in the Classroom," about how mysteries are taught at the college level. Half-hour autographing sessions after panels were a popular feature, allowing fans to get books signed without missing the program. This has now become accepted practice at most mystery conventions.

The funniest moments of the 1990 Omaha occurred in the lobby Saturday night after the banquet. At least four honeymoon couples appeared, in full wedding regalia, though all drove up not in limousines, but in red 4x4 trucks. Ronnie Klaskin asked what drew honeymooners to this Holiday Inn and was told they had big Jacuzzis. Using my best Raymond Chandleresque voice, I repeated "The Big Jacuzzi" to sound like his *The Big Sleep*. Niebuhr thought it would be a great title for a private eye story and said he would write it.

This convention resulted in more bonding among fans than any other. Cole said, "It was like a family reunion," and Ronnie Klaskin said, "*MDM* is becoming quite a family at these conventions." When, on Sunday morning, a rumor circulated that Mike Nevins had suffered a heart attack, because an ambulance had been called for him during the night, there was genuine concern until he appeared, albeit pale. He had a severe gall bladder attack and was released after treatment.

If the contributors to *MDM* unofficially dominated the first Midwest convention, they were officially recognized at the second, May 24–26, 1991, at the same Holiday Inn. Bob Napier, *MDM*'s publisher-editor was honored, along with Mary Higgins Clark, Guest of Honor. There was an *MDM* breakfast, and *MDM* 72½, a special issue roasting Napier. Niebuhr reported, "We spent the con signing each other's issue as if we were graduating from high school."

The previous year's "How to Get Published" panel, moderated by Parnell Hall, was repeated, with a second hour allotted to it because it had been so popular. At the banquet, for the first time, Hall sang "You Gotta Kill 'Em," his song about methods of murder, one he would repeat at other conventions.

At the third (and last) Midwest convention, May 29–31, 1992, *The Big Jacuzzi* was published, but it was not a novel—or even a story—by Gary Warren Niebuhr. Having difficulty in converting the title into fiction, he agreed to publish it and co-edit it with Ori Hardy-Sayles. Following ground rules Niebuhr laid down, six fans submitted mystery parodies, all of which were titled "The Big Jacuzzi." (Each contributor claimed to have written the title story.) The 1990 event of the brides and grooms pulling up in pickup trucks was part of each story. The entire print run sold out quickly, and it became a short-lived cult classic, with successful authors asking the amateur fan-parodists to autograph copies they bought.

A popular Friday night panel was the first of many to come on forgotten private eyes. Beverly DeWeese spoke of Fredric Brown's Ed and Am Hunter, Mike Nevins discussed Robert Ard's Timothy Dane, and I recalled Thomas B. Dewey's "Mac." Especially popular was "Gat Heat," hosted by Robert J. Randisi, who adapted the format of "The Tonight Show" to the mystery with hilarious results.

George Easter truly became part of fandom while attending his first Omaha convention in 1992. Though a long time collector, he learned the meaning of "booking" and was part of several expeditions to bookstores before the convention began, one that went as far as Lincoln, Nebraska. Meeting other fanatical collectors, he said, "What a relief to know that I am somewhat normal—even if it is only among a very small group of people."

Though most would return to Omaha for Bouchercon in 1993, those who attended the final Midwest in 1992 left with feelings of sadness, though getting to and from Omaha led to many travel horror stories. Ori Hardy-Sayles had her return flights cancelled all three years. In 1992 my luggage spent the first day of the convention in Jackson Hole, Wyoming. Don Cole had been most responsible for the convention, telling Levitt, who chaired it for three years, about fandom in the first place. Calling 1992's convention the "last of an era," Cole said, "We pride our con as being the 'down home' convention," and those who enjoyed its relaxed atmosphere agreed.

23 Bouchercon: 1990s

1990: London

Bouchercon's London site, King's College in The Strand, was not a hotel. Some attendees stayed at nearby hotels, most of which were expensive, while others stayed in college dormitories for under £30 a night and made a daily round-trip to the convention via the underground. Due to excellent publicity, about 1,000 people signed up. Many were from the United States, but people also came from France, Finland, West Germany, Canada, Iceland, Greece, Japan, and Belgium. There were twenty-four booksellers, eight from the US.

There were complaints about the college as a convention site due to unavailability of water and coffee, a scarcity of bathrooms, and the need to climb stairs from one meeting room to another. There was a hospitality suite a block away at the Waldorf Hotel, but it was poorly publicized and many didn't know it existed.

Controversy, an increasing part of Bouchercons, began before the convention officially opened on Friday, September 21st. Booksellers Marion and Robin Richmond, who were chairing Bouchercon, scheduled a pre-convention dinner at the Sherlock Holmes Pub in Northumberland Street. The Richmonds were upset that Maxim Jakubowski, owner of Mystery One bookstore, scheduled an open house at his store at the same time. They claimed he discouraged people from attending their dinner and talked of possible legal action. Jakubowski's lawyers answered the allegations, also claiming that the Richmonds had reserved the best location in the dealers' room for themselves and took the hospitality room for their own use, though Pocket Books paid for it.

If there were problems with the site of Bouchercon 21, there was general agreement that the three-track programming arranged by British fan and scholar Barry Pike was excellent. Panels included one on legal mysteries; another called "Scotland Yard—Past and Present;" a centenary tribute to Agatha Christie, who was born in 1890; "The Detection Club: Then and Now;" and a talk on Sherlock Holmes's foil, Inspector Lestrade. The convention program book, edited by novelist Robert Richardson, was highly praised.

Guest of Honor was bestselling British author P. D. James. Bob Adey, British expert on "impossible" crimes, was Fan Guest of Honor. A Lifetime Achievement Anthony was given to Michael Gilbert. American Sue Grafton was Toastmaster. The sold-out awards banquet at the Waldorf started one hour and forty-five minutes late, with no announcement to those waiting. It was later reported that the delay was caused by security checking due to rumors of an IRA bombing.

In his report on Bouchercon in *TAD*, Ric Meyers used Dickensian language to assess it, saying, "It was the best of Bouchercons; it was the worst of Bouchercons." He praised the varied program and opportunity to meet authors new to him. However, he wrote of the college site's shortcomings and the absence of a central location where fans could gather as they had at American Bouchercons and regional conventions. He wrote of missing what he called "lobbycon."

1991: Pasadena

Well before Bouchercon .22 (its number altered to the caliber of a bullet) began October 11th at the Pasadena Hilton, the co-chairpersons, Len and June Moffatt, were getting flak over the guests selected. All—Guest of Honor: Edward D. Hoch; Lifetime Achievement Award: William Campbell Gault; Fan Guest of Honor: Bruce Pelz; Toastmaster Bill Crider—were male.

Ronnie Klaskin and Sandra Scoppettone complained in *MDM*. Len Moffatt replied that the honorees were picked by a gender-split committee. "We are hurt that you would think that June and I would be part of a plan to deliberately exclude women from Bouchercon honors." Not placated, Scoppettone said, "I think the people who run Bouchercons must make a conscious effort to include women at this time in history." Calling her point "too much like tokenism," the Moffatts pointed out that one of the original guests chosen was female, but turned the committee down.

There were also complaints about Bouchercon having accepted a bid for 1994 from Austin, Texas, which most did not consider in the Pacific Coast region. (That region was entitled to put on the 1994 convention.) As the Moffats pointed out, at the time Austin was the only bidder. Not to accept their bid meant no 1994 Bouchercon. Furthermore, the rules had "no set boundaries" for the three regions: Pacific Coast, East Coast, and Midwest.

Bob Napier of Tacoma, Washington, was insistent that Austin's bid was inappropriate since he felt it could not be considered part of the Pacific Coast. On the other hand, James Reasoner of Texas felt that the current three-region rotation was unfair to people in the South and Southwest who had considerable distances to travel to all Bouchercons. Austin was certainly not in the East or Midwest. Eventually, Seattle, Washington, bid for the 1994 Bouchercon just before the deadline. Later changes in Bouchercon bylaws would assign each of the 50 states (parts of Canada) to one of the three regions.

Bouchercon .22 was put on by the Southern California Institute for Fan Interests, a nonprofit corporation which had previously sponsored science fiction and fantasy conventions. 1,300 attended, with the Hilton sold out and the overflow at nearby hotels. The weather, out of the committee's control, was close to 100 degrees and smoggy.

The program book was outstanding, including a reproduction of the entire program for the first Bouchercon. For the first time, there was a listing of writers and fans who had died recently. As mystery's unofficial "obituarian," I provided that. The program also included a copy of the Bouchercon bylaws, much needed in view of contention regarding location and finances. The first American publication of a short story by Guest of Honor Hoch was also included. Part of the registration package was a bibliography of the complete works of Hoch, compiled by June Moffatt and Francis M. Nevins.

There were three full days of programming, with three tracks. A highlight, called "The Panel from Hell," was scheduled at the hellish time of 9 AM Saturday. Sharyn

McCrumb moderated, and she and her panelists, Joan Hess, Wendy Hornsby, Ann and Evan Maxwell, and Conrad Haynes, prepared skits and other hilarious material about the lives of mystery authors publicizing their books. Hornsby displayed a sign: "Will Sign Books for Food."

Another outstanding panel, on Sunday, was about true crime as told through the viewpoints of Bob Samoian, an Assistant District Attorney in Los Angeles, Paul Bishop, a police detective, and Leila Dobscha, a police dispatcher.

1991 was the fiftieth anniversary of *Ellery Queen's Mystery Magazine*, and a panel celebrated it. Editor Eleanor Sullivan had just died; there was a tribute to her by Hoch in the program. Janet Hutchings, the new editor, was introduced as one of the panelists.

My interview of Hoch went smoothly, though we hoped for larger attendance. Perhaps a relatively small crowd was inevitable since it was scheduled for noon and was also in competition with two panels and a reading. It was immediately followed by Richard Moore's interview of Gault, which was embarrassing because Gault's memory was failing. Moore did his best to prompt Gault, but he was unsuccessful. Moore called it "one of the worst experiences I've ever had."

The lobby was a good one, spacious enough for fans to gather for conversation. Some people remained in their rooms to watch the Supreme Court nomination hearing of Clarence Thomas, with questioning of him and Anita Hill. Paul Bishop arranged a tour of the LAPD that included their police academy and firing range.

The Moffatts had asked for a financial report from the London Bouchercon and, according to them, "received an unsatisfactory reply—to say the least." They only received money from the San Diego and Philadelphia conventions. Because of the committee's experience in budgeting and running conventions, Pasadena turned a profit of $20,000, $15,000 of which they turned over as "seed money" to the next three Bouchercons. They also gave $5,000 to the two Bouchercons following those. This profit was despite reimbursing panelists for their registration fees once it was determined that Bouchercon .22 would be profitable. Napier summarized the majority opinion about Bouchercon .22 when he wrote in *MDM*, "Hats off to the Moffatts and their group for their honest and responsible work."

1992: Toronto

1,500 people, more than at any previous Bouchercon, attended October 8–11 at Toronto's Royal York Hotel. The chairman was Al Navis, a native-born Torontonian. Peter Sellers (the Canadian short story writer and anthologist, not the late movie comedian) did the programming.

Visitors arrived early for sightseeing in Canada. They found a clean and safe city, though it had its share of homeless people. There were good restaurants, underground malls, and live theatre. I finally saw *The Mousetrap* and *The Phantom of the Opera*. The local baseball team, the Blue Jays, was in the World Series.

Registration did not go smoothly, and there were long lines before attendees received their packets. There were even longer lines for people to sign up for tables at the banquet. At Thursday night's opening cocktail party a free copy of *Cold Blood II*, an anthology of Canadian short stories edited by Sellers, was given out. Beginning

Friday morning there were three (four on Saturday) tracks of programming.

The program did not have pictures or biographies of the participants, but it did have a good history of the short story by Edward D. Hoch; a short story set at the 1991 Bouchercon by English-born writer Peter Robinson, who lives in Toronto; and an article on Canadian crime fiction by David Skene-Melvin.

Panels included a slide show of covers of Doubleday Crime Club mysteries, the subject of a forthcoming book by Ellen Nehr. Art Scott did another of his slide shows on sexy paperback mystery covers.

People who had attended past Bouchercons said that panel subjects were becoming "old hat," and some seemed to brag about how many panels they did *not* attend. "Done to Death" was different. It was a panel with Gary Warren Niebuhr, Bob Samoian, Orietta Hardy-Sayles, Don Sandstrom, and I describing some of the worst clichés in the mystery. This was the funniest and most popular panel in Toronto. A crowd of 125 people filled a small room, some even sitting on the floor and others standing in back and outside the door. (The panels were taped and this one sold more copies than any other.) The microphone was one step below the dais, and I tripped over that step and fell returning to my chair. There was so much laughter during the panel that some people were convinced I had taken the pratfall deliberately.

Two other unusual events were a panel on "Murder in Traditional Folk Music," with two folk singers to give examples, and an afternoon tea party and hat contest, with Professor B. J. Rahn winning with her mystery-decorated *chapeau*.

Mystery fans were increasingly referring to themselves as part of a "family," and Toronto provided a perfect example. Naomi Hoida of Japan attended though she did not speak English well and did not know anyone there, except through correspondence in *MDM*. She was welcomed warmly, and when she returned home she wrote, "Now I am… truly missing Bouchercon XXIII and *MDM* family I met. I heartily enjoyed my first Bouchercon for their warm friendliness. *MDM* members are my great family."

Guest of Honor Margaret Millar, born in Canada though living in Santa Barbara, California, broke her hip shortly before Bouchercon and was unable to attend. Dorothy Salisbury Davis succinctly summed up Millar's contributions. Also succinct—and humorous—were Toastmaster Otto Penzler and Lifetime Achievement Awardee Charlotte MacLeod, another Canadian living in the US. For the first time since 1983, there was no Fan Guest of Honor. Chairman Navis decided to create suspense at the banquet regarding the vote for the 1995 Bouchercon. Nottingham, England, was competing with two American cities: Miami and Washington, DC. Navis kept postponing the decision until Ric Meyers, who reported on Bouchercon for *TAD*, threatened to come up on stage and force the issue. Finally, Navis announced that Nottingham had won, with almost twice the votes of its competitors combined.

1993: Omaha

Omaha, Nebraska, may have seemed an unlikely spot for Bouchercon, but not to fans who attended enjoyable Midwest Mystery & Suspense conventions there from 1990 through 1992. About 1,000 people attended the 24th Bouchercon October 1–3 at the Holiday Inn Central, the hotel that had become infamous at those gatherings because of its maze of corridors.

Charles "Chuck" Levitt, responsible for the regional Omaha conventions, was chairman, and almost everyone had a great time there, though an unusual number of mistakes caused some to label it "Botchercon." The PWA Shamus Awards were given out at the same time as the auction was held. Attendees were not given up-to-date information about which authors would attend, so some brought books for signing by authors *not* there and failed to bring books for those attending. Some panelists were unaware they had been scheduled. The program book had so many errors that Bob Napier nicknamed the convention "Typocon."

Don Sandstrom of Indianapolis was Fan Guest of Honor. On Friday morning his fellow correspondents in *MDM* had a breakfast honoring him. He was pleased and then shocked when he saw several dozen people performing what appeared to be a strip tease. It was merely to show that they were all wearing t-shirts proclaiming "I'm a Fan of the Fan Guest of Honor." In keeping with the weekend's typos, the convention's name on the shirts was spelled "Boucheron." At that breakfast, there was also the release of *Farewell, My Lobby*, the second book of parodies by mystery fans. Typically, the final paragraph of one story, by Bob Samoian, had been omitted. Casting gloom on Sandstrom's weekend was the fact that his daughter, Karen Sandstrom Muir, was undergoing major surgery that weekend and couldn't attend. Fortunately, the operation was successful.

The Guest of Honor was Evan Hunter, better known under his Ed McBain pseudonym. Also honored with Lifetime Achievement Awards were Hammond Innes, the British thriller writer, and Ralph McInerny.

Panels included one called "The British Are Coming," evidence that more British writers were coming to American Bouchercons. Two panels, "How to Get Published" and "Promotions," were geared toward the increasing number of new or hopeful writers attending. Wisely, Levitt continued his regional convention practice of scheduling panels so that there was one half-hour between panels to obtain autographs.

The Saturday night banquet was brief, which to some was a plus. However, not allowing the winners of the Anthonys to make acceptance speeches, a major reason for brevity, was unsatisfying recognition of their achievements. Mistress of Ceremonies Ori Hardy-Sayles explained, "The dais was so narrow, with wires and uneven planking, it was best to keep the traffic down." Being one of the few to make it to the dais, to introduce Sandstrom, I can testify I had to be careful not to repeat my tumble in Toronto. The awards were handed out in front of the dais by Naomi Hoida, who again came from Japan. One Anthony, for Best Critical Work, went to fan Ellen Nehr, for her monumental *Doubleday Crime Club Compendium*. Mystery writers who had died recently were recognized though, in an oral "typo," Levitt called the late creator of The Saint "Leslie Chartreuse" (Charteris).

After the banquet, music was provided by mystery writer, Max Allan Collins and his "Cruisin' Band." In keeping with this convention, several dancers fell while jitterbugging.

To a veteran Bouchercon-goer, one of its joys is seeing the pleasure derived by first-time attendees. Gayle Lovett came from Australia. Barry W. Gardner, the retired Dallas Fire Department captain who became an outstanding fan reviewer, was thrilled when at Sunday breakfast I introduced him to Allen J. Hubin, who he later confessed was "my idol."

1994: Seattle

The consensus was that the 25th Bouchercon, October 6–9 at Seattle's Stouffer Madison, was one of the best organized. Thom Walls was chairman, and he had an outstanding committee (with one exception). Andi Shechter and Alan Rosenthal did especially good jobs of programming. 1,400 people attended and another hundred were turned away. Even the notorious Seattle weather cooperated; the entire weekend was sunny.

The 140-page program was the best to date, thanks largely to Stu Shiffman, who also provided drawings. As one of several innovations, pocket programs were distributed, which attendees could easily carry to determine which panels to attend. This innovation has now become routine at conventions, and fans complain if pocket programs are not distributed. The program made it clear that writers were welcome, but that Bouchercon was not a writers' conference or workshop. Long-time Bouchercon attendees had been noticing more writers, would-be writers, and editors promoting their own work. The program contained good articles on Anthony Boucher, Guest of Honor Marcia Muller, Fan Guest of Honor Art Scott, Lifetime Achievement Honoree Tony Hillerman, and Toastmaster George C. Chesbro.

Panels were enjoyable and occasionally innovative. For example, on the first morning, at "Bouchercon 101," Don Sandstrom tried to ease the way for new attendees awed at attending so large a convention. Another panel, "Women Who Love Cops Too Much," recognized the increase in mysteries with amateur detectives who have affairs with police detectives. The humor panel with Donald E. Westlake and Parnell Hall provided Bouchercon's first "pie-in-the-face," with Hall the gracious recipient.

A panel on forgotten writers produced arguably the greatest coincidence in Bouchercon history. In suggesting Thomas B. Dewey who wrote about Chicago and was sympathetic to the young, I said, "If you like Sara Paretsky, you'll like Dewey." At that exact moment Paretsky walked into the room and wondered about the gasps of surprise that greeted her. I was asked if I had arranged that with her; I hadn't, barely having spoken to her at prior Bouchercons.

The last-named panel also showed the danger of political correctness carried too far. William DeAndrea, Jeff Marks, Maxim Jakubowski, and I recommended many forgotten writers, including Pat McGerr, Craig Rice, and Lee Thayer. A woman in the au-

Thom Walls, chairman of the successful 1994 Seattle Bouchercon.

dience asked when we were going to discuss more female writers. It became clear that she didn't know enough history to realize that, despite androgynous first names, McGerr, Rice, and Thayer were women.

Because the banquet was sold out at 500 attendees, the committee arranged to have it telecast by closed circuit to hotel rooms. The feature of the banquet was the best speech ever by a Fan Guest of Honor, one in which Art Scott delivered a tribute to fandom, recounting his twenty years as an active fan. He told of friends he had made and the enjoyment fandom had brought him. He concluded by recommending Bouchercon attendees become more involved, "there are all sorts of things you can do in fandom, interesting people you can get to know, 'zines you can write for, mystery events you can get involved in. Start to connect with people. I assure you that you will find yourselves sucked into it; it's almost impossible to resist, and it's my advice that you go with it; you'll be glad you did."

Even as near-perfect a Bouchercon as Seattle had a few negatives. The Stouffer Madison was too small a hotel to handle so many people, and there were crowds, especially riding the elevators. Some rooms were too small, shutting out people from panels they wanted to see. The committee tried dealing with problems as soon as they became aware of them.

Another negative was one over which the committee had no control, an article in the British newspaper *The Independent* by crime writer Michael Dibdin. He gratuitously attacked fans at Bouchercon, calling them "nerds" and claiming that fans are mainly interested in getting autographs for mercenary reasons. He quoted mystery authors, whom he said chose to remain anonymous, who claimed that authors have nothing in common with fans. Descending to his nadir, Dibdin quoted an anonymous publisher as to how the Fan Guest of Honor is chosen. "They look for the *biggest nerd* in the place." Andi Shechter was so angry and embarrassed that she responded to Dibdin for the Bouchercon committee, saying they were sorry they had invited him.

Another post-Bouchercon problem was getting its treasurer to file a financial report. Threats were made to bring the matter before Washington State authorities. Finally, more than a year later, a report was rendered showing that this well-attended Bouchercon had a net profit of under $5,000.

1995: Nottingham

Bouchercon returned to England, to Nottingham, where its chairman, Adrian Wootton, had successfully mounted "Shots in the Dark" conventions since 1991. As early as 1992, objections were raised to another Bouchercon in England so soon. The most valid argument was the expense for Americans. Geoff Bradley reminded those objecting that Bouchercon was the "World Mystery Convention," and that different people would be organizing it.

Though Nottingham was considered by some the current "crime capital of England," the Bouchercon committee emphasized the area's legendary past, especially Robin Hood. The convention was held September 28th through October 1st at the Broadway Media Centre, with events held at other locations, all within a short walk. Because there was no hotel large enough for almost 1,000 attendees, people were scattered at six hotels, but a shuttle bus service minimized inconvenience.

For the first time, brief cases were given with registration material. The program, in the form of a trade paperback, was the most unusual in Bouchercon history, including twenty-seven short stories, to be published later as the anthology *No Alibi*, edited by Maxim Jakubowski. Among the important writers in it, all attendees at Nottingham, were Edward D. Hoch, John Harvey (also in charge of programming), Peter Lovesey, and Val McDermid. It also reprinted an Anthony Boucher short story. Unfortunately, due to health reasons, Phyllis White missed this Bouchercon.

There was much discussion during Bouchercon about P. D. James, who had cancelled her appearance. A few months before, she had been interviewed on BBC radio and made remarks some interpreted as her saying that only the middle class was educated enough to make the moral choices that translate into good crime fiction. She drew protests in the media, and a flyer for an upcoming anthology, *Fresh Blood*, edited by Jakubowski and Mike Ripley, promised to "feature stories from most of the leading 'anti-establishment' British crime authors, who assert that in today's mystery writing, realism is far more important than outmoded questions of morality." James said later she was talking of an author's choice of fictional setting, and the detective novel "works best for me when the setting is orderly and law-abiding and the criminal is intelligent and capable of moral choice."

Nottingham "Criminal Masterminds" (l. to r.) Martin Edwards, Sarah Mason, Ed Hoch, Marv Lachman.

There were two Guests of Honor. Colin Dexter, creator of Inspector Morse, proved to be congenial and likable. The American Guest of Honor, James Ellroy, using four-letter words whenever he could, seemed intent on shocking but only managed to bore. Ruth Rendell received a Lifetime Achievement Award, Reginald Hill was Toastmaster, and Geoff Bradley, publisher and editor of *CADS* was Fan Guest of Honor. There was more of an international flavor than at most Bouchercons, with attendees from Japan, Australia, Finland, and Ireland. Twenty-four booksellers were there, unfortunately given a cramped area, but that did not deter many buyers.

Some of the panels showed considerable originality. Friday began with "How to Enjoy Bouchercon and Retain Your Sanity," a light-hearted introduction, like 1994's "Bouchercon 101," for newcomers. For "Two by Two," teams of writers discussed themselves and their work, while interacting. Among the combinations were Sue

Grafton–Walter Mosley and Donald E. Westlake–Lawrence Block. Other panels discussed romance in crime fiction and "The Roots of Crime," with an interesting philosophical discussion of evil. Bill Deeck gave another of his hilarious dissections of the work of James Corbett.

Trivia quizzes from past Bouchercons were trivial indeed compared to the "Criminal Masterminds Quiz," based on a popular British television program, presented at the Royal Concert Hall. Edward D. Hoch and I represented the United States, and we could claim that we were awed by the surroundings and had trouble understanding British pronunciation, but the simple fact is that the team of Sarah J. Mason and Martin Edwards, two young English mystery writers who are also highly knowledgeable fans, was far too good for us.

For the banquet, attendees were bused to the East Midlands Conference Centre. In keeping with the Robin Hood motif, suitably dressed henchmen of the Sheriff boarded the buses, announcing that they were looking for "that villain Robin Hood." A sword fight was conducted during the banquet, and musicians played period music. Unfortunately, most of the winners of the Anthonys did not appear to receive their awards. There had been considerable lobbying by one member of Sisters in Crime, apparently without that group's approval, for Sharyn McCrumb, who won Anthonys for Best Short Story and Best Novel. As Geoff Bradley said, "the really sad aspect of the whole affair is that [McCrumb] will never know if she won fairly." The convention ended with an event that has occurred at several mystery conventions. At 11:00 PM in my hotel the fire alarms went off, forcing people in various stages of dishabille to tramp downstairs to the lobby, only to learn it had been a false alarm.

1996: Saint Paul, Minnesota

Bouchercon returned to the Twin Cities of Minnesota in a convention with its share of sadness. The Fan Guest of Honor Ellen Nehr died in December 1995. Barry Gardner, who had already written an article for the program, died in July 1996. William L. DeAndrea, a frequent Bouchercon attendee, died the day before Bouchercon began.

This 27th Bouchercon almost never took place. As of 1993 there had been no firm bid, though Jimmie Butler talked of possibly holding it in Colorado Springs. MWA was not supportive, and there was also fear of a boycott. Other organizations had already cancelled plans to meet in Colorado due to a state amendment perceived as anti-gay. It was reported that Atlanta was considering a bid, but they never submitted one. In 1994 Bruce Taylor and Thom Walls called Once Upon a Crime mystery bookstore in Minneapolis to ask the owner, Steve Stilwell, and his employee, Dennis Armstrong, whether either would be willing chair the 1996 Bouchercon. Stilwell refused but ended up playing an important role by giving Armstrong the time off necessary to run it, paying his health insurance, giving advice, and handling the bookdealers' room. Armstrong had the further assistance of co-chairman Bruce Southworth. Furthermore, Dennis Armstrong's mother, Jane Armstrong, edited the 160-page program book.

About 1600 people attended, October 10–13, at the Radisson Hotel. One aspect of St. Paul emphasized throughout the convention was its past as a "safe city" for the underworld, with gangsters of the 1930s, including John Dillinger and "Baby Face" Nelson, spending time there.

Most of Thursday was devoted to the "First Black Mystery Writers Symposium," with seven panels discussing topics pertaining to African-American writers and readers. A reception and fund-raiser followed, with Walter Mosley as keynote speaker, at the Landmark Center. Bouchercon was co-sponsor.

The Bouchercon Welcome Reception was on Thursday night, and the kindest word that can be applied to it is "unfortunate." It began with the playing of "The Star-Spangled Banner," which mystery writer Polly Whitney interrupted in a mock French accent, saying that since this was an international conference, the French National Anthem should be sung. She proceeded to sing "Frère Jacques." She continued in this vein, much to the embarrassment of the emcee, Alan Russell. The acoustics were so bad that many people could not hear her, which may have been a blessing. Many left before Parnell Hall sang his hilarious "Signing in the Waldenbooks." However, Stilwell was pronounced "off the hook" for the 1987 magician.

A Friday breakfast sponsored by *Deadly Pleasures* magazine launched the third set of fan parodies, titled *The Lady in the 10,000 Lakes* to go with the Minnesota location. There were a dozen stories by contributors to *MDM*. Gary Warren Niebuhr published this booklet, which he called "A Deep But Still Meaningless Collection of Shallow Short Stories."

The Guest of Honor was Mary Higgins Clark, who spoke graciously at the banquet Friday night. Ellen Nehr's husband, Al, spoke about her, as did writer Joan Hess who was a good friend of Ellen. The program book contained a touching article by Art Scott describing Ellen's diffident entry into fandom when she adopted the "I'm-just-an-ordinary-housewife-from-Ohio-who-likes-mysteries" guise. As Scott further said, "At her death she left behind a host of friends and a solid legacy of scholarship."

The Toastmaster was Jeremiah Healy, who didn't need a microphone to be heard. *The Armchair Detective* was recognized with an Anthony as Best Magazine. Though I had contributed to *The Armchair Detective Book of Lists*, I was embarrassed that it won the Anthony as "Best Critical Work" over outstanding biographies of John Dickson Carr and Jim Thompson by Douglas Greene and Robert Polito respectively. After the banquet, a Dixieland band played, and Sara Paretsky and Parnell Hall drew applause for their dancing skills.

In keeping with the opening symposium, there were two panels on minority writers. Several panels concerned the internet, then in its relatively early days. One called "To Boldly Go" was about the DorothyL e-mail group. Having apparently found a niche, I was again on a "forgotten author" panel, this one called "The Best Author You've Never Heard Of." I selected *Whistle Up the Devil* (1953) by Derek Smith, a book published only in England, after which Smith apparently disappeared. It is an admirable detective story in which two seemingly impossible murders are solved ingeniously and fairly. To my surprise I was told after the panel by a Japanese fan that the type of Golden Age puzzle Smith wrote is still popular in Japan and that Smith's second book, *Come to Paddington Fair*, which he was never able to get published in England, would be published in Japan in 1997 in English!

There was a mass signing on Sunday morning by all the authors, so fans would not have difficulty getting books autographed. However, there were stories on Doro- thyL after Bouchercon of fans pursuing authors into rest rooms for autographs. Some wondered whether it was necessary to have "autograph-free zones" at Bouchercon, as they had in Seattle, but wiser heads suggested it was not possible to change human nature and that the few guilty parties were jerks, not fans.

1997: Monterey, CA

There were complaints when the original site of this Bouchercon, co-chaired by Bruce Taylor and Bryan Barrett, was changed from San Francisco to Monterey. A few people questioned the extra travel and expense from the San Francisco or San Jose airports. However, the combination of perfect weather and the loveliest setting in Bouchercon history removed most objections. From October 30th through No- vember 2nd, about 2,000 people, the largest attendance ever, were at the Monterey Conference Center, with the attendees (and some of the panels) spilling over into three nearby hotels. Programming consisted of seven simultaneous tracks, and there were fifty-one bookdealers.

Sara Paretsky was Guest of Honor, and Bob Napier was Fan Guest of Honor. Don- ald E. Westlake received a Lifetime Achievement Award. An additional honoree was Ross Thomas, who had died in 1995. Some of the people who regularly played poker with Thomas at Bouchercons (including Jan Grape, Jeremiah Healy, Gayle Lynds, and Bob Randisi) staged "The Ross Thomas Memorial Poker Game."

Another popular panel was on the "Hypermodern Mystery," those recent books that were so collectible their value had gone into four figures. Other panels were the opposite of "hypermodern." Burl Barer discussed The Saint, about whom he had written an Edgar-winning book, and Ted Hertel covered Ellery Queen, once the most popular American detective, but in 1997 largely forgotten.

My wife Carol and I presented a program that was new to Bouchercon, "Just in Crime: the Musical." Longtime fans of show music, we combined two interests by playing crime-related music from Broadway. Among the numbers were "The Bal- lad of Lizzie Borden" from *New Faces of 1952*, "All You Have to Do Is Wait" from the private eye musical *City of Angels*, and "Suppertime" from *As Thousands Cheer*. Carol also sang a little, and I did my Monty Woolley impression, reciting "Miss Otis Regrets," Cole Porter's song about a lynching.

Don Sandstrom, probably the most popular of all mystery fans, had died of leu- kemia twelve days before Bouchercon. Because we knew he would not be able to attend, Carol and I had flown to Indianapolis where, with a few other friends and one of his daughters present, we performed "Just in Crime" for him at what some- one called "DonCon." Gary Warren Niebuhr represented the mystery-fan aspect of Don's life at his funeral. In Monterey, Don was sorely missed, and people remarked that when they saw, from a distance, a distinguished-looking gentleman with white hair, they imagined they were seeing him. Don was honored at a special Bouchercon breakfast, and as tributes were paid to him, many a tear was shed.

A cocktail party honoring Paretsky and Napier at the Maritime Museum was a success, though the line to greet them (and go inside for free wine) was long. Less successful was the banquet at which the Anthony winners were again asked not to give speeches, a mistake that many felt devalued those awards. Also, failing to seat Napier on the dais (or even at a table near the dais) was unfortunate.

Booksellers and frequent convention hosts Steve Stilwell (l.) and Bruce Taylor.

Some attendees were distressed by the sheer size of this Bouchercon, and there was debate, especially in the pages of *MDM*, on the subject. Many fans, as Bill Deeck said, "wanted to make sure Bouchercon did not become a combined writers' conference and author-publisher business meeting." Yet, a proposed by-law change to call Bouchercon a "fan convention" failed to pass. Some fans, especially Lorraine Petty, complained that the Bouchercon business meeting, held at 10:00 PM on the day before the convention started, was perfunctory and not conducive to getting new people involved in putting on Bouchercons since people were tired, having traveled that day. Napier even proposed reserving the name Bouchercon for smaller, more fan-oriented conventions. However, Gary Warren Niebuhr, co-chairman of the forthcoming Milwaukee Bouchercon, was in favor of attracting as many people as possible. He said that there was room for fan-oriented panels, even if they were apparently not what most attendees wanted. He gave as example no more than thirty people attending a panel on fan magazines, while 400 to 500 attended a panel in which published authors of first novels were interviewed. Clearly, there were more would-be writers who wanted to know how to get published than fans.

This Bouchercon was successful, with a net profit of $50,000. Money was passed on to future Bouchercons, though Deen Kogan, chairing Philadelphia in 1998, opted not to accept any and not to pass any along. Writing in *MDM*, Niebuhr said, "The time has come to abandon the concept that anyone can force the sharing of profits and seed money.... Each committee should be left to disperse its funds as it sees fit."

1998: Philadelphia

There was difficulty getting a bidder for this year. Otto Penzler was willing to run a New York Bouchercon, provided he could keep any profits. He withdrew his proposal when Deen Kogan was willing, and she mounted a successful Bouchercon October 1–4 at the Wyndham Hotel in Philadelphia. The Mayor of Philadelphia proclaimed "World Mystery Week," and this was a more international Bouchercon than others. More than 1,650 people registered, and they came from sixteen countries, plus the United States. Testament to the popularity of mysteries was the presence of a record sixty-nine book dealers.

Bouchercon 1998 honored more people than past conventions. Janwillem van de Wetering, who was International Guest of Honor, attracted many by talking about his Zen Buddhist philosophy. The American Guest of Honor was Carl Hiaasen of Florida, as amusing in person as in his environmental mysteries. Tom Fontana, writer-producer of television's *Homicide: Life on the Street* was Media Guest of Honor. Hal and Sonya Rice were Fan Guests of Honor. Jonathan Gash was the Honorary Host for the Anthony Brunch; an additional honoree was Ruth Cavin, esteemed editor.

There was an opening night reception at the Free Library of Philadelphia, plus other events away from the convention hotel, including a tour of a former penitentiary. The International Association of Crime Writers (IACW) played an important role. They had a reception, four panels, and the North American Branch presented their annual Hammett Prize. Mystery Readers International presented its Macavity Awards.

The program book was 128 pages, four of which were devoted to the latest Bouchercon bylaws. They provided for bids in three US regions, causing unhappiness in England. However, they were amended to permit an international bid every fourth year. There were also articles by writers titled "Why I Write Mysteries."

One of the first panels during three-and-one-half days of five-track programming was on "The History of Mystery," and there was discussion of the Golden Age between the World Wars. It was not as popular as the panel featuring a Philadelphia fire marshal and his arson detection dog.

A silent auction raised $7,000 for three Philadelphia branch libraries. Friday evening featured a play written by Simon Brett. There was a "Bouchercon Ball" with a jazz band Saturday night. The Mummer's Band, a Philadelphia specialty, performed before the Anthony Awards Brunch Sunday.

Ten years after George H. W. Bush awakened Bouchercon attendees in San Diego, President Bill Clinton arrived at the Wyndham for a political fundraiser. Secret Service guards, with guns, could be seen on rooftops, and the elevators were shut down, stranding people in the lobby or in their rooms during his stay of several hours. I wondered whether inconveniencing Bouchercon attendees for political reasons wasn't an impeachable offense.

1999: Milwaukee

If the 30th Bouchercon was, as longtime attendee John Apostolou said, "the best organized convention I've ever attended," it was due to Conference Coordinators Gary Warren Niebuhr and Ted Hertel, who devoted three and a half years to make three and a half days run smoothly. "Mischief in the Midwest" was held September 30–October 3 at the Milwaukee Hilton, known when Bouchercon was held there in 1981 as the Marc Plaza. More than 1,200 people attended, and it was noticed that stuffing the brief cases given to each was becoming time-consuming for the committee and helpful fans. Publishers were now giving out many free copies of books and other promotional material, as were writers. There was also the program and a small squeeze cow, appropriate for this dairy state.

Bouchercon began Wednesday evening with the "Edelweiss Cruise" on the Milwaukee River, complete with champagne and hors d'oeuvres, for special guests. Max Allan Collins did yeoman duty as American Guest of Honor. He appeared on panels, presented *Mommy*, a movie he wrote and produced, and his band played throughout the Saturday night dance. Reginald Hill was International Guest of Honor. The Fan Guests of Honor were Mary "Maggie" Mason of San Diego and Beverly DeWeese of Milwaukee. Len and June Moffatt were Lifetime Achievement honorees, receiving a special Anthony. As Toastmaster, Parnell Hall did not sing as he had done at so many Bouchercons, but he did read a short story that hilariously incorporated the names of mystery writers and fans.

The program book (196 pages) was especially good, including pictures and articles by the Moffatts about early Bouchercons. There was also the publication of a story by Libby Fischer Hellmann that won Bouchercon's first short story contest.

There were eight tracks of programming, including a panel about Anthony Boucher, others regarding computers, collecting, plot versus character, cooking mysteries, and cultural diversity. Another panel titled "What Agents Can Do for You" included Dominick Abel, the successful agent who represents many mystery writers and is a frequent Bouchercon attendee. Recognizing that many would like to be published, Bouchercon, in cooperation with the Midwest chapter of MWA, offered a writers' workshop (eleven sessions) throughout the convention.

Some of the convention spilled over to the nearby Midwest Center, which had room for events that drew large crowds. These included a tribute to Ellery Queen on the 70th anniversary of the publication of *The Roman Hat Mystery*, the first Queen novel. It took the form of a radio play, "The Adventure of the Murdered Moths," with Ted Hertel achieving a lifelong ambition by playing Ellery. As the play's official "armchair detective" challenged to deduce the killer's identity, Max Allan Collins solved the case. On Friday night, Carol and I put on our revised, second edition of "Just in Crime: The Musical."

There were two tributes to the late fan Don Sandstrom, in addition to one in writing in the program by his daughter Karen. An auction was held to raise funds for the Sandstrom Memorial Scholarship at Butler University to encourage developing writers; $8,000 was raised. Less serious was the Don Sandstrom Memorial Family Feud, a trivia contest arranged by Ted Hertel's brother Harry. One of the contestants was another of Sandstrom's daughters, Bibi.

When I wasn't speaking as a panelist during a discussion of "The Golden Age," I looked out at the audience and saw that Phyllis White had dropped off to sleep, her head practically resting on the shoulder of my wife. It seemed understandable. She was over eighty and traveling across two time zones is not easy, even for younger people. She was ill, and shortly after Bouchercon mystery fans learned that Phyllis had inoperable brain cancer.

24 Left Coast Crime (1991–)

One convention a year was not enough for fans, and people thought of regional conventions that would be more intimate than Bouchercons and involve less travel. The East Coast had had Malice Domestic since 1989, and a successful Midwest Mystery & Suspense Convention was held in Omaha in 1990. Bryan Barrett decided to chair a San Francisco conference for 1991.

There was indecision as to what to call it. Early ads called it "Crime-One," but it was later referred to variously as West Coast Crime Conference, Western Regional Mystery Conference, and Left Coast Crime Conference before the simpler "Left Coast Crime" (LCC), which has proven popular, was arrived at.

The program book said it was celebrating two important events in the mystery: the 150th anniversary of what is generally accepted as the first detective story (by Poe) and the 50th anniversary of *Ellery Queen's Mystery Magazine*. However, the program also acknowledged the growth of mysteries set on the Pacific Coast, "Perhaps the freshest crimes are being committed in the imaginations of our New West writers, in the solid traditions of Poe and Queen, to be sure, but also on the firm basis of Chandler and Hammett…. It is today's Western states inheritors of the tradition—authors, readers, collectors, and critics—that we intend to celebrate here."

The first LCC, February 15–18, 1991, at the Sir Francis Drake hotel in San Francisco, invited two residents of nearby Sonoma County, Bill Pronzini and Marcia Muller, as Guests of Honor, and Bruce Taylor, owner of San Francisco's leading mystery bookstore, as Toastmaster. Panels dealt with such local issues as the environment and gay and lesbian detectives. The banquet was held in John's Grill, a restaurant Sam Spade visited *in The Maltese Falcon*. A popular attraction during LCC, as at San Francisco Bouchercons, was Don Herron's Dashiell Hammett Walk.

That fewer than 200 people attended was due to several factors. The LCC committee did not have access to a mailing list of attendees at prior conferences. Also, the Gulf War, with threats of terrorism, had made many reluctant to fly. Perhaps the small size of the conference made it so enjoyable for many. As Len Moffatt reported, "Left Coast Crime was fun mostly because we got to visit with friends who stepped right off of the pages of *MDM* and *DAPA-EM*." LCC was a reunion for many of those who had attended Omaha in 1990.

Donna Rankin, treasurer for the first Left Coast Crime, chaired the second in 1992. It remained in San Francisco but moved to the Holiday Inn in Union Square. On Saturday night, the Chinese New Year's parade could be seen from the windows of the room in which authors were autographing books. Two Washington State writers, Earl Emerson and J. A. Jance, were Guests of Honor, and James Lee Burke came from Montana to be Toastmaster. Peter Davison, then playing Albert Campion on *Mystery!*, attended and was very accessible. Another attendee was Sara Paretsky, wearing a button saying, "Don't judge a book by its movie," recognition of the poor reception given *V. I. Warshawski*, the film version of her work. Lia Matera chaired a panel on social issues, always a popular topic in San Francisco. "Fireside Chats," intimate interviews and readings with individual authors, was also popular; attendance at each was limited to fifty people.

Though some hoped LCC would remain in the Bay area, others were anxious to have it in their backyards, and LCC #3 moved in 1993 to the Hyatt Regency Alicante, near Disneyland in Anaheim. Kevin Moore and Kathy Johnson were co-chairwomen. Sue Dunlap and Julie Smith were the Guests of Honor, and Ann and Evan Maxwell were Toastmasters. Attendance reached 400. A Sunday night banquet was unpopular with some people because it ended too late for their trip home, and they felt they were forced to spend for an extra night's lodging.

Left Coast Crime returned to the Anaheim location in 1994, with Kevin Moore again as chairwoman. Aaron Elkins was Guest of Honor, with Carolyn G. Hart as Toastmaster. Programming was limited to two tracks, allowing people to see more without having to make difficult choices. Sex in the mystery was discussed at many panels. In what was becoming a LCC tradition, there was a group autographing session of authors. The un-popular Sunday night banquet was held again, and at 3 AM Monday morning, those staying in the hotel were awakened by an announcement telling them to remain in their rooms because there was a power outage. Some realized the hotel might be legally required to do that, but they wondered why awaken people who were sleeping in the dark. On a prior night during the convention, there was a 4 AM false alarm to awaken people.

Left Coast Crime had been meant for locations in the Pacific and Mountain time zones, but some Californians questioned

Bryan Barrett, who chaired the first Left Coast Crime in 1991 and LCC 2002.

the non-coastal location of the 1995 LCC at the Old Town Holiday Inn in Scottsdale, Arizona. Barbara Peters of the Poisoned Pen Bookstore there managed the convention, with Jean Hanus as chairwoman. Writer-fan Jim McCahery, scheduled to attend, died of a heart attack in New Jersey shortly before LCC began. Bob Samoian, who had recently had brain surgery, attended his final mystery convention, dying of a heart attack three days after he returned home. He had been as enthusiastic as ever.

Others attending were among the walking wounded. Parnell Hall was on crutches due to a torn Achilles tendon, and Don Sandstrom fell down a flight of stairs at the hotel and had to walk with a cane.

Two Albuquerque writers were honored. Tony Hillerman was Guest of Honor, and Judith Van Gieson was Toastmaster. Robert B. Parker was also a Special Guest. P. D. James was in Scottsdale on a book tour but didn't attend LCC. Neither she nor Parker was at the authors' signing Saturday night. Again, there were only two tracks of programs. In line with the Southwestern location, three panels under the general title "The Modern Gunslinger" were held, but they dealt with mysteries, not Westerns.

Left Coast Crime moved further inland in 1996, to the Clarion Hotel in Boulder, Colorado. Tom and Enid Schantz of Rue Morgue Books there chaired it. Because Boulder is at 7,000 feet, they called this LCC "Murder with an Altitude." Over 450 people attended. The location provoked some controversy because Boulder had probably the strictest non-smoking code at that time in the United States. Ann Williams of Denver registered, but cancelled when she learned the only place she could smoke was in her room. She said, "The pious majority in Boulder has zero tolerance for minority rights." Barry Gardner also railed against the Boulder City Council. Ironically, both Williams and Gardner died in 1996, in their fifties, with cigarette smoking apparently a contributory factor. Others who attended said they enjoyed the absence of second-hand smoke and it was the only mystery convention at which they felt free to go into the bar, normally a smoke-filled place.

Kinky Friedman was Guest of Honor and Nevada Barr Toastmaster. A cabaret was held Saturday night at the Boulder Theater. Parnell Hall was a hit with one of his songs, and Alan Russell and Jeremiah Healy serenaded Left Coast Crime's first Fan Guest of Honor, Mary "Maggie" Mason. Some thought Friedman's performance (including a song about mucous) was tasteless and walked out on him.

For the first time the "Lefty" Award was given. Saluting the best humorous mystery of the previous year, it was given to Russell for *The Fat Innkeeper*. The award took the form of a plaster impression of a left hand, "posed" for by Enid Schantz. Panels in Boulder, which had three tracks, included "Collecting the Hypermodern," then at its peak. I explored another aspect in a one-man panel, "Book Collecting for Po' Folks," describing the fun (and bargains) found at library sales, garage sales, and second-hand stores.

In 1997, LCC came to the Stouffer Renaissance (formerly Madison) in Seattle, where 1994's Bouchercon was held, with Andi Shechter as chairwoman. There were joint Guests of Honor, the husband-and-wife team of Jonathan and Faye Kellerman. Lia Matera was Toastmaster. Because the Kellermans are Orthodox Jews, their participation at LCC was limited to Sunday when their speeches at the brunch were well received. Attendees were disappointed when Jonathan, due to carpal tunnel syndrome, couldn't sign his books, though he had a stamp of his signature.

About 400 people attended. Again, the timing did not please everyone. Advertised as running from Thursday through Sunday, LCC had few Thursday panels. By Sunday afternoon, there were only two panels remaining. Some said that had they but known, they'd not have booked for Sunday evening. At the auction, emcees

Bruce Taylor and Parnell Hall raised $1,700 for the Northwest Literacy Foundation and a battered-women's shelter.

In 1998 Left Coast Crime was at San Diego's Bahia Hotel and Resort in the Mission Bay area. Elizabeth George, the Southern Californian who writes about England, was Guest of Honor, and local author Alan Russell was Toastmaster. A noted San Diego book collector, Willis Herr, was posthumous Fan Guest of Honor. A Lifetime Achievement Award went to another local, novelist-reviewer Robert Wade.

Left Coast Crime started at Albuquerque's Hyatt Regency Friday, March 5, 1999, but for me it started the night before when, reliving my Mystery Readers' bashes in the Bronx, I had a party for a dozen mystery fans at my home in Santa Fe, seventy miles away. John Dunning was LCC Guest of Honor; Deborah Crombie, a Texan who (like George) sets her mysteries in England, was Toastmaster; Tasha Mackler, formerly a mystery bookstore owner in Albuquerque, was Fan Guest of Honor. Harlen Campbell, who had recently published his first mystery, was chairman.

The theme of this LCC was "the literary mystery," and Dunning tried to stick to this topic in his Saturday night banquet speech. It proved unsatisfying since Dunning couldn't seem to decide whether the mystery should be "escape" or "great literature." The same indecisiveness was present in Campbell's interview with him, in which he opined that the mystery can be "literature," but because it is essentially plot-driven and has rules, it doesn't permit the freedom to explore character that mainstream fiction does. The success of Dunning's own *Booked to Die* (1992), a highly collectible "hypermodern" book, was due to its combination of old-fashioned detective story and book collecting lore, gathered by Dunning in the years he owned a Denver bookstore.

Panels on publishing again proved popular as LCC invited a new group of hopeful mystery writers. Increasingly, as lobby space at hotels seemed limited, the book room was the place fans gathered to talk, a trend not unpopular with dealers.

In 2000, Left Coast Crime returned to Arizona, at Tucson's Holiday Inn City Center, and the weather in mid-March was hot. Sue Grafton, author of the popular alphabet series, was Guest of Honor. Harlan Coben came from New Jersey to be Toastmaster. George Easter, editor-publisher of *Deadly Pleasures,* was Fan Guest of Honor. Maggie Mason organized "The Easter Egg Caper," gathering egg-shaped pantyhose containers and having George's friends insert notes to him. In what was proving a regular event, Mason's team won the trivia contest, one patterned after the TV show *Jeopardy.* She modestly claimed her success was due to naming her team "The Golden Retrievers," her favorite breed of dog.

More than a dozen fans had an enjoyable dinner at a local Cajun-Creole restaurant owned by Elmore Leonard's son Chris and his wife. A large committee made this LCC a success, with Ellie Warder handling four different functions. The program was varied, though Friday's panels leaned in the direction of police procedure, with two DNA Fingerprinting Workshops. Literacy continued as the charity of choice, and there were both silent and live auctions to help Literacy Volunteers of Tucson.

Alaska in mid-February seemed a dubious attraction, but there was general agreement that Left Coast Crime at the Anchorage Hilton in 2001 was a good convention. Even the weather cooperated, with temperatures generally in the twenties.

Many attendees took the opportunity of their first Alaska trips to spend a few extra days seeing scenery and wildlife; some reported seeing moose on the streets of downtown Anchorage. To encourage Alaska's native population to read, the local branch of Sisters in Crime organized a project called "Authors to the Bush," in which writers volunteered to go in small planes to remote settlements to promote reading. Linda Billington chaired this convention in which Michael Connelly was US Guest of Honor, Lindsey Davis was British Guest of Honor, and Andi Shechter was Fan Guest of Honor.

Recognizing Portland, Oregon's damp climate, Left Coast Crime 2002 at the Columbia River Doubletree Hotel was called "Slugs and Roses." Bryan Barrett and Thom Walls were co-chairmen. Laurie R. King and Steven Saylor, known primarily for their historical mysteries, were Guests of Honor. Don Herron was Fan Guest of Honor, and G. M. Ford of Seattle the Toastmaster. Mary Mason saw fewer collectors in the book room, though many who attended took the time to visit the world-famous Powell's bookstore. Few hospitality suites received as high ratings as the one at the Doubletree.

Left Coast Crime returned to the Pasadena Hilton in 2003. One 1991 problem that had not been solved was annoying spillover of sound when the main ballroom was split into two meeting rooms without soundproof dividers. Otherwise, this LCC was a success, enjoyed by its largest crowd to date, about 600 people.

Robert Crais was Guest of Honor; Sue Feder was Fan Guest of Honor; Jerrilyn Farmer was Toastmaster. The famous radio play "Sorry, Wrong Number" was recreated at the Pasadena Library, with attendees bused there and back. Los Angeles writer-fan Paul Bishop had an interesting conference. After a panel "Cops vs. Coppers," regarding the US police and their British counterparts, he went to compete in the Los Angeles Marathon, finishing the twenty-six-plus miles in three hours forty-three minutes. He also received "hate mail" from the wife of a judge who was in attendance at his panel. She thought he was being disrespectful to the law, despite his twenty-six years service as an LAPD officer.

The Doubletree Hotel in Monterey, scene of 1997 Bouchercon, was the locale for the equally successful 2004 Left Coast Crime, with about 850 attending. Bill and Toby Gottfried were co-chairs. Sharan Newman and Walter Mosley were the Guests of Honor. Newman did a slide show on the art, history, and costuming of 12th century France, the setting for her historical mysteries. Bryan Barrett and Thom Walls were Fan Guests of Honor. Gillian Roberts was Toastmaster, and Richard Lupoff received a Lifetime Achievement Award. A new award was instituted, the Bruce Alexander History Mystery Award, in honor of the writer who had died three months before LCC. The committee also instituted a one-time award, the Otter, for the best mystery set in the Monterey area. The auction benefitted the Friends of Sea Otters, and the opening reception was at the renowned Monterey Bay Aquarium.

25 ClueFest (1992–2003)

ClueFest, first held at the Radisson Suites Hotel in Dallas during Easter weekend, April 17–19, 1992, came as close to being a true fan convention as any. Caryl Thompson underwrote it to please her mother, Terry Thompson, a mystery fan who bemoaned the fact that other conventions were too far away and expensive to attend. Wilson Tucker was Toastmaster, Bill Crider was Literary Guest of Honor, and Carlton Stowers was Non-Fiction Guest of Honor. Mari Hall called it a "relax-a-con" as no one seemed to worry about preparation for panels, which Hall said "were decided when we arrived; most were audience participation… wherever two or three people gathered we had a panel."

There *was* some planning as local actors performed a *Shadows* radio script and a Sherlock Holmes performance that was interrupted by a "murder," with attendees asked to solve it. Attendance, according to some who attended, was sparse, perhaps thirty people. Writer James Reasoner said, "I went as a fan, not as a guest, and there were times I felt like I was the only paying customer there. Everybody else was either a guest or a member of the convention staff."

My involvement with ClueFest began in 1993 when it was held, July 17–18, at the Holiday Inn Park Central Hotel. I was Non-Fiction Guest of Honor due to my writings about the mystery. Susan Rogers Cooper was Fiction Guest of Honor. Jan Grape was, according to ClueFest, "Toast Mistress." Sandy Cupp was its first Fan Guest of Honor, though she admitted her interest was limited to supporting her husband, Scott Cupp, a serious fan, collector, and bookseller.

Though in *MDM* she had criticized Caryl Thompson's lack of mystery convention experience the year before, Mari Hall was chosen to handle 1993 programming. Once more ClueFest's panels were non-structured, with participants recruited at the last minute. Attendance again was meager. I doubt I saw more than thirty-five people, and few were from out-of-state. Perhaps some felt as did Bob Napier, who said, "I've been to Dallas in the summer and I'd rather vacation in Hades than do that again."

ClueFest began growing in 1994, when it was held at the Ramada Park Central, August 5–7. Barry Gardner jokingly predicted "The audience might actually outnumber the panelists on occasion this year." About 150 attended, with Joan Hess and Stuart Kaminsky as Guests of Honor and Bill Crider as Toastmaster. Book Tree, a Dallas bookstore operated by brothers Barry and Terry Phillips, co-sponsored with Thompson. Two highlights were ClueFest's first charity auction, with Geraldine Galentree as auctioneer, and a Friday night pizza party at Gardner's home. ClueFest was getting more out-of-state attendees, and Gardner's party guests included Len and June Moffatt and Bruce Taylor from California and Steve Stilwell of Minnesota.

During its first three years there had been complaints about all three ClueFest hotels. The 1994 meeting room even lacked air conditioning! In 1995 ClueFest was held at the Harvey Hotel in suburban Addison, and there was general approval of that site. Barry Gardner was Fan Guest of Honor in 1995 and again invited visitors, more than a dozen, to a Saturday night barbecue at his house. Judith Van Gieson of Albuquerque was Fiction Guest of Honor, and two Texas authors, A. W. Gray and Carole Nelson Douglas, were respectively Non-Fiction Guest of Honor and Toastmistress. At the Sunday banquet, Douglas famously introduced Gardner as Barry "Gordon." Attendance at ClueFest was not huge, though there were at least 100 people.

Pat Hawk, the reigning expert on pseudonyms, moderated what was probably the first panel on that subject. I moderated a panel on mystery fandom that created some controversy; there was more when Gardner later wrote about the subject to *MDM*. Initiating what was possibly the first major discussion of the *future* of fandom, I noted the aging of fans and wondered if younger fans would provide the convention organizing and writing for fan journals that fans of two decades before had. My fellow panelists, Don Sandstrom, Gardner, and the Moffatts, were no more optimistic than I that younger fans were as anxious to participate, and there was discussion of how to encourage them.

Texas fans and writers (l. to r.) James Reasoner, Joe R. Lansdale, and Bill Crider.

The Fan Guest of Honor in 1996 was Terry Klebba of suburban Dallas. Though she was not active in writing about the mystery, few fans were as avid collectors and as supportive of mystery booksellers as she. Carolyn G. Hart and Robert Crais were the Fiction Guests of Honor and Jay W. K. Setliff, editor-publisher of *Mostly Murder*, the Non-Fiction Guest of Honor. Marlys Millhiser of Colorado was a most amusing Toastmistress. This proved to be easily the most successful ClueFest until then, with attendance of about 275. A "Fandom 101" panel on Saturday was designed to encourage the new fans I had feared for in 1995. Other panels included repeats on pseudonyms and collecting, plus a new one called "Sex and Violence: Where I Draw the Line."

Barry Gardner drove visitors to a legendary store in Denton, Texas: Recycled Books and Records. For the third year in a row, he and his wife Ellen hosted mystery fans. After ClueFest, he drove Bruce Taylor and Steve Stilwell to various Texas bookstores. Then, only four days after ClueFest, Barry died at his desk of a heart attack. Though he only became part of mystery fandom in 1992, he had, in the words of Art Scott, become "a dear friend, now irreplaceable" to fandom. Barry had informed his wife and his cardiologist that, as a smoker, he was going to live his life the way he wanted to. In the last week of his life he smoked, enjoyed himself at a mystery convention, went booking with friends, and wrote reviews. He went as he wanted to.

Attendance in 1997 was 242, but a few people, including Bruce Taylor, said that Barry's death made it too sad an occasion to attend. Jeremiah Healy and Joyce Christmas were Fiction Guests of Honor. Christmas had been a big supporter of ClueFest in the past, flying down from New York. Pat Hawk was Non-Fiction Guest of Honor, and Dr. Karen Ross, a pathologist, was Fan Guest of Honor. Parnell Hall was the amusing Toastmaster. At the banquet, Bill Crider paid a touching tribute to Gardner. Gardner's widow, Ellen, attended for the first time. She had become active in fandom because it was important to Barry.

ClueFest 1997 remained, in the words of Don Sandstrom, a "laid-back and friendly convention," with only two tracks of programming. Popular panels included "Tough Guys and Dangerous Dolls" and "They Made Me This Way—Books That Shaped Me." The annual auction to help the Dallas Public Library was a success.

Walter Satterthwait and Charlaine Harris were the Fiction Guests of Honor at ClueFest in 1998. Dean James and Jan Grape were Non-Fiction Guests of Honor. Barbara Burnett Smith was Toastmistress, and Richard Centner was Fan Guest of Honor.

After ClueFest had announced its 1999 dates, July 7–9, EyeCon 1999 in St. Louis, organized by Robert Randisi of PWA, said it had selected the same weekend. Randisi said this was not deliberate, just a scheduling mistake. Predictably, attendance at ClueFest in 1999 was down. There are only so many fans to attend mid-summer mystery conventions in hot, humid locations. Bill Crider was Non-Fiction Guest of Honor for his fan writing. Carole Nelson Douglas and Peter Robinson were Fiction Guests of Honor. Tony Fennelly was Toastmistress and gave a hilarious talk at the luncheon banquet. Fan Guest of Honor Teresa Loftin moderated six panels!

Dianne Day and Steve Brewer were Guests of Honor in 2000. Maxine O'Callaghan was Toastmistress. Lauri Hart was Fan Guest of Honor. Reed Andrus, recently moved from Arizona to the Dallas suburbs, attended his first ClueFest and moderated two panels and participated on a third. Though Brewer and O'Callaghan write of private eyes, Andrus felt most authors attending were a bit too cozy for his taste. Still, he enjoyed it "despite the hats and cats and amateur sleuths."

Bill Crider, who had attended every ClueFest, was Special Decade Guest of Honor at its tenth anniversary in 2001, held at the Harvey Hotel in another suburb, Plano. Deborah Crombie and Joe R. Lansdale were Fiction Guests of Honor. M. E. Cooper was Non-Fiction Guest of Honor, Joyce Christmas was Toastmistress, and Frances Butt was Fan Guest of Honor. New authors and hopeful, non-published authors were in attendance along with small publishers. One author refused to acknowledge the term "small press," substituting "independent press" when possible. There was discussion of the increasing separation between new electronic publishing and traditional books with advances and print runs.

The popular Jan Burke was chosen for Fiction Guest of Honor in 2002, but the invitation was withdrawn by Cluefest's organizer because Burke had agreed to be Guest of Honor at Deadly Ink. Though Deadly Ink is in New Jersey and was scheduled a month prior to Cluefest, her appearing there was regarding as a conflict of interest by Caryl Thompson. Joyce Spizer, who was the Non-Fiction Guest of Honor, has written fiction as well as true crime, and doubled as Fiction Guest of Honor. Bill Mark was

Fan Guest of Honor, while Texas private eye writer Rick Riordan was Toastmaster.

Tony Fennelly was the popular Fiction Guest of Honor in 2003, while Bill Crider, wearing another hat, was again recognized, this time as Fan Guest of Honor, the fourth time ClueFest honored him. Attendance, at about 100, was down from the high point in the 1990s. ClueFest was cancelled for 2004 and 2005 because Terry Thompson was in poor health.

26 Deadly Pleasures (1993–)

With *The Mystery Fancier* in its last stages, Bill Deeck contemplated editing and publishing a replacement. He considered *Mysterious Maunderings* as a title but later changed it to *The Criminous Connoisseur*. However, it became academic because his announced plans in *MDM* and *TMF* failed to draw much response, let alone the balance of two-thirds articles and checklists and only one-third reviews that he hoped to achieve. The material Deeck had received was turned over to George Easter, a lawyer and publisher of a discount-coupon magazine who lives near Salt Lake City, for *Deadly Pleasures*, which he launched with the Spring 1993 issue.

The first issue of Easter's quarterly magazine contained twenty pages. By his second issue, he doubled that number. In the early issues, articles about and reviews of older books took up considerable space. Bill Deeck's review column, "The Backward Reviewer," took four pages in the first issue and five in the second. Easter quickly put together a stable of leading fan writers, including Philip Scowcroft and Martin Edwards from England. His early reviewers and writers also included Allen J. Hubin, Don Sandstrom, Sue Feder, Barry Gardner, Carol Bird, and Maryell Cleary, who wrote "Vintage Crime." Ubiquitous as ever, I moved my "It's About Crime" column from *TMF*. Each issue had interviews, usually with the author who was the subject of its cover article.

Early in his publishing career, Easter started two participatory features that make *Deadly Pleasures* distinctive. One is his "Quarterly Question." In his third issue he started what is arguably *DP*'s most popular feature, "Reviewed to Death." Easter obtains multiple copies of new books and sends them to various reviewers. It is fascinating to see how differently six or more people review the same book. Another feature enjoyed by many readers was "Atlantic Asides," a column by Mat Coward, like Edwards a British fan-reviewer as well as a writer of fiction.

Deadly Pleasures kept growing, to fifty-six pages in #4 (Winter 1994), to sixty-four pages in #10 (Fall 1995), reaching eighty-eight pages in #38 (2003), though it has since reverted to eighty-four pages. It soon became apparent that what its readers most wanted was reviews of current books. Articles on older writers and books became far less frequent. Mary (Maggie) Mason, who wrote a column on collectible books of the 1990s, switched to a review column. *DP* developed a new crew of reviewers, including Mason, Ted Hertel, and Dr. Larry Gandle, who reviewed first mysteries and also evaluated each year's Edgar nominees.

There was controversy in the early issues, and not merely disagreements over books. When Don Sandstrom denigrated some reference works as "non-books," many disagreed with him. Joe Christopher raised a small storm by calling John Dickson Carr "second-rate." I called the Anthony Awards mere popularity contests in #15, and Rick Robinson disagreed in the next issue. In #22 Maxim Jakubowski criticized fellow bookseller Lewis Buckingham, including his prices.

Gradually, the number of new reviews (and previews) increased, taking up more than seventy percent of *Deadly Pleasures*. With the exception of Philip Scowcroft, hardly anyone wrote about older books, though I usually included reviews of them in my column. The new reviews were invariably positive, something that did not jibe with my own reading of many new books. Finally, I stirred up some debate with a letter Easter published both on his web site and in his letters column. I said there was not enough about past mysteries, too many current reviews, and too little controversy in *DP*. I also criticized Mat Cow-

George Easter, who founded *Deadly Pleasures*, and Mary "Maggie" Mason, mystery's trivia ace.

ard's column for being less about crime fiction than about politics and the criminal justice system, usually discussed from a decidedly anti-American viewpoint. Eight readers responded; they all said I was wrong and that they liked *DP* as it is.

Since 1997 Deadly Pleasures has given out the Barry Awards, honoring one of its most popular reviewers, the late Barry Gardner. These awards, which recognize Best Novel, Best First Novel, Best British Crime Novel, Best Paperback Original, and Best Short Story, are handed out at Bouchercons.

27 Magna Cum Murder (1994–)

Fandom mixes gracefully with academia at Magna Cum Murder, the popular name for the Mid-America Mystery Conference of Ball State University in Muncie, Indiana. It was the idea of Joanna Wallace of its School of Continuing Education and has been organized since the beginning by Kathryn Kennison. Magna has proved popular despite being held in October, the traditional month for Bouchercon. Muncie is different from other convention sites. A small Midwestern city, it was the basis of "Middletown," the classic sociological study in the 1920s and 1930s by Robert and Helen Lynd.

The first Magna was held October 28–30, 1994, with Ralph McInerny as Guest of Honor. 265 people attended. *The Armchair Detective* helped promote it by giving a $500 prize for the outstanding critical/biographical work of 1993. Peter Wolfe won for his book on Eric Ambler. Don Sandstrom praised the convention site, the Hotel Roberts, especially its lobby, but some events were across the street at Muncie's convention center. Outstanding was "The Panel from Hell," with Joan Hess and Sharyn McCrumb reprising their 1991 Bouchercon panel, aided by Les Roberts, Parnell Hall, and Jeff Abbott.

From the beginning Magna has honored many people. Hess and McCrumb were "Luminaries," and Michael Z. Lewin was labeled "Mystery Master." Instead of being called banquet emcees, Don Sandstrom and Nancy Pickard were Master and Mistress of the Revels. Sandstrom, to whom Kennison gives much credit for helping Magna get off the ground, was also the Fan Guest of Honor, a title Magna sometimes calls Reader Guest of Honor.

Gary Warren Niebuhr was Fan Guest of Honor at the second Magna, in 1995, when over 350 attended, and he started the conference with his slide show on the history of the private detective in fiction. Emphasizing that fans use their time and money to attend conferences and buy books, Niebuhr said, "Every author should realize that the fans who attend these conferences are their support organization and their safety net, as well."

Mary Higgins Clark was Guest of Honor. Donald E. Westlake, as "Mystery Master," was interviewed by Sandstrom, who was given the academic-sounding title "Host Emeritus," and Parnell Hall. Later, Hall sang "If It Ain't Fried, It Ain't Food," using lyrics from Westlake's *Baby, Would I Lie?* Hall and Dorothy Cannell were Master and Mistress of the Revels. A radio mystery contest was held, with the winning play performed live at the banquet and also over the local Public Broadcasting System station. Maggie Mason, fandom's outstanding trivia player, won the Trivia Bowl. Sandstrom and Neil Albert reprised their EyeCon 1995 panel called "Big Macs," discussing John D. MacDonald and Ross Macdonald respectively. B. J. Rahn and Jeanne M. Dams were outstanding in a panel on the "Golden Age." In keeping with the academic setting, one track consisted of papers presented by professors or doctoral candidates, for example one by Jan Steffensen on Scandinavian mysteries.

At the third Magna, in 1996, Sara Paretsky was Guest of Honor, with Peter Lovesey as Mystery Master. Bill Spurgeon, the Fan Guest of Honor, led a Sunday morning walking tour of downtown Muncie, pointing out scenes of crime. Attendance was 360, approaching the 400 limit which the organizers have set. The convention started with a hilarious panel: "Overdunnits: An Irreverent Look at Trite, Hackneyed, Effete, or Just Plain Silly Plots," with Sandstrom, Niebuhr, and Roberts.

Though 1997 Magna ended only a few days before the Monterey Bouchercon, its loyal fans did not forsake it. James Crumley was Guest of Honor and Lawrence Block was Mystery Master. The Arsenic and Oolong Society of Indianapolis, a mystery reading group supportive of Magna, was collectively Fan Guest of Honor. Sadly, one of their most active members, Don Sandstrom, died shortly before Magna began.

Magna occasionally changes the subjects it honors, extending its appeal. In 1998, Jerry Bledsoe was True Crime Luminary. Sue Grafton was listed as Mystery Master Guest of Honor. In both 1999 and 2000, Mickey Spillane was slated to be Mystery Master Guest of Honor, but he had to cancel both years due to illness. Anne Perry and Carolyn G. Hart were respectively Guests of Honor in those years.

In 2001, Clark Davenport and Jim Ebert became Magna's first Forensic Guests of Honor. The Fan/Reader Guest of Honor that year was Phil Momberg, who has attended every Magna and is the greatest fan of Ralph McInerny; he has eighty books by him, all autographed.

In 2002, Magna joined other American conventions in having an International Guest of Honor (Frances Fyfield) to go with the American Guest, Michael Connelly.

Charles King, an expert in detecting arson, was supposed to be co-Forensic Guest of Honor in 2003, along with his wife, mystery novelist Shelly Reuben, whose series character is an arson investigator. Unfortunately, King died a few months before Magna. Magna had its first Keynote Speaker that year, Carolyn Gilbert, founder of the International Association of Obituarists.

A coup for Magna in 2004 was getting Alexander McCall Smith, the enormously popular Scottish writer, as Guest of Honor. The True Crime Guest of Honor was Don Hale. Keynote Speaker at the banquet was Dr. Elliot Engel whose talk on Poe was surprisingly funny, considering the subject.

Magna invariably sells out the Hotel Roberts, its site since the first year. Unlike other conventions, Magna publishes a quarterly newsletter, *Pomp and Circumstantial Evidence*, to keep loyal attendees informed. The secret of Magna's success was succinctly stated by Lev Raphael, Master of Revels in 2001, when he compared it to a weekend house party with several hundred close friends.

28 Other Conventions

Spurred by the popularity of Bouchercon, many people have decided to put on conventions, especially in the latter half of the 1990s and early 21st century. There are many worth mentioning, in addition to those covered in separate chapters. Most of those discussed are general conferences for mystery fans, although sometimes a specific sub-genre such as the "cozy" or private eye is celebrated. There are also conferences not strictly for mystery fans, though their subjects have the mystery as an important component.

Many fans are aspiring authors and are welcome at such writer-oriented conventions as Of Dark and Stormy Nights in South Bend, Indiana; Murder in the Grove in Boise, Idaho; Love Is Murder in the Chicago area; and Sleuthfest in Florida.

Mid-Atlantic Mystery Book Fair and Convention (1991–)

Deen and Jay Kogan, responsible for the 1989 Philadelphia Bouchercon, put on the Mid-Atlantic Mystery Book Fair and Convention, November 8–10, 1991, at Philadelphia's Holiday Inn on City Line Avenue. More than 200 attended. There were no banquets or award ceremonies, but there were good panels and lots of socializing. William L. DeAndrea said in *TAD*, "It had that same kind of neighborhoodly block-party feeling that the World Convention [Bouchercon] has grown out of."

The second Mid-Atlantic in 1992 moved to a different Holiday Inn, in Philadelphia's Center City, near Independence Hall. Ronnie Klaskin found it "relaxed and intimate." Real crime intruded on crime fiction when author Tony Fennelly had her fur coat and cash stolen from her hotel room.

The third Mid-Atlantic was obviously difficult for Deen Kogan because Jay died November 5, 1993, less than a week before it began. However, she bravely helped to make it a fine convention for 334 who registered, plus 80 daily admissions. Later, in *MDM*, Deen thanked those who had offered condolences and said, "Jay thoroughly enjoyed the genre and it was an important segment of our life." Ann Williams called the convention "a mellow blend of people" but commented on the presence of 350 noisy teenagers at the hotel; they were among 7,000 in Philadelphia for a Catholic Youth Organization convention. When a priest in the elevator apologized to her for their noise, she wittily replied, "That's all right Father; I forgive you."

In 1994, Deen Kogan capped membership at 400 to allow "lots of interaction in an informal setting." At the convention she sold *The Mid-Atlantic Mysterious Cookbook* to benefit the Friends of the Free Library in Philadelphia. The popularity of Mid-Atlantic forced her reluctantly to raise the membership limit to 450 in 1995. 1996 saw the first official reception, a Friday night cocktail party. In 1997 Mid-Atlantic, which had always been held in November, moved to October 3–5 to avoid conflict with Bouchercon. Due to Kogan's work in running the 1998 Philadelphia Bouchercon, Mid-Atlantic was not held in 1998 or 1999.

Resuming October 13–15, 2000, Mid-Atlantic had a different hotel, The Wyndham Franklin Plaza, site of 1998 Bouchercon. There was now a Sunday lunch, with special guests Warren Murphy, S. J. Rozan, and George Pelecanos honored. Gordon Magnuson found it the "best organized of all conventions." Because of the proximity of Washington, DC, site of the 2001 Bouchercon, Mid-Atlantic was not held that year.

The 9th Mid-Atlantic, September 27–29, 2002, opened with a Friday night reception dinner. It included presentation of the IACW North American Branch's Hammett Prize to Alan Furst. An unusual panel, on *Feng Shui*, demonstrated how to structure an office to help one's writing. On Sunday Jonathan Gash conducted a writing workshop, and there was a "High Tea" to honor the mother-son writing team of Caroline and Charles Todd, who publish under the latter name.

Deen Kogan's involvement with Bouchercons in 2003 and 2005 has caused her to put Mid-Atlantic on hold, though she plans to resume it in the fall of 2006.

Shots on the Page (1992–1997) and Crime Scene (2000–)

The growth in conventions was not restricted to the United States. In Nottingham, England, where plans were being made for a Bouchercon, the committee organized conventions to give them experience, beginning with **Shots in the Dark**, a two-week 1991 festival of crime films that included the British premiere of *Silence of the Lambs*. Organized by the staff of the Broadway Media Centre in Nottingham, it proved a success. In 1992, they added a three-day mystery convention, **Shots on the Page**, to run concurrently, and went to Toronto and bid successfully for 1995 Bouchercon. Julian Symons was Guest of Honor, but praise also went to a panel with Barry Pike and Stephen Leadbetter on writers such as John Rhode, who had been called "humdrum" by Symons. That panel was so popular it lasted one half-hour past its allotted time and only ended when the cleaners for the conference room arrived. For those attending this first "small" British convention, the pleasure came from meeting and chatting with other fans.

At the 1993 Shots on the Page, Sara Paretsky was Guest of Honor, and Michael Gilbert British Guest of Honor. In addition to the panels, there were "Extra Shots," a popular supplementary series of talks by writers, organized by Peter Lovesey. In 1994 James Crumley was Guest of Honor. At the mystery quiz, now an annual event, Geoff Bradley was made scorer because, as Ethel Lindsay said, "It was felt that any team that had him would have an unfair advantage."

Shots on the Page lasted through 1997, though the last convention was a more limited event, despite yeoman efforts by Maxim Jakubowski, who put together the entire program. Financial aid in the form of grants had ceased.

Adrian Wootton, principal organizer of "Shots" and the Nottingham Bouchercon, moved to an important position at the National Film Theatre on London's Southbank. In 2000, with Jakubowski, he organized **Crime Scene**, a London film festival that had a mystery fiction component. Attendance was about 650, with movie fans far outnumbering mystery readers. Crime Scene, which continues, features celebrations of mystery writers whose work has been adapted for film and television, including Agatha Christie and Georges Simenon.

Southwest Mystery/Suspense Convention (1993)

Some assumed the **Southwest Mystery/Suspense Convention** was a continuation of Omaha's Midwest Conventions of 1990–1992, but this gathering, called "Deep in the Heart of Texas," was put on by different people at Austin's Hyatt Regency, May 28–30, 1993. Elmer and Jan Grape, then owners of Austin's mystery bookstore (she is also a writer), were co-chairs. Jan also served on seven committees, and her hard—though seemingly effortless—work resulted in a smooth convention for about 250 people.

Loren D. Estleman and D. R. (Doris) Meredith were Guests of Honor. Lifetime Achievement Awards went to Robert J. Randisi, founder of PWA, and Joan Lowery Nixon, winner of many Edgars for young adult mysteries. (Estleman, Meredith, and Randisi all write in the Western genre as well as mystery, while Nixon writes a historical series set in Missouri that might be considered Western as well.) The Toastmaster, Sharyn McCrumb, was called "Mystress of Ceremonies," and the banquet featured a Texas barbecue. Parnell Hall was ready to sing "Achy Breaky Heart" at the banquet, but fortunately no one asked him.

One panel, part of three-track programming, was a dance demonstration of the Texas Two-Step. As one member of a panel of fanatical collectors, Richard Moore got off the best line of the convention when he said, "I wanted my wife to know, I may be bizarre, but I'm not unique." During a reviewers' panel, Carolyn Banks upset several fans by giving away the ending of a mystery. In the dealers' room, Pat Hawk introduced the first edition of his compendium of pseudonyms, covering over 10,000 authors, including many mystery writers.

Shortly before this convention, someone committed suicide by jumping from the 16th floor of the atrium. This didn't keep people from frequenting the bar in the atrium, but the outdoor terrace overlooking the Colorado River was so delightful it attracted more fans for talk and drinks each night. One night, a saw-whet owl perched on a small potted tree on the terrace and remained for a half hour, long enough for identification by mystery fans who were also birders. The hotel was also near a bridge, from under which emerged, each evening at dusk, over a million bats, reputedly the largest urban concentration in the world.

This was the first mystery convention for Barry Gardner, and he was overjoyed to put faces to the names he had only encountered in fan magazines. He summed up his experience by writing, "the real highlight was just sitting around and talking and listening to you all, and I wouldn't have missed it for the world."

St. Hilda's Crime & Mystery Weekend (1994–)

Beginning in 1994, Oxford took advantage of empty dormitories in summer for St. Hilda's Crime and Mystery Weekend. Registration fees have been unusually reasonable; in 1999 bed and breakfast was only £26 per day. Each conference has a different theme. In 1998, it was "Men and Women in Blue: The Police Detective in Fiction." The conference has been chaired by distinguished writers, including Robert Barnard and Natasha Cooper. Writers speak on favorite subjects. For example, Barnard has spoken about Margery Allingham, and Simon Brett covered the Detection Club. There are often day trips before and after the weekend. One year, some who attended had tea in the garden of mystery author Kate Charles.

BuffCon (1995)

A convention in Buffalo, New York, BuffCon, was held only once, in May 1995. It was organized by Douglas Anderson, who published a detective novel with a Buffalo setting in 1993. The Guest of Honor was Lawrence Block, who was born in Buffalo.

EyeCon (1995, 1999)

Some fans, and even writer Donald Westlake, were wondering whether the private eye story had grown stale, even moribund, in the '90s. Gary Warren Niebuhr, its most dedicated fan, put on EyeCon, the first convention devoted to that sub-genre, in Milwaukee June 15–18, 1995. Sue Grafton was Guest of Honor, and Les Roberts the Toastmaster. There were three auctions during the convention to raise funds so Milwaukee County libraries could purchase copies of Hubin's bibliography. Almost all who attended thought EyeCon was a great convention, justifying eighteen months of work by Niebuhr and his committee. Attendance was 325, including Naomi Hoida from Japan.

There were panels called "Dead Folk's Dues," about dead writers, and an Art Scott slide show. Much attention centered on the EyeCon debate between George Kelley and Barry Gardner on whether the private eye story was dead; Kelley said it was. Bob Napier officiated and even wore a bow tie, as do boxing referees. Kelley was preaching to the uncommitted since people attending a private eye convention, especially writers in that field, were not especially open to his idea. He hoped to prove his point by giving out paper for the audience to list their favorite

Cap'n Bob Napier (r.) declaring Barry Gardner the winner of the great 1985 EyeCon debate.

private eye stories. He planned to use a timeline to show most favorites were not recent. Unfortunately, some of the audience grew restive at what they perceived as a pedantic approach and became rowdy, with several turning the sheets into paper airplanes, which they threw. Some who were more open to being convinced, such as John Apostolou, felt that Kelley might have had a better chance of proving his point if he had stated, as Westlake once did, that it has lost its vitality, not that it was totally dead. Referee Napier said afterward that he regretted not explaining the ground rules in advance but that he had assumed both participants were there to debate, not lecture, as he felt Kelley had done. Letters about the debate filled pages in *MDM* afterward, with Kelley and Michael Seidman criticizing each other. This led Gardner to comment, "The debate about the debate is turning out to be a hell of a lot more interesting than the debate was."

Jane Ellen Syrk and Don Newhouse of Murder & Mayhem Bookstore in Indianapolis planned another EyeCon convention for July 25–27, 1997; Marcia Muller and Bill Pronzini were to be Guests of Honor. There was a conflict between the planners and Private Eye Writers of America over who would get space in the dealer's room. PWA wanted more of a voice in deciding which dealers were included and threatened to withdraw from EyeCon, though it had not provided financial or other support. What seemed negotiable got out of hand. Syrk and Newhouse realized they could not have EyeCon without PWA, so they decided to cancel it. Niebuhr wrote in *MDM*, "I just wish someone could have mediated between PWA and EyeCon '97 so that those who love this form of writing could have had a place to go in July."

A second EyeCon *was* held (sponsored by PWA this time), July 8–11, 1999 at the Adam's Mark in Randisi's home city, St. Louis. Loren D. Estleman was Guest of Honor, and Maxine O'Callaghan, whose Delilah West in 1974 anticipated more famous, later female P.I.s, received The Eye for lifetime achievement. "Friends of the P.I." Awards were given to Michael Seidman and Joe Pittman.

Historicon (1995, 1999)

Recognizing the growing popularity of historical mysteries, Tom and Enid Schantz of Rue Morgue Books put on **Historicon** in Boulder, Colorado in 1995. Edward Marston was Guest of Honor. A second Historicon was held there in 1999, with Steven Saylor Guest of Honor. Attendance at each was limited to 100 people. Though no date has been set, the Schantzes plan to put on another Historicon in the future.

AZ Murder Goes… (1996–)

In the United States, as well as England, booksellers, for obvious reasons, sponsor conferences. After organizing a 1995 Left Coast Crime, in 1996 Barbara Peters and Robert Rosenwald of the Poisoned Pen bookstore and publishing company started an annual Scottsdale, Arizona event **AZ Murder Goes….** After the ellipse is a word or two telling the theme of that year. For example, in 1998 it was "AZ Murder Goes… Alternatively," a conference devoted to gay & lesbian mysteries.

Dead on Deansgate (1998–2003)

Dead on Deansgate, which took its name from a local street, began in Manchester, England, in October 1998 as a replacement for Shots on the Page. It was first organized by Britain's Crime Writers Association and Waterstone's bookstore (located on Deansgate). There were no other dealers; Waterstone sold books written by the participating authors. The panelists were mainly authors. Fans were relatively few, though Geoff Bradley of *CADS* was among about 300 who attended. Deansgate adopted the practice of having an American Guest Author, in addition to an

International Guest of Honor. Those honored have included Ruth Rendell and Janet Evanovich. It was not held after 2003.

Other Regional Conventions (1999–)

Since the 1980s, virtually every mystery novel has a strong regional component. Mysteries are no longer set only in large cities such as New York and Los Angeles. No region is too far off the beaten track to be a mystery setting. The same has happened to conferences, with fans and aspiring writers everywhere.

The **Bloody Words** Conference started in Toronto in 1999, moving to Ottawa in 2003, with about 225 in attendance. The guests of honor have usually been Canadians and have included L. R. Wright, Medora Sale, Howard Engel, and Peter Robinson. However, American Loren D. Estleman has been honored, and in 2003 Val McDermid was International Guest of Honor.

Omaha, Nebraska, was a center of fandom in the early 1990s with the regional conferences and Bouchercon previously discussed. Though, inevitably, a few of the people who worked on the earlier Omaha conferences were involved, **Mayhem in the Midlands**, started in 2000, made it clear that they were in no way related to the Midwest Mystery & Suspense Convention. It was sponsored by the public libraries of Omaha and Lincoln. Guests of Honor, such as Dennis Lehane and Jan Burke, have come from outside the Midwest. A highlight of the 2003 banquet was Burke singing "Makin' Mayhem" to the tune of "Makin' Whoopee." The organizers of this conference eschewed the maze-like Omaha Holiday Inn, holding their conferences at the Sheraton.

A one-day conference, **Deadly Ink**, in New Jersey, starting in 2000, has been described as a "small, friendly conference." Its first Guest of Honor was Parnell Hall, who lives in New York, but in more recent years Jan Burke of California and Steve Hamilton of Michigan have been honored at this conference, first held in Mount Arlington, and then in Parsippany, New Jersey.

Cape Fear is not only the title of two movies based on a John D. MacDonald novel but also site of **Cape Fear Crime Festival**, held since 2001 in nearby Wilmington, North Carolina. It is a joint effort of local publishers and New Hanover County Library. Margaret Maron, North Carolina's most famous mystery writer, was keynote speaker at the first conference, but later events have had Carolyn G. Hart of Oklahoma and Parnell Hall in that capacity.

Though recent (it only began in 2003), the **Harrogate Crime Writing Festival** in northern Yorkshire seems destined for great popularity. This "brainchild" of popular author Val McDermid, who added a crime-fiction strand to an existing arts festival, pleased fans by returning to single-track programming, obviating difficult choices. Though it has its share of panels and interviews, Harrogate emphasizes entertainment, and there were two quiz programs and a "Cabaret of Crime" in which writers provide the show.

The Southern branch of Sisters in Crime, Crosshaven Books, and the Homewood Library jointly sponsor **Murder in the Magic City**, which started in 2003 in Birmingham, Alabama, and is held at Homewood Library. 2004 Guests of Honor were Rhys Bowen and Charles Todd.

The **Great Manhattan Mystery Conclave** was not expected to be a continuing conference, since it was held in 2004 to celebrate the centennial of the Manhattan, Kansas, Public Library. Among the guests were Nancy Pickard (of Kansas), Carolyn Wheat, and Margaret Maron for "A Golden Celebration of the Small Town Mystery." It was such a success that another Conclave is planned for 2005.

The people in Austin, Texas, who put on the 2002 Bouchercon are launching a new convention, **ConMisterio**, in July 2005. Kate Derie, who operates the famous mystery website Cluelass.com, is slated to be Fan Guest of Honor.

Other Fan Magazines & Organizations: 1990s & 21st Century

Australian Fan Magazines (1990–2003)

Distance and expense keep Australian fans from attending many mystery conventions, though I have met Graeme Flanagan, Gayle Lovett, and Graeme Windsor in the United States. Much of the interest in Australian mysteries is in the hardboiled school, and that was the main focus of *Mean Streets*, the Australian quarterly journal that started in October 1990 and had an unfortunately short life. It was edited and published by Stuart Coupe of the Bondi Beach suburb of Sydney. Its first issue featured articles on Alan Yates, Australia's most prolific mystery writer under his "Carter Brown" pseudonym. However, much of the magazine was devoted to American writers, though Coupe had an interview with a hardboiled new Australian writer Marele Day. There were also articles on the "mean streets" of Los Angeles, Sue Grafton, Elmore Leonard, James Crumley's Milo Milodragovitch, and paperback cover art, mostly from US books. The last was balanced by an article by Graeme Flanagan on Phantom Books, Australia's leading paperback publisher of the 1950s and early 1960s. There were two short stories, including one by Peter Corris about his private eye Cliff Hardy and an article by him. Australia's leading anthologist, Stephen Knight wrote an overview "Old Crime in New Form: Australian Thrillers Today."

Flanagan, from Canberra, started his own magazine, *PI News*, in the early 1990s, and as the title indicates it was mainly about that sub-genre. It included news, checklists, and interviews. It is no longer published. Another Australian magazine, now defunct, was *Crime Factory*, which lasted for nine issues between 2001 and 2003. It covered worldwide English-language crime writing, with an emphasis at the hardboiled end of the spectrum. To the usual mix of articles, interviews, and reviews was added occasional fiction and a continuing "graphic fiction" storyline.

Mostly Murder (1990–1998)

The name of the publisher, Mostly Book Reviews, Inc., of this quarterly tabloid newspaper tells everything about its goal. Jay W. K. Setliff of Dallas was editor-publisher of this periodical that began in 1990 and contained mostly reviews, except for the occasional interview. Its reviewers included Barry Gardner, often considered the best fan reviewer, as well as Dallas booksellers Geraldine Galentree and Barry and Terry Phillips. *Mostly Murder* lasted until the May/June 1998 issue according to its website.

Perry Mason Fandom (1990–2000)

About 1990, long after Erle Stanley Gardner died and his best-known sleuth was no longer a staple of network television, Jim Davidson, a thirtyish word processor from Berkeley, California, founded The National Association for the Advancement of Perry Mason. In 1987 two other fans, Brian Kelleher and Diana Merrill, published *The Perry Mason TV Show Book*, describing every case seen on the small screen until then. Davidson had at least 125 members who paid $10 yearly and received the *NAAPM Newsletter*. After running the club for ten years, Davidson gave it up due to other "personal commitments."

Mystery Review (1992–2003)

This was a Canadian quarterly, started in 1992 by Barbara Davey of Ontario, that lasted about ten years. In addition to reviews, it published articles and interviews. A feature was its history of Canadian mystery writing. It stopped in 2003 due to Davey's illness; she died in 2004.

Murder & Mayhem (1993–1994)

I am reminded of Mickey Rooney and Judy Garland famously saying, "Let's put on a show in the barn," when I think of *Murder & Mayhem*, the publication of Kansas City couple Fiske and Elly-Ann Miles. It started in the spring of 1993 as a pocket-sized (4″ x 9¼″) publication, subtitled "A Mystery Fiction Newsletter." In October 1993 they gave away sample copies of the first three issues at the Omaha Bouchercon. I met them, and their enthusiasm was engaging, so I subscribed.

They finished their first volume with three more small issues, now referred to as "A Pocket Guide to Mystery Fiction." With their second volume (and seventh issue) they converted *Murder & Mayhem* to a slick-covered, full-sized magazine and began to publish visually appealing articles, including in that issue a well-illustrated one on New York City mystery bookstores and the Malice Domestic convention. *M & M* was now designated "The Mystery Reader's Guide." The eighth issue had features on ClueFest and Seattle mystery bookstores. The ninth contained an impressive article on the 1994 Bouchercon.

Possibly the most memorable aspect of *Murder & Mayhem*, a decade after its disappearance, is the brief Fiske Miles held for the concept of "objective reviewing" standards. He claimed, "The path to a more objective review is for reviewers to separate the question of whether they like a book from the question of whether that book is well-written." He never was able to explain to my satisfaction—or that of anyone to whom I spoke—the criteria for deciding a book is well written, or why anyone should continue to read a mystery he or she didn't like. Many letters in *M & M* responded to Fiske Miles's unfavorable review of Michael Connelly's *The Concrete Blonde*, which most readers liked but which Fiske criticized for reasons that seemed merely politically correct: Connelly's having an overweight lawyer and a female whose actual first name was "Honey." It appeared that Miles had never heard of a woman so named, not even the Ficklings' detective Honey West.

The dispute was fun, but just when things were getting interesting, publication ceased after that undated ninth issue, and the mystery was whether *M & M* would ever resume and whether subscribers would receive the rest of their issues or a refund. A decade after it disappeared, with some internet detective work, I got in touch with Fiske Miles through a still-active e-mail address on the *Mayhem* web site he had established but not updated since 1997. He said that "We stopped publishing because it was running us into bankruptcy.... I realize some subscribers may imagine we somehow absconded with the funds, took a trip to Tahiti, whatever. The fact is that the subscription money paid for only a small portion of the publication expense. We ended up having to make financial arrangements with our printer to repay production expenses (which ran into thousands of dollars). We regret that people who subscribed to the magazine did not receive all of the issues for which they paid. However, the financial resources for the publication have long since been depleted." Obviously, Fiske and Elly-Ann didn't realize what was involved in putting on a fan magazine in the barn.

Shots (1994–) and Crime Time/CT (1995–)

Two British magazines joined *CADS* in the 1990s. *A Shot in the Dark*, titled to connect it with the popular Nottingham festival, started in June 1994. After fourteen issues it was renamed *Shots* by its editor Mike Stotter in 1999. In 2002, after ten quarterly issues, it became an online "e-zine" that included much crime fiction. *CT (Crime Time)*, which began in 1995, also includes fiction and material regarding films and remains alive in print in 2004, with Barry Forshaw as editor.

Mystery Collectors' Bookline (1995–1999) and Firsts (1990–)

Fans are often collectors, and many were caught up in the "hypermodern" book craze of the early 1990s, in which recent books such as Sue Grafton's *'A' Is for Alibi*, Patricia Cornwell's *Post Mortem*, and John Dunning's *Booked To Die* sold for enormously high prices. In February 1995, David M. Brown of San Rafael, California, started *Mystery Collectors' Bookline*, a magazine designed to identify the authors of "hot" books, usually their first since these, due to relatively small first print runs, become most valuable.

Though there were reviews in *Mystery Collectors' Bookline*, the language used more often related to books' value than to their quality. For example, regarding one recommended book, it said, "the buzz on this title is loud and clear and coming from every direction." Many of the authors *Mystery Collectors' Bookline* recommended are forgotten only a few years later. The hypermodern era soon died out (and with it *Mystery Collectors' Bookline*) as collectors, some of whom tried to be sellers, found they couldn't get their investment back—let alone make a profit. Meanwhile, *Firsts: The Book Collector's Magazine*, published by Robin Smiley of Tucson, Arizona, remains viable, perhaps because its scope is all literature, though it has issues devoted to mystery fiction.

Tangled Web (1995–1999)

Tangled Web, the magazine, was not connected to the similarly-titled web site. Andrew Osmond was the publisher and also contributed articles. Like *CADS*, another British fan magazine, *Tangled Web* did not offer subscriptions. Osmond notified those on his mailing list when an issue was available, and if interested, they sent money. It began in 1995 and lasted through 1999, with nine issues published. There were no replies to inquiries regarding issue #10, so apparently it never appeared.

Mysterious Women (1995–)

Late in 1995, Kathleen Swanholt of Walnut Creek, California, began *Mysterious Women*, "A Quarterly Newsletter for Fans of Women Mystery Writers." It includes articles, reviews, interviews, and bookstore information. Swanholt may have been the only editor whose mother, Alma Connaughton, wrote articles. She said in her second issue that she was expecting an article by her mother on Lilian Jackson Braun, but "Mom decided to do Amanda Cross instead. I may be Managing Editor but, let's face it, in this life Mom will always outrank me." *Mysterious Women* is still published, though now by Sara Berger of Amherst, Massachusetts.

Murder Most Cozy (1995–2004)

This bimonthly newsletter on "cozy" mysteries and creators was published by Jan Dean of Diamondhead, Mississippi, who also offered an annual "Cozy Crimes, Cream Teas & Books, Books, Books" tour of the British Isles. As its title indicates, it offered considerable time for booking. When she ceased publication, she offered subscribers the choice of refunds or back issues.

The Ngaio Marsh Society International (1996–2004)

Nicole St. John of Midland Park, New Jersey, founded this group in 1996 to celebrate the work of the famous New Zealand writer. It had a semiannual newsletter *Harmony* and an annual journal, *Promptbook*, the latter recognizing that Marsh was once an actress and later a well-regarded theatrical director. The society was discontinued in 2004.

Francis M. "Mike" Nevins, fan of Harry Stephen Keeler and more..

The Friends of Chester Himes (1996–)

Also established in 1996, in Oakland, California, was a group to honor this mystery writer. They hold an annual conference, presenting papers, panels, and films that focus on African-American writers such as Himes. They give the annual Chester Himes Award, and have a writing contest for high-school students.

The Harry Stephen Keeler Society (1996–)

Once, Francis M. Nevins seemed to be Harry Stephen Keeler's only fan, as he kept his memory alive with amusing articles such as "The Wild and Wooly World of Harry Stephen Keeler." Nevins was really recommending Keeler's work, despite its convoluted plots and its inordinate length (some books are over 700 pages). If he was ever alone in his enthusiasm, Nevins no longer is. Since 1996 there has been the Keeler society, founded by Richard Polt of Cincinnati, which issues *Keeler News* five times yearly. At the same time, Ramble House, a small publisher, has been reprinting the entire oeuvre of the prolific Keeler.

Daphne du Maurier Festival of Arts and Literature (1998–)

Mention Cornwall and one thinks of Daphne du Maurier, author of *Rebecca* and other novels, some of suspense, set there. Since 1998 there has been an annual festival with guided walks, exhibitions, talks, and entertainment. In 2004 it lasted for ten days.

Dastardly Deeds (1999-2000)

Another late, lamented publication is *Dastardly Deeds,* a colorful newsletter whose contents displayed a sense of humor. It described itself as "A Tainted Newsletter for Readers, Collectors, Booksellers and yes, even Authors, gasp!" Paul Petrucelli was publisher, and Diane Plumley was called "Editor-in-Grief." Its contents included columns on collecting "hypermodern" books and writers of the past. There were interviews with popular writers such as Dennis Lehane, and also with some who are underrated, for example, Alan Beechey.

The International Sister Fidelma Society (2000–)

Peter Tremayne is the pseudonym of Peter Berresford Ellis. His 7th century nun-detective is the subject of a group started in 2000 by David Robert Wooten of Little Rock, Arkansas. Ellis has said in praise, "The Fidelma Society seem to know more about the books than I do." Three times a year Wooten puts out a journal, *The Brehon*, its name taken from the system of law in which Sister Fidelma was trained. He sells Fidelma-related material to keep the organization going.

The James Hilton Society (2000–)

Also founded in 2000, in England, was a group to celebrate the work of a best-selling author who also wrote one detective novel, as by "Glen Trevor," and a handful of criminous novels and short stories.

Partners in Crime (2002–2005)

In the summer of 2002, Gill Roberts and John Curran of England started *Partners in Crime,* but they are no longer partners, Curran leaving after about a year. Roberts has announced that due to his ill health the magazine will cease publication after its 12th issue (Spring 2005). This should not be confused with *Partners in Crime,* a newsletter published by Susan Wittig Albert and her husband Bill, who publish mysteries under the pseudonym "Robin Paige."

Old-Time Detection (2002–)

A welcome visit to the past is this fan journal Arthur Vidro started in the autumn of 2002. It has the unusual alternate name *(Give Me That) Old-Time Detection.* (Think of the gospel song "Give Me That Old Time Religion.") Vidro's interests rest in the great writers of detective fiction's "Golden Age," including Rex Stout, Ellery Queen, and Ngaio Marsh, but he is also a fan of the suspense writer Cornell Woolrich. Asked why he started the magazine, he replied, "Because after years of immersion in the subject matter, it was time to be more than just a fan. I wanted to contribute to the cause."

The magazine that Vidro, who lives on New York's Long Island, publishes three times a year is reminiscent of the early days of fan magazines. Vidro types every article himself, apparently without a word processor. Unlike other publisher-editors, he doesn't have a web site. His love for the great books of the past shows throughout his magazine. The classic detective puzzle is its main focus, with in-depth articles on Philip MacDonald, T. S. Stribling, and C. Daly King. However, besides reviews, there are also articles on Hillary Waugh, whose detection was in an outstanding series of police procedurals, and Julian Symons, known for his psychological suspense novels.

Though all opinions are Vidro's, *Old-Time Detection* is an official publication of a special interest group of American Mensa, the high IQ society.

Crime Spree Magazine (2004–)

Started by Jon and Ruth Jordan of Milwaukee in 2004, this is the most recent print publication to come to my attention. It is a bimonthly that attempts to attract a diverse group of readers. Each issue includes short stories, true crime (one had an interview with a private detective), articles about small press publishers and bookstores, and interviews with current writers. That Jon Jordan would include many interviews is not surprising; in 2003 he published an Anthony-nominated book, *Interrogations*, that contained twenty-five interviews with leading current writers. However, *Crime Spree* also has delved into the past with an article by Ted Hertel on Ellery Queen, and Ruth Jordan's piece on Father Brown, a sleuth created almost a century ago.

One of the best things *Crime Spree* does is report on smaller conventions. "I Was a Mystery Convention Virgin" by Sue Kelso told about her first convention: Omaha's Mayhem in the Midlands. Ann R. Chernow's report on the Harrogate Crime Writing Festival showed the same enthusiasm demonstrated when people wrote about early Bouchercons and included that oft-used line "You had to be there!" when words are inadequate to capture a delightful experience.

# Bouchercon: 21st Century

2000: Denver

Because it can snow in Denver even in late September, Tom Schantz and Rebecca Bates, co-chairpersons, wisely scheduled the 2000 Bouchercon for September 7–10. (There is debate over when the 21st century began, but for convenience I have placed the 2000 Bouchercon in that century.) The setting was the Adam's Mark Hotel, and attendance was about 1,250. Elmore Leonard was Guest of Honor, and Jane Langton received a Lifetime Achievement Award.

The program book recognized that the primary interest of many (possibly most) attendees was recent mysteries. However, it said in the welcome, "Even if you never read anything published before 1990, come prepared to learn something about what has gone before." Panels among the eight tracks such as "Forgotten Paperback Writers of the 1950s" drew surprisingly good crowds. Most panels *were* directed at new writers, especially those still unpublished. I counted twenty-one panels about the "business" of writing and being published, including "After Your First Book Is Published," "Studio Publishing: Self and Small Presses," "Foreign Rights and International Markets," "E-Publishing Roundtable," and "Self-Publishing."

Steve Stilwell was Fan Guest of Honor, and his reputation for "chatting up" attractive females made him an ideal target for a hilarious, standing-room-only "Roast." Of course, his allegedly lecherous instincts received much attention, but Bill Deeck got the biggest laugh when, recalling the 1987 Bouchercon, he uttered two words: "The Magician."

In addition to the Anthonys, awards were given out by a virtual alphabet of organizations, including IACW(NA), PWA, MRI, and DP. The last named, *Deadly Pleasures* magazine, gives out the Barry Awards, honoring the late Barry Gardner. There were several receptions and a Bouchercon Ball, with a jazz quartet, though it was sparsely attended because it was scheduled opposite the popular auction and a Colorado Rockies baseball game at which a block of seats had been reserved for Bouchercon attendees. Probably no one gives more at auctions to be "Tuckerized" in future mysteries than Maggie Mason. Even pets were an excuse to give to charity. After Denver, Deen Kogan said, "I am well on my way to having my Doberman, Miata, become the most Tuckerized animal in detective fiction."

This seemed the best attended Anthony banquet because its price was included in the cost of registration. Unfortunately, the food was possibly the worst of any Bouchercon banquet. A mystery was identifying the "yellow glob" on the plate; it turned out to be risotto. Val McDermid was a popular Toastmaster, singing a Scottish murder ballad while accompanying herself on the guitar. I paid tribute to Phyllis White who was too ill to attend. One of the Anthony categories, for Best Critical/Biographical work, mixed literary apples and oranges when it pitted two fan magazines against two biographies and the third edition of Willetta Heising's bibliography, *Detecting*

Women, which won. In addition to the Anthonys, there were "Millennium Awards" voted on by fans for the best series, mystery writer, and novel of the 20th century. The winners, respectively, were Hercule Poirot, Agatha Christie, and *Rebecca*.

2001: Washington, DC

Many things changed after September 11, 2001, including Bouchercon. At the end of July 2001, more than 1,400 had signed up for the convention due to be held November 1–4 at the Hyatt Regency in Arlington, Virginia, only about a mile from the Pentagon, one of the terrorists' targets. Some people canceled, but attendance was still healthy at over 1,300, and that included a large contingent of British writers and fans. One of the most moving moments was a toast to Americans by International Guest of Honor Peter Lovesey. Co-Chairmen Adolph Falcón and Bill Starck said in the program book, "We thank you for your understanding and patience... These have been difficult times for the Washington, DC, area and by attending "A Capital Mystery" you are helping to make a capital difference in restoring the region's well-being."

The American Guest of Honor was Sue Grafton. Book dealers Lew and Nancy Buckingham were Fan Guests of Honor, though they had a minimal record of true fannish activity. Edward D. Hoch received a Lifetime Achievement Award, and Michael Connelly was Toastmaster.

Halloween night, before the convention's official opening, saw one of the worst events in Bouchercon history, one comparable to the infamous happenings in the Twin Cities, previously described. Billed as "An Edgar Allan Poe Halloween," it disappointed most who had come to see David Keltz's one-man performance as Poe. There were flashing strobe lights and blaring sound, making it difficult to watch a preliminary costume contest. Keltz's appearance was delayed so long, I left with a headache before he arrived.

Thursday night, on the other hand, was memorable for me. Presentations were made of three awards, the Herodotus for Best Historical Mystery, the Macavity from Mystery Readers International, and the Barry from *Deadly Pleasures*. I won the Macavity for my critical work, *The American Regional Mystery*, and received an even greater surprise during the Barry presentations. George Easter gave me the first Don Sandstrom Memorial Award for Lifetime Achievement in Mystery Fandom. Because Don had been a good friend, it was especially appreciated.

There were seven tracks of programming on Friday and eight on Saturday. Taking advantage of many British writers present, there were panels called "Cops: Brits vs. US," "British Crime at the Cutting Edge," "Today's Traditional British Mystery," and a panel on British royalty in mysteries. There was a "Meet the Brits Reception" on Friday night, sponsored by the Crime Writers Association.

There were also panels on publishing trends, two panels on forensics, and an interview with the daughter and granddaughter of Dashiell Hammett. Called "Down Memory Lane," there were three panels regarding writers of the past, and the enthusiastic panelists brought so much material, someone described them as "over-prepared." One panelist, John Apostolou, said, "It helped that none of us was trying to sell his or her latest book." He was recognizing that most authors at Bouchercon were there to promote their work, not as fans. Bouchercon had become an important event in "the industry," and almost one-fourth of the program book was taken up by advertisements, mostly from publishers. Publishers also provided fifteen free books, leaving registrants who were travelling by air wondering how to fit them all in their luggage.

2002: Austin, Texas

Texas, scene of other mystery conventions, had its first Bouchercon in Austin October 17–20, at Marriot's Renaissance Hotel. Subtitled "Longhorns of the Law," it was co-chaired by Karen Meschke and Willie Siros. George Pelecanos and Mary Willis Walker were the Guests of Honor. Following a lead from the Malice Domestic convention, this Bouchercon honored someone who was dead, designating Barry Gardner of Dallas as Fan *Ghost* of Honor. Though a prolific professional author, Bill Crider of Alvin, Texas, was Fan Guest of Honor. He had been a true fan long before he was published. Crider, with Judy, his wife, won an Anthony for Best Short Story. When Richard Moore could not attend due to a shoulder fracture, Crider stepped in for him on a panel on short notice. Crider's interview, by Joe Lansdale, was one of the highlights of the convention.

Still another Texan, Elmer Kelton, was "Special Guest," though he is mainly a Western writer, with only one criminous title in Hubin's bibliography. George Easter of *Deadly Pleasures* presented the second Don Sandstrom Award to Gary Warren Niebuhr, arguably the most enthusiastic of all fans.

With attendance at 1,438, there were long lines to register. The free books from publishers had so increased, they filled two bags. The many glitches in this convention began even before it opened. The committee was confused as to when the bookdealers room would open. Not only were some panelists not told of their assignments, but even some moderators weren't informed. Len Moffatt arrived at 4:00 PM Thursday and was told he was on a "History of the Mystery" panel at 4:30 PM. The program book only gave the names of panels, not telling who the panelists were. Luckily, some attendees got that information from the Bouchercon website. Despite often chaotic conditions, the committee members weren't always

Chris Aldrich (l.) and Lynn Kaczmarek (r.), publishers of *Mystery News,* at Bouchercon 2002 in Austin, Texas.

Forgotten "Forgotten Authors" panel (l. to r.) John Apostolou, Ted Hertel, and Bill Crider.

present when problems needed to be solved.

There were several "Forgotten Authors" panels. Mine did not have a moderator, so I stepped into the breach. Ted Hertel found that his "Forgotten Authors" panel had been forgotten. There was a meeting from an entirely different convention in his room. He got another room, but it had no chairs at all, let alone a table for the panelists. Posting signs and helping to move furniture in, he and his panelists (John Apostolou and Crider) persisted and gave a good presentation, albeit to only about twenty people.

The dichotomy between panels that active fans attended and those popular with people who are mainly readers grew. Hertel jokingly described the latter as having panelists who say, "Hi. My name is Big Name Author. My new book is called *Bestseller*. It's available in the dealers' room." "Trufans," a term borrowed from science fiction, were to be found, in far smaller numbers, at panels in which S.S. Van Dine, R. Austin Freeman, Philip MacDonald, George Harmon Coxe, Robert Reeves, and Day Keene were discussed. "Trufans" also went to the panel about such old time radio detective shows as "The Adventures of Ellery Queen."

Some were perturbed at the $50 per person banquet when, after having made their choices of meat or vegetarian dishes in advance, they found they had to get in line for a buffet. The banquet was far briefer than most and rather bland. Sparkle Hayter, as Toastmistress, did not sparkle.

Despite problems, reactions among the attendees were positive. For many, Bouchercon remained about people, old and new friends. Also, the hotel was comfortable, the weather mild, and good shopping and restaurants were a short walk away. Many went on a combined bus and boat tour of Austin called the "Duck Adventure" and were given duck whistles. Later, in the spacious hotel atrium, one could hear the duck callers serenading each other.

2003: Las Vegas

The 34th Bouchercon came to Las Vegas October 16–19 with a predictable emphasis on gambling. Attendees were even given rolls of nickels in their registration package, and most spent some time at the "slots." Gambling metaphors abounded in the program, and a separate booklet, *The Gleam in Bugsy Siegel's Eye* by Barry T. Zeman, a bibliography of mystery fiction about Las Vegas and gambling, was distributed. The site was the Riviera, one of Las Vegas's oldest hotels. Many attendees found it run-down, and signs in bathrooms offering "free needles" didn't inspire confidence that they were intended for diabetics.

1,641 people registered, and many found this hotel with its multiple towers confusing. There were long walks, through corridors filled with cigarette smoke, to the meeting rooms. There was no place to sit and chat near the meeting rooms or even on the way except, of course, in the casino. Also, there was no hospitality suite. Everyone paid a 3% "energy fee" on their hotel bill to allow Las Vegas to keep its lights on twenty-four hours a day.

Deen Kogan, who had put on two Bouchercons in Philadelphia, saved this one by agreeing to chair this one in the Western region, but her nerves seemed somewhat frazzled throughout. A live-cast radio mystery during the opening reception was almost impossible to hear, not surprising at what essentially was a cocktail party with several bars. It should have been presented as a separate production. The highlight of the reception was the third Sandstrom fandom award to Mary "Maggie" Mason.

The dealer's room was more crowded than at any previous Bouchercons, and there was wonder that the fire marshals didn't close it. Some potential book buyers avoided it. One person suggested that whoever planned the dealers' room forgot people needed aisles in which to walk.

James Lee Burke was American Guest of Honor, and Scottish writer Ian Rankin was International Guest of Honor. Ruth Rendell was saluted for her "Exemplary Body of Work," and Janet Hutchings, editor of *EQMM*, was cited for her "Contribution to the Field." Jeff and Ann Smith of Baltimore were Fan Guests of Honor. They represent what is most generous in fandom. Unlike some honored in the past, who have also written for pay, they are not involved in the commerce of the mystery. They are devoted readers, contributors to *DAPA-EM*, and loyal Bouchercon attendees. In Las Vegas, they threw their suite open to mystery fans every night.

On the Wednesday before Bouchercon officially opened, there was a Writer's Workshop conducted by Jeremiah Healy and Gayle Lynds. During Bouchercon, there were again many panels on the "business" of writing and being published. Other panels were about Las Vegas, its history, and gambling scams. There were true crime panels including another with a police dog and its handler. Two panels were about the internet, and another on audio books. Perhaps the most unusual panel was "Walter Sickert Is Innocent, OK!" in which two British academics disputed Patricia Cornwell's book in which she "identified" that British painter as "Jack the Ripper." Highly popular was "Wanted for Murder," a show in which Liza Cody, Peter Lovesey, and Michael Z. Lewin amusingly demonstrated how a mystery is developed.

The annual auction benefited the libraries of Las Vegas and Clark County. People were bidding up to $2,000 to be a character in an Ian Rankin or Lee Child book.

Mostly thanks to Beth Fedyn, it was a great success, raising $22,347. Child was Toastmaster, but he was in no way responsible for the Sunday brunch that featured barely edible steak. Again, flaws did not prevent attendees from enjoying the awards ceremony or Bouchercon.

2004: Toronto

Disagreeing with Thomas Wolfe, many who enjoyed the 1992 Toronto Bouchercon found that they could go home again—or at least enjoy another Bouchercon there. Once again Al Navis stepped in when there were no other bidders, assuming financial risk. With no "seed" money from prior Bouchercons, Navis used his own money for expenses until registration money arrived. 1,350 people attended at the Metropolitan Conference Centre on October 7–10. Most people stayed at the new Intercontinental Hotel, adjacent to the Centre, but some of us were at 1992's site, the Royal York, and ate at Marché, the delightful restaurant that attracted so many 1992 attendees.

Navis's choice of Fan Guest of Honor Gary Warren Niebuhr was an inspired one. Not only was he deserving because of more than two decades of activity, but also he provided the most entertaining moments during the convention, especially when interviewed by Ted Hertel. In 1992 Gary had entertained some of us with a brief dance from *The Wizard of Oz*. In 2004 he did a hilarious five-minute reprise of the entire movie. Gary was also amusing and gracious in his acceptance speeches when winning the Macavity and Anthony for his critical work *Make Mine a Mystery*.

The professional Guests of Honor were Lindsey Davis (British), Jeremiah Healy (American), Peter Robinson (Canadian), and Bernard Cornwell (Lifetime Achievement). Natasha Cooper was Toastmistress and amusing if a trifle effusive. Despite not being a private eye writer, Donald E. Westlake won PWA's The Eye for lifetime achievement. Ted Fitzgerald was the fourth winner of the Don Sandstrom Award. The award for best fan magazine is not given every year. It was in 2004 and was won by *Mystery Scene*, edited by Kate Stine.

"Been There, Done That" was the title of one of the panels, and one must admit that in thirty-five years of Bouchercons most topics have been covered—many times. However, Navis and his programming chairman Peter Sellers did come up with some unusual topics, including a live production featuring jazz music and a demonstration/seminar by a professional fighter. At two panels "All-Nighters: Books You Can't Put Down" and "Precious Gems" (about underappreciated writers) one could see the audience busily taking notes for future reading. I first spoke about regional mysteries at the 1974 Bouchercon. This year, I led a panel with five regional novelists. I stirred up some controversy by raising the question of whether we have now gone too far in the direction of regional realism at the expense of detection and plotting.

There was four-track programming, plus another experiment called "20 on the 20" in which every twenty minutes a different author spoke about his or her work or read from it. All that was missing in three and a half days of full programming was a lunch hour.

31 Famous Fans

It is highly unlikely you will see famous fans at a convention. There are so many security problems, and they are so busy they cannot attend. However, because every aspect of their lives is covered in the media, their reading of mysteries often has a significant influence.

The first famous fan emerged less than two decades after Edgar Allan Poe wrote what is considered the first mystery in 1841. In an 1860 campaign biography, William Dean Howells wrote of Abraham Lincoln: "he is therefore pleased with the absolute and logical method of Poe's tales and sketches, in which the problem of mystery is given, and wrought out into everyday facts by processes of cunning analysis. It is said that he suffers no year to pass without a perusal of this author."

Few remember Arthur B. Reeve now, but his scientific sleuth Craig Kennedy was so popular, especially in the second decade of the 20th century, that he was known as "the American Sherlock Holmes." When Reeve learned that Theodore Roosevelt liked his work, he sent the former president a specially bound set.

An alert White House reporter spotted Woodrow Wilson reading J. S. Fletcher's *The Middle Temple Murder* (1919) and reported it. His report turned it into a book that sold far better than it might have.

Franklin Delano Roosevelt was probably the best-known mystery fan. He is the only president who appears in Hubin's bibliography as an "author." During a White House supper, FDR told his guests of an idea for a story that he had not been able to write: "How could a man disappear with five million dollars and not leave a trace?" One of his guests was Fulton Oursler, editor of *Liberty*, and, as "Anthony Abbot," a popular American detective story writer. Enlisting six other writers, each of whom contributed a chapter, Oursler serialized *The President's Mystery Story* in his magazine in 1935. It was also published as a book that year and was reissued in 1967 as *The President's Murder Plot*.

In December 1941, Roosevelt and Winston Churchill watched the film version of *The Maltese Falcon*, starring Humphrey Bogart, at the White House. After Roosevelt's death in 1945, it was reported that the book he had been reading in bed the night before he died was *The Punch and Judy Murders*, which John Dickson Carr wrote as Carter Dickson. The Dickson series character, Sir Henry Merrivale, is reported to have been based, at least in part, on Churchill. Roosevelt was also a fan of Sherlock Holmes, as was his successor Harry S Truman.

John F. Kennedy is often credited with promoting the popularity of the James Bond novels in the US The publicity director for Ian Fleming's paperback publisher was surprised at how much better sales went after another of those alert reporters spotted JFK with a Bond novel and was told that he loved Fleming's books.

Before attention shifted to his sex life, Bill Clinton's reading habits made the news pages. He was revealed to be a fan of Walter Mosley and Michael Connelly. Reporters accompanying Clinton followed him into a Washington bookstore where he bought a copy of Connelly's *The Concrete Blonde*. George W. Bush is said to read his fellow Texan Kinky Friedman. Laura Bush is a fan of Elizabeth Ironside. Bill Crider has reported that at a reception in Austin, she mentioned his mystery set at the state capitol building there.

It is not only in America that political leaders find relaxation from their duties in mysteries. Former Prime Minister Harold Macmillan read them and wrote Peter Lovesey a fan letter. Margaret Thatcher watched *Mystery!* on television.

Love of mysteries is not limited to political figures. Perhaps, as Philip Guedalla, a well-known British historian in the first half of the 20th century said, "The detective story is the normal recreation of noble minds." Some of the great names in culture and literature have been readers—and occasionally writers of or about mysteries. Jacques Barzun, discussed previously, is probably the best known. Russell Kirk, a leading conservative philosopher, also wrote two mysteries, the first of which was highly praised by Anthony Boucher. The Nobel Prize-winning French writer André Gide wrote of his love of the work of Dashiell Hammett. In *Six Men*, Alistair Cooke wrote about interviewing the noted philosopher Bertrand Russell on a train between New York and Washington, DC. After the interview, he observed Russell reading several paperback mysteries before they arrived.

The anti-fan was Edmund Wilson, a noted novelist and essayist, whose series of 1944-1945 diatribes in *The New Yorker*, "Who Cares Who Murdered Roger Ackroyd?" mobilized early mystery fandom to strong response.

Popular entertainers also read mysteries. In the 1950s, *EQMM* advertised that stars as diverse as Steve Allen, Joan Crawford, Eddie Cantor, Ethel Merman, and Beatrice Lillie were among their readers.

32 Scholarship by Fans

There was a time when scholarly writing about the mystery was done by professionals. Yes, Howard Haycraft and Ellery Queen were fans, but they earned their livelihoods writing and editing. Many of the most active Sherlockians, including Christopher Morley, Anthony Boucher, John Dickson Carr, Rex Stout, and Queen, were professionals too.

Beginning with the "fan revolution" of 1967, an enormous number of scholarly articles and books about every aspect of the mystery have been written by fans whose livelihood is earned elsewhere. *JDMB, TMLN,* and *TAD* sprang from people wanting to share information about the subject and the writers they loved. Publishers of fan magazines were lucky if they didn't lose money. Even when fans were paid for their work, the amount was minimal. I speak from the experience of writing three books and hundreds of reviews and articles, as well co-editing and co-writing two books, when I say that financial gain has never been the motive for fan scholarship.

Early articles and bibliographies in fan magazines were about such major names as Agatha Christie, Raymond Chandler, G. K. Chesterton, Harry Kemelman, and Edgar Wallace. So little had been written *about* the mystery, that was a logical starting point. Soon material appeared on less well-known writers, including Freeman Wills Crofts, Margaret Millar, Arthur W. Upfield, and Sax Rohmer who had their champions but were not known to all fans, let alone the general mystery-reading public. Then, more obscure authors—Cleve Adams, Norbert Davis, C. E. Vulliamy, Ernest Savage, and James Corbett—became subjects of articles.

In 1976, Mystery Writers of America established an Edgar category for Best Critical/Biographical Work, but fans were already publishing books. In 1971, Francis M. Nevins published *The Mystery Writer's Art,* the first anthology of articles in twenty-five years. That year, Philip Donaldson, a chemist, published *In Search of Dr. Thorndyke,* about R. Austin Freeman and his detective. Also in 1971, Jacques Barzun and Wendell Hertig Taylor won a Special Edgar for *A Catalogue of Crime.* Barzun is a famous savant who writes widely in many areas of culture, while his friend Taylor was a scientist. They wrote as fans, reprinting forty years of notes they sent to each other on the mysteries they read.

Their book, revised in 1989, is the largest *annotated* bibliography of crime fiction and one about which few are neutral. The authors admit to a bias in favor of fair-play puzzles. This has made it a valuable book for it introduced readers to little known writers, some of whom were never published in America, especially those who wrote in the "Golden Age" years between the World Wars. Other reviewers and fans question their omission of many American hardboiled writers. Their writing is witty and sophisticated, though there are many errors in the first edition, making one suspect that the book was largely printed from the authors' notes, without overly careful review.

This year also saw the publication of *Detectionary*, destined to become a legend. Its origin was in a proposal from Hammermill Paper Company for a book, to be delivered in a few months, to demonstrate their reference book paper. It consisted of brief biographies of the great detectives, helpers, and rogues in crime fiction, as well as brief summaries of important crime novels, short stories, and detective movies. The five author-editors were Nevins, a law professor; Otto Penzler, a writer for ABC's *Wide World of Sports*; Chris Steinbrunner, program director of a New York television station; Charles Shibuk, a school teacher; and myself, an administrator at a New York State agency.

We delivered the book on time and even received our copies. However, before it could be distributed, Hammermill discovered a small defect (a wrinkle) on some pages. It was not fatal to reading *Detectionary*, but was if you were using the book to promote your company's paper, so Hammermill destroyed the remainder of the first printing. A second printing in 1972 proved equally unlucky. Though some copies were distributed, most were destroyed in a warehouse in Pennsylvania when a rainstorm caused the Susquehanna River to overflow. Copies of either printing became collectors' items, though there was a commercial hardcover edition in 1977 and a paperback edition in 1980.

The first "new fan" to win a Special Edgar was Nevins for his 1974 book *Royal Bloodline: Ellery Queen, Author and Detective*. Like his earlier anthology and the Donaldson book, it was published by Bowling Green State University's Popular Press. One of the first universities to make popular culture "respectable," they published books by fans about crime fiction, although they never distributed them widely.

In 1973, a major publisher, McGraw Hill, commissioned the first mystery reference book, *Encyclopedia of Mystery and Detection*, to be written and edited by four perpetrators of *Detectionary*: Steinbrunner, Penzler, Shibuk, and Lachman. It won MWA's first Critical/Biographical Edgar.

There had been no bibliography of crime fiction before the "fan revolution," though while Hubin was deciding to publish *The Armchair Detective*, another Minnesota fan, Ordean Hagen, was writing *Who Done It: A Guide to Detective, Mystery and Suspense Fiction* (1969). Its main feature was Hagen's attempt to list, by author, every mystery book published in English. There were errors and omissions, and Hagen's death April 5, 1969, before his book was published, denied him the opportunity to add to or correct it. Other sections, also incomplete, included a subject guide to mysteries, lists of plays and screen adaptations, a list of geographical settings, a list of series characters, a list of anthologies and collections, and a bibliography of secondary sources. Despite its faults, Hagen's book is a major work, and every feature of it became the basis of later scholarly works by fans.

Shortly after Hagen's death, Hubin began to devote part of each issue of *TAD* to correcting and adding to Hagen's book. He also added many features that made his bibliography easier to use, including separate listings of pseudonymous work, important because so many mystery writers wrote under pen names. Hubin's *The Bibliography of Crime Fiction, 1749–1975*, published in 1979, is generally regarded as the one indispensable reference work. Jon L. Breen said it "has come about as close as humanly possible to achieving the goal of listing every volume of mystery and

CRIME FICTION IV
1749-2000

detective fiction published in English." Later editions updated it, and an edition published in 2003, both as a CD-ROM and in a five-book set, carried it through 2000. Since then, Hubin uses his column in *Mystery*File* to correct and add information.

There are other bibliographies that are enormously useful and enjoyable reading because they are annotated. Breen was a mystery reader from a young age and a fan before, in his twenties, he began publishing fiction and other material in *EQMM*. He later became their reviewer. In 1981 he published *What About Murder? A Guide to*

Al Hubin with his indispensible bibliography at Bouchercon 2003.

Books About Mystery and Detective Fiction, covering 239 books, most of which were published after 1967. This is a short book of 157 pages, but had Breen only included works published before the "fan revolution," it would have been far shorter. So extensive is the later writing about the mystery, much of it by fans, that a second edition, covering only 1981 through 1991, listed 565 books and took up 377 pages.

Detective and Mystery Fiction: An International Bibliography of Secondary Sources (1985) by Walter Albert, a fan and a former Professor of French, goes beyond Breen because he also includes thousands of magazine articles. There are evaluations of many of the 5,200 entries but not in the depth Breen's more limited scope allowed. The first revision, published in 1997, included only the period 1985–1990 but now had almost 7700 listings. A final revision, through the year 2000, on CD-ROM, has 10,715 annotated entries.

Other bibliographies were more specific. In 1992, Ellen Nehr published her Anthony-winning *Doubleday Crime Club Compendium 1928–1991*, a lavishly illustrated history of the longest-lasting line of mysteries from any hardcover publisher. She listed every book they published and described plots and even dust jackets.

There are also bibliographies of individual authors. In addition to working on one for John D. MacDonald, June Moffatt, with the help of Francis M. Nevins, produced a bibliography of the prolific Edward D. Hoch. She updates it each year. By 2004, Hoch had published almost 900 short stories, as well as novels and non-fiction.

Nevins, with Ray Stanich, compiled *The Sound of Detection* about the Ellery Queen radio mysteries. The first edition, in 1983, was useful but contained gaps.

With old-time radio expert Martin Grams, Jr.., Nevins brought it up to date in 2002. Another successful Nevins bibliographic project was reprinting Anthony Boucher's 1940s reviews from the *San Francisco Chronicle.*

Annotated bibliographies have increasingly taken the form of "Companions," books that also treat an author's work in considerable depth and provide biographical material. Perhaps the earliest was *The Agatha Christie Companion* (1984), which authors Dennis Sanders and Len Lovallo called a "four-year labor of love." Sometimes the emphasis is on the author's character, as in *The Cadfael Companion* (1991) by Robin Whiteman, about Ellis Peters' Brother Cadfael. A major part of *The Tony Hillerman Companion* (1994), edited by Martin Greenberg, is a 200-page "concordance" of all the characters in Hillerman's fiction by Elizabeth A. Gaines and Diane Hammer.

Another example is Sharon A. Feaster's *The Cat Who... Companion* (1998) devoted to the cat mysteries of Lilian Jackson Braun. It includes an interview with Braun, plot summaries of her books, an alphabetical list of characters in the series, and even a map of its setting, fictional Moose County. The format of *The Dick Francis Companion* (2003) by Jean Swanson and Dean James is similar to Feaster's, but they added some features appropriate to a guide to Dick Francis: a gazetteer to the racing locations mentioned, a list of the horses in the books, and, fittingly for an author who so often grabbed readers with his first sentence, a list of memorable opening lines in the Francis canon.

While the Cold War was still hot, Andy East published *The Cold War File* (1983), a listing of the work of eighty authors of spy novels. His range was great, from the literary espionage novels of John Le Carré to such sexy novels of Ted Mark as *The Man from O.R.G.Y.*

One of the most ambitious of all fan-bibliographers was Michael L. Cook of Evansville, Indiana. His first "project" was *Murder by Mail: Inside the Mystery Book Clubs* (1979) with histories and complete lists of offerings of the Detective Book Club, the Mystery Guild and the Unicorn Mystery Book Club. A revision in 1983 updated the offerings of the first two clubs, still active, and added several lesser-known clubs.

The long title of *Cook's Monthly Murders: A Checklist and Chronological Listing of Fiction in the Digest-Size Mystery Magazines in the United States and England* (1982) aptly describes his bibliography of about one hundred periodicals. For the computer age, William G. Contento updated this work in the CD-ROM *Mystery Short Fiction Miscellany: An Index* (2003), adding to it information from his *Crime and Mystery Anthologies,* compiled with Martin H. Greenberg, first published as a book in 1990.

Two somewhat-related 1983 bibliographies of Cook's were *Mystery, Detective, and Espionage Magazines* and *Mystery Fanfare: A Composite Annotated Index to Mystery and Related Fanzines 1963–1981.* The first book included descriptions of fan magazines, along with hundreds of pulp and digest-sized fiction magazines. The second book covers almost fifty fan magazines.

Arguably, Cook's most daunting indexing project, one undertaken with Stephen T. Miller, was *Mystery, Detective, and Espionage Fiction: A Checklist of Fiction in US Pulp Magazines, 1915–1974,* published in two volumes in 1988. Cook died June 14, 1988, at age fifty-eight, shortly before it was published. The first volume is a chronological listing of each magazine, beginning with *Ace Detective Magazine* and extending to *Zeppelin Stories*. (Yes, in 1929 there was a magazine with the latter title, and it included some mysteries.) The second volume is an alphabetical author listing.

Steven A. Stilwell indexed the first ten years of *The Armchair Detective*, and William F. Deeck updated it through *TAD's* demise in Vol. 30. Alone, Deeck indexed *The Mystery Fancier, The Poisoned Pen, Mystery Readers Journal, CADS,* and *Deadly Pleasures.* With Deeck's death in 2004, the last three, still active, cry for some fan to bring them up to date. Deeck's indexes are invaluable to scholars.

John Nieminski was another tireless bibliographer, and his work is more impressive because its 4,212 entries were done with index cards, not a computer. In 1974 he published an index to *Ellery Queen's Mystery Magazine,* covering its first 350 issues. Nieminski was proud of his complete *EQMM* collection, including the fact that all the issues were in mint condition. Not willing to trust his copies to the Postal Service, he bought them at newsstands. (As another fan with a complete collection of *EQMM,* I have continued his index for the magazine, beginning where he left off in January 1973.) Nieminski also did a complete index for *Saint Mystery Magazine,* and his death prevented a similar index for *Alfred Hitchcock's Mystery Magazine.*

As the mystery became increasingly popular, it was apparent that a high percentage of readers (demographic studies say about seventy percent) are women. It was also clear that many female readers enjoy reading about female characters. Once, scholarly works were gender-neutral, but then fans began writing books about female authors. Perhaps the first of these was *Silk Stalkings: When Women Write of Murder* (Black Lizard, 1988) by Victoria Nichols and Susan Thompson. Their subjects were female mystery writers, but they did not restrict themselves to those with female characters. Thus, P. D. James and her Adam Dalgliesh are included. A new edition in 1998, *Silk Stalkings: More Women Write of Murder* (Scarecrow Press) added many new writers. Incidentally, the title "Silk Stalkings" was so clever that a cable television network purchased it for a series with female sleuths.

Jean Swanson and Dean James's *By a Woman's Hand* (1994; second edition 1996) is a guide to over 200 female authors and their characters. In *Mystery Women: An Encyclopedia of Leading Women Characters in Mystery Fiction* (in three volumes, published between 1997 and 2003), Colleen Barnett wrote of over 1,100 female series characters. Her numbers testify to their increase since 1980. Between 1860 and 1979, there were 392 female series characters. Between 1980 and 1989, there were about 250 new ones, and then more than 500 emerged from 1990 through 1999!

Willetta L. Heising first published *Detecting Women* in 1995, listing living female authors that write mystery series, with biographical information about them and a listing of the books in which their series characters appear. Proving she was an equal-opportunity bibliographer, Heising published *Detecting Men* in 1998. By 2000, *Detecting Women* was in its third edition, having added 225 authors since the second edition in 1996.

The growth of female series detectives was a reflection of a huge increase in mysteries published. Readers wanted recommendations, not only in magazine reviews but also in books. This led to a growth in guides that were not restricted to authors or series characters of one sex. G .K. Hall employed six fans for their Readers' Guide series. First, Susan Oleksiw, who became series editor, wrote the book that was the prototype: *A Reader's Guide to the Classic British Mystery* (1988). It included brief plot descriptions of about 1,000 British mysteries. There were also appendices that listed settings, occupations, and the period in which the mystery takes place. Finally, Oleksiw picked 100 outstanding books in her field. Her book was followed by my *A Reader's Guide to the American Novel of Detection* (1993), Gary Warren Niebuhr's *A Reader's Guide to the Private Eye Novel* (1993), Jo Ann Vicarel's *A Reader's Guide to the Police Procedural* (1995), Nancy-Stephanie Stone's *A Reader's Guide to the Spy and Thriller Novel* (1997) and Mary Johnson Jarvis's *A Reader's Guide to the Suspense Novel* (1997).

No subject seems too obscure for fans wishing to share their enthusiasm with others. John Kennedy Melling's *Murder Done to Death* (1996) is the definitive book about parody and pastiche in detective fiction. John E. Kramer wrote *Academe in Mystery and Detective Fiction* (2000) concerning mysteries set on college campuses. Jon L. Breen's *Novel Verdicts* (1984) is an annotated listing of courtroom mysteries. Though a non-lawyer, Breen shows a remarkable knowledge of the law as well as wide reading. He analyzes eighty-six Erle Stanley Gardner novels that have court-room sequences. With the growth of legal mysteries following the success of Scott Turow's *Presumed Innocent* (1987), Breen published a second edition of his book in 1999. The number of courtroom mysteries had risen from 421 in 1984 to 790 fifteen years later.

Combining a love of sports and mysteries stories, I wrote a series for *TAD*, beginning in 1972, about mysteries with sports backgrounds. It was an idea inspired by an earlier article I published in *World Tennis*, "Tennis and the Mystery Story." Tom Taylor's *The Golf Murders* (1996) is the ultimate book about golf mysteries.

Scholarship is not all humorless. Bill Pronzini, as those who know him are aware, is as much a fan as a writer of fiction. He's a collector of pulp magazines and other mysteries and searches for examples of funny, bad writing, what he calls "alternate classics." He uses these in his "Gun in Cheek" series, one book of which is subti-tled "An Affectionate Guide to More of the 'Worst' in Mystery Fiction." Illustrations include: "The next day dawned bright and clear on my empty stomach," from Mi-chael Avallone's *Meanwhile Back at the Morgue,* and "He poured himself a drink and counted the money. It came to ten thousand even, mostly in fifties and twenty-fives," from Brett Halliday's *The Violent World of Michael Shayne.* Bill Deeck, to whom I previously referred, captured the best of the worst of James Corbett in his *The Complete Deeck on Corbett* (2003).

Cover art can be an important bonus to mysteries. A feature of Nehr's book on the Doubleday Crime Club was the color reproduction of ninety-four of their best dust jackets. John Cooper and Barry Pike compiled two books with some of the best British dust jacket art. Art Scott is one of the leading experts on American paperback art and conducts popular slide shows, with examples, at Bouchercons. Scott is the leading expert on the work of Robert McGinnis, arguably the best artist to illustrate the covers of paperback mysteries. With Dr. Wallace Maynard, he published the well-illustrated *The Paperback Covers of Robert McGinnis* (2001). Equally beloved is the artwork that was on the covers of mystery pulp magazines. Among the best collections of these are Lee Server's *Danger Is My Business* (1993) and Robert Lesser's *Pulp Art* (1997).

Definitive biographies of writers have been written by fans. After writing a book about the "normal" authors Frederic Dannay and Manfred B. Lee, who wrote as Ellery Queen, Francis M. Nevins won an Edgar with his biography of Cornell Woolrich, *First You Dream, Then You Die* (1988). Nevins had been writing about Woolrich for fan magazines for twenty years and edited collections of Woolrich's stories. In addition to describing Woolrich's ability to write suspenseful prose, Nevins conveys the unusual life led by Woolrich, a recluse full of self-hate who spent most of his life living in hotels with his mother.

Doug Greene, expert on John Dickson Carr and founder of Crippen & Landru Publishers..

Another unhappy life is documented by Jeffrey Marks in *Who Was That Lady?* (2001), the biography of Craig Rice. Marks discusses the question of whether it was Rice who "ghosted" Gypsy Rose Lee's *The G-String Murders*. Known for her screwball comedy-mysteries, Rice died at age forty-nine, her death hastened by alcoholism.

John McAleer spent years researching his definitive, Edgar-winning 1977 biography *Rex Stout*, being fortunate to have interviewed Stout before he died. Equally worthy of an Edgar was Douglas G. Greene's *John Dickson Carr: The Man Who Explained Miracles*, but he did not win it or any of the three other awards for which he was nominated.

J. Randolph Cox wrote an exhaustive article on his almost-namesake, George Harmon Coxe, for *TAD*. He later published *Man of Magic and Mystery*, a guide to the work of Walter Gibson, creator of The Shadow.

Richard Martin was a fan of Margery Allingham since he first read her at age seventeen. His 1988 biography of her, *Ink in Her Blood*, is appropriately titled because she came from a family who thought writing the only suitable way to earn a living. There is biographical material about Allingham in *Campion's Career* (1987) by B. A. Pike, but the focus of this British fan is her detective, Albert Campion. Ray B. Browne published *The Spirit of Australia* (1988), about the crime fiction of Arthur W. Upfield. B. J. Rahn edited *Ngaio Marsh: The Woman and Her Work* for the 1995 centenary of Marsh's birth. Marsh wrote her own autobiography in 1965, but since she lived another seventeen years, there was much that was not included in it but was in *Ngaio Marsh: A Life* by Margaret Lewis, a 1991 biography that involved two round trips from England to New Zealand for research by Lewis. Biographies of Golden Age writers are seldom published, but a fortunate exception is Malcolm J. Turnbull's *Elusion Aforethought: The Life and Writing of Anthony Berkeley Cox* (1996), a book about the author better known as Anthony Berkeley and Francis Iles.

Since the 1980s, almost every American mystery has a strong regional element, with detailed descriptions of the geography, speech, dress, and life style of their locations. At times, it seems that this lengthy description overwhelms the mystery plot. My complaint is ironic since in 1970, in *The Mystery Reader's Newsletter*, I started a series of articles on how the regions of the United States are depicted in mystery fiction. I said then that there weren't enough mysteries with good regional descriptions. My series was completed in 1977, having moved to *TAD* when *TMRN* ceased publication. Eventually, despite the vast number of new regional mysteries, I finished revising and updating my articles and published them in a 542-page book, *The American Regional Mystery* (2000). Steve Glassman and Maurice J. O'Sullivan have been more pragmatic in writing about smaller areas, with books on mysteries set in Florida and the Southwest.

Many mystery readers and writers have remarked on the influence of the Nancy Drew and Hardy Boys series on their future tastes. An unscientific poll indicates the Drew influence was greater, perhaps because more women read mysteries than men. Fans of these two young detectives series have written respectively *The Nancy Drew Scrapbook* (1993) by Karen Plunkett-Powell and *The Mysterious Case of Nancy Drew and the Hardy Boys* (1998) by Carole Kismaric and Marvin Heiferman.

Scholarly fans like to play detective when they can, and one of the most fertile areas concerns pseudonyms. Reading the books of two different authors and finding similarities of style, they are wont to guess that one is a pseudonym, and they are often right. Nevins in 1968 demonstrated that two well-known British authors, John Rhode and Miles Burton, were really Major Cecil John Charles Street, writing under both names. More than thirty years later, in *CADS*, Tony Medawar revealed another pseudonym for Street. When Jon L. Breen speculated in 1974 that Emma Lathen and R. B. Dominic were both the creations of the same authors (Mary Jane Latsis and Martha Henissart), Patricia McGerr was able to confirm that in the next issue of *TAD*. The most active scholar of pseudonyms is Texas fan Pat Hawk whose *Authors' Pseudonyms* (1992) has gone through three editions, with 1,600 pages and more than 61,000 pseudonym attributions, a significant percentage of whom are of mystery writers, in the third.

A unique and useful reference book is *The Deadly Directory*, which was started by Sharon Villines in 1995. Kate Derie, creator of Cluelass.com, took over in 1999 and edited it until its last annual edition in 2004. Accurately subtitled by Derie as "A Resource Guide for Mystery, Crime and Suspense Readers and Writers," it provides information regarding mystery booksellers, organizations, periodicals, internet websites, and events.

As the next two chapters will demonstrate, mystery scholarship remains alive and well, though it and fandom are changing in the cyberspace age.

33 Mystery Fandom in Cyberspace

Woody Allen famously joked that the trouble with instant gratification is that it takes too long. Things are seldom as fast as some would wish, but in cyberspace fans are able to communicate with each other quickly, and that has changed the nature of fandom.

Many of us are Luddites and have gone figuratively kicking and screaming into the age of technology. A first step for fans who write letters, articles, and books is the realization that writing is much simpler with a personal computer. Revisions are more easily made, and mistakes can be corrected without the sometimes-messy use of correction fluid. I acquired my first computer in 1984 and quickly joined the fan chorus asking, "How did I ever write anything before I got a computer?" Still, there are many fans uncomfortable with reading lengthy material on the computer screen, so the hard copy is important, and we are far from the "paperless society" once predicted.

By the mid-1990s virtually everyone contributing to *DAPA-EM* and *Mystery & Detective Monthly*, to name two fan groups involving written participation, was using a computer and had electronic mail ("e-mail"). Whereas once I wrote many letters, I now have only two correspondents to whom I regularly send what is called—pejoratively, by some—"snail mail."

Most of the magazines still in print maintain a website, and others, including the publication of the Agatha Christie Society, have gone online. Similarly, fans purchase many of their mysteries from online sellers.

The letter column of *The Armchair Detective* was once the liveliest place for fans to communicate. They were satisfied that their letters would appear in the following issue. When *TAD* was no longer edited and produced by Al Hubin, the wait to see one's letter was sometimes nine months, so fewer readers wrote.

MDM solved the problem temporarily with its almost monthly appearance and lively letters. However, after almost twenty years its regular contributors were down to about a dozen. It seemed clear that it would be replaced by internet chat groups, including the most famous and largest "list-serve," DorothyL. One can write to DorothyL, see one's posting published later that day, and get responses the next day. That is as close to instant gratification as one can get in fandom.

DorothyL was created in July 1991 by two librarians, Diane Kovacs and Ann Okerson. When Ann dropped out soon after, Kara Robinson, a reference librarian at Kent State University in Ohio, where Kovacs used to work, became co-moderator. There are almost 3,000 members located in twenty-five different countries. Every day the members can download an average of fifty to seventy-five messages, either singly or in the form of several daily digests. A relatively small number of people are responsible for most of the messages; if all members wrote, it would be an impossible task for the moderators.

What makes DorothyL an interesting discussion group is the variety of the postings. There are lists of favorite books or movies, reviews of books, and details of personal lives, generally presented discreetly. Betty Webb has described members as "sort of a family," wording previously applied to *DAPA-EM* and *MDM*.

Though most reviews tend to be positive, there is plenty of room for disagreement, for example about the bestselling *The Da Vinci Code*. However, criticism of other members is often regarded as personal and leads to postings supporting the target.

Some topics are considered taboo, primarily politics and religion, and most members stick to the guidelines, though at the end of 2004 moderator Kovacs strongly chided people for straying too far into religion, saying on December 14, "One more religious post and that person gets removed." Occasionally, members have engaged in disputes with Kovacs and other members, notably Kevin Burton Smith, who admits rubbing people the wrong way with his criticism of some postings. Kovacs deemed his language inappropriate.

The moderators walk a fine line regarding what they call "BSP (Blatant Self Promotion)." Many published writers are members, and they often mention their own books. Some routinely list their book credits after their "signature" line in a posting. Others offer advance review copies. Though some readers refer to it as "spam," BSP seems to be tolerated as long as it doesn't go too far, and the author otherwise contributes to the discussion.

Though there were DorothyL events at several 1990s Bouchercons, recognition of the work of Kovacs and Robinson did not really come until 2005 when it was announced that they would receive MWA's Raven Award for their activities and, coincidentally, would be Fan Guests of Honor at Left Coast Crime in 2007.

Though possibly the best-known mystery activity in cyberspace, DorothyL is only one of many. The *Mysterious Home Page (MHP)*, created and formerly owned by Jan B. Steffensen of Denmark, was the first general mystery website, established in May 1995. It is now operated by Kate Derie of Cluelass.com, who calls it "a streamlined 'just the links, ma'am' jumping off site for the mystery world online." The Cluelass site, which began in June 1995, also includes a calendar of events, a list of forthcoming books, answers to frequently asked questions (FAQ), and advice to mystery writers. While Steffensen listed website links only, Derie has annotated each link with a de-

Kate Derie, better known as Cluelass.

scription of the site. She keeps track of over 1500 web sites, hundreds of which belong to individual mystery authors. When Jon Jordan interviewed authors for his book *Interrogations*, twenty-four of the twenty-five interviewed listed their own websites.

Keeping track of websites is not easy as sites spring up and become defunct with great rapidity. For example, only five of fourteen sites listed in the 1998 Bouchercon program were still in operation in 2004.

The range of fan websites is wide. *The Gumshoe Site* by Japan's Jiro Kimura, established in January 1996, is one of the best for news. He is especially good regarding information on deaths of writers, awards, and publication of short story collections. He also publishes pictures he takes at Bouchercon.

With the short story market having shrunk to a handful of magazines, the web has partly filled the gap, at least in the hardboiled area. An example is Russel D. McLean's *Crime Scene,* which started as a bookselling site but evolved into an "intermittent internet journal," including short stories. Kevin Burton Smith's *Thrilling Detective* website has been active since 1998. It includes short stories (authors are paid $7.50 per story), reviews, and some essays that would not have been out of place in *TAD,* for example Marcia Kiser's "Nero Wolfe: A Social Commentary on the US."

The Short Mystery Fiction Society is an e-group like DorothyL, though it is hosted by Yahoo.com, rather than a university. About 850 people belong. They give the Derringer Awards annually for excellence in short mystery fiction. Bob Tinsley of Colorado Springs started The ShortOfIt.blogspot.com in late 2004. Tinsley, who reviews short stories on his site, predicts that the future of the mystery short story rests in "e-zines," and there are at least a half-dozen such magazines publishing crime fiction—mostly hardboiled—that fans of this new form of magazine consider exceptional. Among these is *Plots with Guns,* which, despite paying little, attracted "name" writers such as Laura Lippman and Steve Hamilton to contribute to a special issue.

Jeff Cohen's e-zine *Mystery Morgue,* in addition to reviews, articles, and interviews, features "Murder by Committee," an ongoing serial mystery written by various writers, including Julia Spencer-Fleming, Rhys Bowen, and Robin Burcell. All were asked to write it in the style of the mystery writers who had inspired them.

If anything, there is greater enthusiasm for the short story online than there is for it in conventional print media. One of the leading advocates is Sarah Weinman who edits fiction for the e-zine *Shots.*

Bonny Brown of Edmonds, Washington, is webmaster of *Stop, You're Killing Me,* which she describes as "A Site to Die for... If You Love Mystery Books." There is information on new books and pages on hundreds of authors, including lists (generally not complete) of their books. *Tangled Web,* the UK's leading website, uses similar language, calling itself "A Web Site to Die For." It provides news, reviews, author profiles, lengthy interviews, often by Bob Cornwell, and essays. In a recent issue, Natasha Cooper had an essay on Josephine Tey. Many of these sites have links to or ads for on-line bookseller Amazon.com, providing a source of income for sites that are accessible without charge.

Though most of the interest in current magazines and websites is in current mysteries, there are sites for fans of older detective stories. *Golden Age Detection,* run by Jon Jermey of Australia, has had more than a thousand electronic "issues." Its members are often polled, with questions such as what were the best and worst "last bows," allowing members to vote on the best and worst final novels of writers. Another poll concerned the best short stories of all time. Members frequently discuss forgotten writers such as Anthony Wynne. All is not sweetness and light, and one member clearly had annoyed others with his attacks. Someone wrote, "I finally had a bellyful and stopped being diplomatic. I unloaded on him."

As one who decries the lack of interest on the part of many 21st century fans in the history of their favorite genre and their lack of knowledge of past writers, I am made more optimistic because two knowledgeable contributors to Golden Age Detection, Xavier Lechard of France and Nick Fuller of Australia, are in their twenties.

Michael E. Grost calls his *Classic Mystery and Detection* "an educational site containing reading lists and essays on great mysteries, mainly of the pre-1965 era." He also publishes his own short stories on its "mystery fiction page." His essays show considerable knowledge and reading by Grost, who also operates *Classic Film and Television* and *Classic Comic Books* sites.

"Blog"—short for "web log"—is a word that wasn't in any dictionary before the web, and now there are millions of these personal websites in the US, many operated by mystery fans. These personal journals have become another way to communicate in cyberspace. One of the most popular blogs is Sarah Weinman's *Confessions of an Idiosyncratic Mind,* with its combination of news, quotes from articles about writers, reviews, and lively opinions about controversial topics such as mystery awards. Another outstanding blog, by a writer who is also a fan, is *Bill Crider's Blog.* He reviews books and writes articles about old paperbacks and radio mysteries, as well as telling about his personal life, for example, a trip to Peru.

34 The Future of Mystery Fandom

Twenty-five years ago, many mystery writers and editors were pessimistic about their future. In 2005 the mystery is far healthier, and this improvement has proven rewarding to fans also. There is more for them to read and more avenues in which to pursue fandom.

The growth of Bouchercons in the 1980s and 1990s has not been reversed, though Bouchercons have not gotten larger than, say, Monterey in 1997. The more intimate conventions that began with Malice Domestic in 1989 have grown but still are small enough, compared to Bouchercon, to provide pleasant contrast. Regional conventions, especially Left Coast Crime, continue to thrive, and have been joined by conventions in Alabama, Arizona, Florida, Idaho, Indiana, Nebraska, New Jersey, and North Carolina, among other states. There are also smaller conventions in Canada and England.

At a 1995 Cluefest panel, I questioned where we would find young fans willing to perform the scholarship and organizing that had been done since 1967. In *MDM*, editor Bob Napier echoed the pessimism of my panel, wondering if active fans weren't an endangered species. However, he and others wisely suggested that with so many mystery readers, there had to be "New Blood." Ronnie Klaskin and Len Moffatt were prophetic in predicting that the internet would be the source of future fans.

There are now more than 800 mystery-related websites, allowing an unprecedented level of communication by fans. If the scholarly articles in magazines such as *TAD* are no longer being written, knowledge is exhibited on the web in the form of bibliographies and essays that speaks well for the future. Though material on the internet may seem ephemeral to older people such as this writer, one must remember that different generations have different means of communicating. For example, there is enthusiasm about short fiction published online that I seldom find about short stories published in magazines or book anthologies.

More mysteries than ever are published—and by more publishers, and that is without tapping the full potential of print-on-demand services. In the late 1940s, about 250 new mysteries a year were published. Early in the 21st century, estimates are of about 1,250 new mysteries. Some worry that quality is not keeping up with quantity, but reviewers on the web and in magazines have no trouble finding many books to recommend.

The books being published are not all modern. Two publishers—who are also fans—have found niches reprinting material from the past. Doug Greene's Crippen & Landru Publishers, in its Lost Classics Series, brings out short story collections by writers in danger of being forgotten, including Helen McCloy and T. S. Stribling. Rue Morgue Press, the offspring of Tom and Enid Schantz, reprints in paperback neglected novels, most more than fifty years old, that most readers never expected to find except at high prices in used bookstores or on eBay. To cite one example,

Margaret Scherf's *The Gun in Daniel Webster's Bust* (1949) is most welcome to fans of "the old stuff." As mentioned in prior chapters, there are also magazines and websites devoted to the past, especially the Golden Age between the World Wars.

Perhaps the best sign of a healthy future for fandom is the number of mystery discussion groups, probably hundreds, in every part of the United States. Examples include the Cloak & Clue Society in Milwaukee, active since 1980. In addition to discussing books, its members have been active in putting on conventions, including two Bouchercons. Mystery Readers International's Northern California reading group is going into its 30th year. "Murder in Sin City" has monthly meetings in Las Vegas. The members include an engineer, a lawyer, and retired teachers, and they have bonded into a congenial group that goes to conventions, plays, author appearances, and dinners together. Other popular and cleverly named groups include Clews and Brews of St. Paul, Minnesota; Scotland Yard in Winnetka, Illinois; and the Society of Sedentary Sleuths in central New York State. Yahoo sponsors an online discussion group with more than 100 members. Peter Lovesey and D. R. Meredith, among others, have written mysteries about reading groups, and in a case of things going full circle, groups have read and discussed these books.

The future of mystery fandom will continue to follow technology, as it has done on the internet. In this era of pay-per-view television, we may expect a time when people will "attend" mystery conventions from their homes. This may be beneficial to people for whom travel is either difficult or overly expensive, but I suspect that the personal contacts one enjoys at conventions will never become a thing of the past. Similarly, though reading material will be increasingly available on the internet, I doubt that the desire to hold a book (or a fan magazine) in one's hands will ever vanish.

About the Author

Marvin Lachman won a Raven Award from the Mystery Writers of America in 1997, for his fan-related activities. MWA calls the Raven a "special award given for outstanding achievement in the mystery field outside the realm of creative writing." Lachman won the MWA's Edgar Award for Best Critical/Biographical Work in 1997, for *Encyclopedia of Mystery and Detection* (with co-authors Chris Steinbrunner, Otto Penzler, and Chris Shibuk) and was nominated for the same award in 1994 for *A Reader's Guide to the American Novel of Detection*. His *Reader's Guide* was also nominated for an Agatha, an Anthony, and a Macavity Award. Lachman won a Macavity Award in 2001 for *The American Regional Mystery*, which was also nominated for an Anthony and an Agatha. In 2001 he also received the Don Sandstrom Memorial Award for Lifetime Achievement in Mystery Fandom. He lives in Santa Fe, New Mexico, with his wife, Carol.

Index

CPSIA information can be obtained at www.ICGtesting.com
Printed in the USA
LVOW11s1949211014

409832LV00001B/209/A